D1265779

1939: Baseball's Pivotal Year

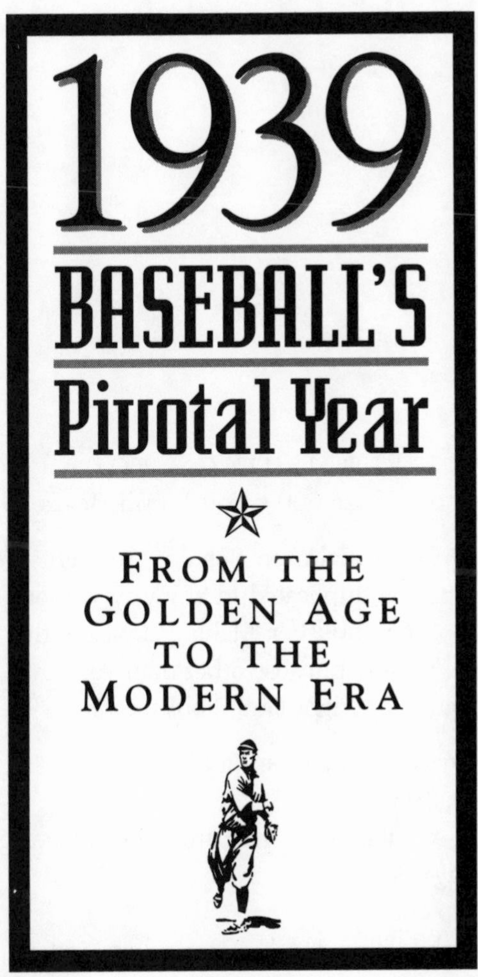

by

Talmage Boston

THE SUMMIT GROUP • FORT WORTH, TEXAS

THE SUMMIT PUBLISHING GROUP
1227 West Magnolia, Suite 500 • Fort Worth, Texas 76104

 Published in 1994.

Library of Congress Cataloging-in-Publication Data
Boston, Talmage, 1953-
1939, baseball's pivotal year: from the golden age to the modern era/by Talmage Boston.
p.cm.
Includes bibliographical references and index.
ISBN 1-56530-143-9: $22.95
1. Baseball—United States—Histoyr—20th century. I. Title. II. Title: 1939.
GV863.A1B64 1994
796.357'0973—dc20 94-37021
CIP

To the memory of Bart Giamatti

and to all who attempt to
"conserve something of purpose in a world of confusion...

and to praise something other than the giddy headlong rush."

CONTENTS

FOREWORD

BASEBALL'S HISTORY IS REALLY AMERICA'S HISTORY. Sometimes it's easy for us to forget how events that happened years ago have shaped where we are today, and will continue to affect us in the future.

The season of 1939 has never really filled up a book before, and I was surprised at the number of important events in baseball history which happened during that one year. Talmage Boston has written a wonderful book that draws together all the different parts of the game as it was in '39. I was part of some of the events he writes about, and I pretty much knew all the people he describes on these pages. The players, the managers, the owners, the sportswriters, and even the umpires combined for one of the greatest years ever in baseball.

I have said many times, "There's nothing greater for a human being than to get his body to react to all the things one does on a ball field. It's as good as anything. It fills you up." As far as baseball goes, the next best thing to playing the game or watching it is reading about it. Talmage's book jogged my memory of so many wonderful people and times. In my mind, I can still recall Satchel Paige's hesitation pitch, Bobby Feller's fastball, Josh Gibson's power, Joe DiMaggio's smoothness, and feisty Leo Durocher. They are some of my favorite memories.

For those of you who didn't get to see the baseball stars of 1939 play the game, reading Talmage's book is almost as good.

I've recently been part of a television documentary with Ken Burns that I hope will make Americans understand better just how much baseball and America are part of each other. Talmage's book might do that, too. I hope so.

This book is *true*. I know, and once you read it, you'll know, too.

Buck O'Neil
Kansas City, Missouri
July 21, 1994

PREFACE

THESE TWELVE MONTHS CHANGED our national pastime. Looking backward, 1939 vitalized the game's first one hundred years of history with the June 12 dedication of the National Hall of Fame and Museum at Cooperstown and centennial festivities, which occurred throughout the summer all over the country. Looking forward, for the first time all sixteen major league teams had radio broadcasts, night games were played in both leagues, baseball appeared on television, and a novelty called Little League began in Williamsport, Pennsylvania.

Between the past and the future was the 1939 season itself, marked by the ending of Lou Gehrig's consecutive game streak, Ted Williams's explosive rookie year, Leo Durocher's debut as a manager, Joe DiMaggio's greatest season, Red Barber's moving to Brooklyn's "Catbird Seat," Bill McKechnie's becoming the first manager to take three different teams to the World Series, Bob Feller's first 20-win season, and Lombardi's infamous snooze highlighting the fourth consecutive World Series of Yankee superiority. Bill "the Old Arbitrator" Klem and Al "the Clown Prince of Baseball" Schacht stayed in the headlines all year, while Satchel Paige, Josh Gibson, and black journalists led the Negro leagues toward the day of integration.

This book started subconsciously when my wife and I traveled to Cooperstown in 1989 with our friends Peter and Liz Haveles for the induction of Carl Yastrzemski[1] into the Hall of Fame. Given my last name, I had always been a Red Sox fan, and Captain Carl had been my hero since childhood. Peter and I had made a pact more than a decade before that when Yaz got into the Hall, we would be there, not knowing his induction would coincide with the Hall of Fame's celebration of its first half-century.

Cooperstown's lure was powerful. Before July 1989, I had never written anything about baseball. Since leaving the village, as my work schedule permits, I have not stopped researching and writing about baseball history.

At the induction ceremonies, Yastrzemski's speech closed with the following familiar words:

> "The race doesn't always belong to the swift... It belongs rather to those who run the race, stay the course, and fight the good fight."

Yaz's words apply to our national pastime. Compared to basketball, football, and other games controlled by a clock, baseball is not swift. Yet it has stayed the course past its centennial and sesquicentennial, and prospered amidst its recreational competitors.

The game's politics, economics, agents, and organized labor player structure now threaten its future. Rather than focus on the dissidence and greed in today's game, this book attempts to visualize 1939's manifestation of baseball's greatest stories: Lou Gehrig's quiet dignity, Ted Williams's brash debut, Leo Durocher's aggressiveness, Bill McKechnie's paternal leadership, Joe DiMaggio's magnificent play, Red Barber's vivid professionalism, Bob Feller's pitching dominance, Buck O'Neil's remarkable serenity amidst adversity, the Doubleday myth, the Little Leaguer's hopeful joy, and the lush paradise called Cooperstown, where I like to think it all started.

---

[1]Yastrzemski's date of birth is August 22, 1939

In 1992, newscaster Jane Pauley observed, "Remembering is more than good; it is important. The more remembering we do, the better." My sentiments exactly.

—TALMAGE BOSTON
Dallas, Texas

The Iron Horse. (Copyright: Mark Rucker; Transcendental Graphics)

CHAPTER ONE

THE IRON HORSE CORRODES

Lou Gehrig as "The Luckiest Man on the Face of the Earth"

HERO. It is a word now considered overused and inaccurate for describing the role of an athlete in our society. *Webster's* defines it as "a man admired for his achievements and noble qualities." Once upon a time, fifty-five years ago, people called athletes "heroes" and no one winced. Using *Webster's* definition, Lou Gehrig became baseball's greatest hero in 1939 and reminded the nation that life is fragile, even for an Iron Horse.

Gehrig's headlines in 1939 started in March with a spring training marked by stumbles and falls, weak hitting, and poor fielding. Sportswriters publicly wondered and teammates privately asked, "What's the matter with Lou?" In April, he started the opening eight games of the season and hit an anemic .143 with no extra-base hits. On May 2, Gehrig ended his 2,130-consecutive-game streak. In June, the Mayo Clinic transmitted the fateful report that the Yankees captain had amyotrophic lateral sclerosis, "a form of chronic poliomyelitis—infantile paralysis." On the Fourth of July, the "quiet hero" delivered baseball's Gettysburg Address on Lou Gehrig Appreciation Day to the standing-room-only fans at Yankee Stadium, telling them he considered himself "the luckiest man on the face of the earth." In October, the Yankees paid tribute by putting Gehrig alone on the cover of the

World Series program. In December, baseball writers waived the eligibility rules' mandatory waiting period and inducted him into the Hall of Fame. He would die June 2, 1941, before reaching the age of thirty-eight.

Since his death, Gehrig has served as the subject of at least six biographies, thousands of articles, two motion pictures, and a United States postage stamp. His uniform number 4 (received to reflect his clean-up position in the Yankees batting order) was the first ever retired by a major league team. Gehrig's monument, dedicated July 4, 1941, still stands at Yankees Stadium. Today, amyotrophic lateral sclerosis is a medical term known only by the medical profession, while Lou Gehrig's Disease is a malady recognized by virtually the entire population as a terminal degenerative illness.

Two of the most respected sportswriters who covered the Yankees during the Murderer's Row era, Joe Williams of the *New York Telegram* and Frank Graham of the *New York Sun*, described the essence of Lou Gehrig with the same phrase. The Yankees first baseman was "whole-souled." The many accounts of his life portray the same virtuous personality characteristics—accomplished, courageous, honest, humble, persistent, pure, sensitive, strong, and unselfish. An only child, Gehrig focused his short life on unconditional devotion to his parents, coaches, teammates, and wife.

Although fans and friends saw Gehrig as being essentially flawless (roommate Bill Dickey called him "the greatest guy that ever lived"), the Yankees captain had his share of human faults. Raised in poverty by immigrant parents, his frugality evolved into stinginess, and his desire for income outside of baseball made him abandon his dignity to pose as Tarzan and later attempt to act in a second-rate film. Gehrig's joyless steamroller mother so dominated "the only egg in her basket" that he became perpetually insecure about himself, causing wife Eleanor to describe him as "a man trapped by a poignant sense of personal inadequacy." The Iron Horse handled adversity poorly. An inopportune fielding error or failure to deliver a timely hit produced sulking and extended moodiness. Perhaps Gehrig's least-recognized limitation was his notoriously slow mind. He once humbly acknowledged, "Every time I think, the ball club suffers."

Despite Gehrig's human imperfections, experts agreed that the Yankees first baseman's virtues substantially outnumbered his flaws. Noted baseball historian Donald Honig designated him as "one of the game's few inviolable saints." Legendary sportswriter Grantland Rice observed that Gehrig had "a quality of character that certainly no one I ever knew has topped... a mixture of strength and gentleness, of courage and complete cleanness in everything he did." Finally and most eloquently, author Paul Gallico ended his 1942 biography on the *Lou Gehrig: Pride of the Yankees* by suggesting Gehrig's "light that shines like a friendly, beckoning beacon, is that of a clear, honest, decent, kindly fellow gleaming through the darkness of a dispirited, disillusioned world." The events of 1939 made Lou Gehrig a legend and focused his permanent place in the American Dream.

The 1938 Season: A Forewarning

DURING THE TWELVE YEARS PRECEDING 1938, Gehrig assembled an unmatched record for offensive consistency. After a solid 1937 season, the two-time American League Most Valuable Player entered 1938 approaching age thirty-five, a point when even the greatest ballplayers normally begin the tapering-off process. Statistics from 1938 reflected a definite decline, yet nothing worthy of panic.

	1926-1937	1937	1938
HITS	200	200	170
RUNS	141	138	115
2B & 3B (COMBINED)	52	46	38
HR	37	37	29
RBI	149	159	114
BA	.347	.351	.295

Gehrig's mild off-year did not concern his Yankees teammates. Said Joe DiMaggio, "Nobody that I spoke to seemed too alarmed. At thirty-five, a guy was entitled to go back a bit." In his recent autobiography, Tommy Henrich attempted to establish Gehrig's vitality in 1938 by pointing out that he led American League first basemen in double plays that season with 157. Henrich added, "There was never any talk among us that something might be happening to our teammate and leader, because there was no reason for such talk. As far as any of us knew, Lou Gehrig was still Lou Gehrig."

Despite the respectable but declining statistics, problem signs appeared to the careful observer. Pitcher Wes Ferrell left the Senators and joined the Yankees at the end of the 1938 season. He related to historian Donald Honig about a game late in the year: "You know, something happened in that game. I thought it was curious at the time, though now I can understand it. We should've won the game in nine innings, but Gehrig made a bad play on a ground ball and let the tying run in. Instead of going to the plate and throwing the man out, he went the easy way, to first base. It was the kind of play you'd never expect him to make."

The oncoming disease gave other signals. Gehrig's hands trembled unexpectedly. Coffee cups dropped. At least one journalist could see the old power missing in his bat. Late in the 1938 season, the *New York Sun*'s Jim Kahn remarked to friend Toots Shor:

> "I think there's something wrong with him. Physically wrong, I mean. I don't know what it is. I haven't any idea. But I am satisfied that it goes far beyond his ball playing. I have seen ballplayers 'go' overnight, as Gehrig seems to have done. But they simply were washed up as ballplayers. It's something deeper than that in this case, though."
>
> "What makes you think so?" Toots asked.
>
> "This, I have watched him very closely and this is what I have seen: I have seen him time a ball perfectly, swing on it as hard as he can, meet it squarely—and drive a soft, looping fly over the infield. In other words, for some reason that I do not know, his old power isn't there. That's the reason he isn't getting base hits. He isn't popping the ball into the air or hitting it into the dirt or striking out. He is meeting the ball, time after time, and it isn't going anywhere."

Gehrig certainly lacked his traditional power in the 1938 World Series. In his six previous Series, involving a total of 30 games, he always hit for extra bases and drove in runs. In those Fall Classics, Gehrig averaged .386, delivered 21 extra-base hits (out of his 39 total hits), and drove in 35 runs. In the 1938 Series against the Cubs, the Iron Horse hit .286, with no extra-base hits, and no runs batted in. Phil Caveretta played for the Cubs and recalled Gehrig "did seem kind of sluggish in the field. I don't think he ran too well and there was something missing in the way he swung the bat."

Yankees president Ed Barrow decided there was definitely something missing in the way his first baseman swung the bat. After the 1938 season, he submitted a $36,000 contract to Gehrig for the coming year, amounting to a $3,000 pay cut. The Yankees captain signed it without challenge.

Lou Gehrig internalized that something abnormal and wrong was happening to his sturdy body. The man whom DiMaggio said "gave the impression of power as no other ballplayer I ever saw"; whom Claire Ruth said "hit that ball like a Mack truck running into a stone wall at one hundred miles an hour… whose line drives literally screeched as they headed for the outfield or the bleachers"; and whom John Kieran of *The New York Times* described as having "the delicate physique of a railroad locomotive" (hence the nickname "Iron Horse"), sensed a mysterious but disabling corrosion. Gehrig's capacity to play, through concussions, lumbago, and seventeen broken fingers during his consecutive game streak no longer seemed to serve him in trying to combat his mysterious physical deterioration.

Eleanor Gehrig had always thought of her husband as an "adult Eagle Scout." At the Yankees' celebration following the 1938 World Series sweep over the Cubs, a teammate came to Eleanor and told her she had better take care of her husband because Lou was "drinking triples, and he's really bombed." Sensing impending demise beyond his control, this simple, straight-arrow Eagle Scout could think of only one thing to do. Lou Gehrig got drunk.

The 1938-1939 Offseason: The Motor Neuron Deterioration Accelerates

AMYOTROPHIC LATERAL SCLEROSIS (ALS) REMAINS A MYSTERY. Doctors today know neither its cause nor cure. Although not considered contagious, ALS has attacked groups of people. Most notably, a high incidence of the disease has afflicted citizens of Guam and members of the San Francisco 49ers who played for the team in the late 1950s.

A person with ALS usually dies because feeble muscles finally cannot move the lungs to breathe, and the patient strangles. As described in a recent *Sports Illustrated* article by David Noonan, the physical decline comes from the deterioration of the body's motor neurons which "carry the motor impulses from the brain through the spinal cord and to the muscles. They are the critical links in the chain between the mind and the body. They enable you to move." As the disease progresses, Paul Gallico accurately observed, "Iron muscles suddenly turn to useless rags."

Although ALS ultimately destroys the body, the blessing/curse of the disease is that it leaves the mind intact. The brain has full command to observe the corpus reduce to a corpse. Gehrig's most recent biographer Ray Robinson related that having ALS "is like being a participant at your own funeral." Muscles taken for granted suddenly malfunction. Life's simplest routines become traumatic and even dangerous. Such were Lou Gehrig's circumstances following the 1938 World Series.

During the offseason, Eleanor Gehrig noticed her husband stumbling over curbstones and dropping kitchen utensils at their home in New Rochelle. Normally an excellent ice skater, he started falling often. A local doctor diagnosed that a gall bladder problem caused Gehrig's malfunctions and treated it accordingly.

New York journalist Fred Lieb covered the Yankees for more than thirty years and was Lou Gehrig's best friend in the press. In the Gary Cooper movie *Pride of the Yankees*, the journalist played by Walter Brennan was modeled after Lieb. During the offseason following the 1938 World Series, Lieb and his wife lived in St. Petersburg, Florida, where the Yankees conducted spring training. In early 1939, the Liebs received a letter from Eleanor Gehrig. "Lou hasn't been too well, doesn't have the old starch." She then asked the Liebs to find the Gehrigs a rent house in St. Pete with the idea sunshine would restore Gehrig's vitality. The Liebs located a suitable house and the Gehrigs arrived in late January.

In Florida, Lou and Eleanor spent their days fishing and their nights socializing with the Liebs. An innocent game of Ouija one night offered a fateful prediction to Eleanor: "You soon will be called upon to face the most difficult problem of your life." Little did she know.

1939 Spring Training: "What's Wrong with Lou?"

Eleanor's private recognition that her husband lacked "the old starch" became a public spectacle in March 1939, when the Yankees opened spring training. DiMaggio saw Gehrig swing and miss at nineteen consecutive fastballs. Other teammates observed his inability to move away from inside pitches, causing manager Joe McCarthy to fear for his first baseman's life in those days before batting helmets. Tommy Henrich likened his strained base running to that of a man running uphill. At best, Gehrig's bat could only produce pop flies. Most disturbing was his constant falling down—while tying his shoes, walking to the batter's box, and trying to back away from pitches.

Off the field, roommate Bill Dickey saw his best friend losing control of his legs, falling often in their room and bathroom. Wes Ferrell witnessed Gehrig's shuffling gait while in attendance at the St. Petersburg Open golf tournament. Rather than wear the customary cleated shoes on the golf course, the Iron Horse found it safer and easier to drag along his feet by wearing tennis shoes.

Fans did not understand. All they knew was what they saw—Lou Gehrig's play was badly hurting the Yankees. The streak needed to stop. Sportswriter and biographer Frank Graham heard fans yelling at the first baseman, "Why don't you give yourself up? What do you want McCarthy to do, burn that uniform off you?"

Joe McCarthy was torn. His sincere goal throughout his managerial career had been to win every game by as high a score as possible. In an exhibition game against a minor league team won by the

Yankees 19-1, McCarthy told his satisfied players, "Against a team like that you should have made 50 runs." Despite his tough-minded attitude toward his opponents, the childless McCarthy loved his first baseman like a son. Donald Honig recorded:

> Gehrig was McCarthy's favorite, the old skipper finally brought himself to admit at the end of a long interview, after having loyally extolled the virtues of all his star players. "Why not?" McCarthy asked. "He always showed up, didn't cause any trouble, and he hit."

McCarthy, the uncompromising winner, now had to face a team captain whose decaying spring performance threatened the Yankees' ability to repeat as world champions. As a major complication, Joe McCarthy knew Lou Gehrig had become genuinely obsessed during the past few years with maintaining his consecutive game streak, which stood at 2,122 games entering the 1939 season.

During spring training, the Yankees skipper observed he had All-Star strength at the other eight positions on his 1939 team. In particular, second baseman Joe Gordon had exceptional range, thereby reducing the territory Gehrig needed to protect. McCarthy resolved to let his first baseman decide on the timetable for the streak's inevitable end.

Amidst the daily media reports on the Yankees spring training, one main story kept repeating itself. "What's the matter with Lou?" Was he an aging veteran who had finally fallen over the hill? Had the streak worn him down so much, his body was now staging a rebellion? How could any player deteriorate so rapidly? Joe Williams of the *New York Telegram* put it best in his column of March 16, 1939:

> The older newspapermen sit in the chicken-coop press boxes around the grapefruit circuit and watch Lou Gehrig go through the laborious movements of playing first base, and wonder if they are seeing one of the institutions of the American League crumble before their eyes.
>
> They watch him at the bat and note he isn't hitting the ball well; they watch him around the bag and it's plain he isn't getting the balls he used to get; they watch him run and they fancy they can

> hear his bones creak and his lungs wheeze as he labors around the bases. Every mental note they make contributes to the broad conviction of physical disintegration. On eyewitness testimony alone, the verdict must be that of a battle-scarred veteran falling apart.

During his obvious, rapid decline, Lou Gehrig knew only one thing to do: He would try that much harder. After a spring training 7-6 loss to the Cardinals, in part caused by Gehrig's 0-for-five day and failure to drive in the winning run with the bases loaded in the ninth, he said to Fred Lieb, "What in hell is wrong with me? What am I doing wrong? I just need more work, lots of work."

Paul Gallico observed, "He drove himself furiously, castigated, and punished himself. He took it out on the body that had for so long been his willing and sometimes abused slave."

As spring training ended, the gaps kept extending between Gehrig's occasional glimmers of hope. For the first time in his life, hard work was not paying off. Something was destroying the indestructible. The reality that the streak had to end one day was closing in. How long would it take proud, obsessed, bewildered, shuffling, falling Lou Gehrig to place the team above the streak?

The 1939 Season Opens: .143 after Eight Games

THE YANKEES OPENED THE 1939 SEASON against the Boston Red Sox and their ace pitcher Lefty Grove. Earlier in his career, Grove had remarked he feared pitching to Lou Gehrig more than Babe Ruth. That fear was gone on April 20, 1939. In the fifth inning, the Hall of Fame southpaw delivered the ultimate indignity to the Yankees captain. Grove walked DiMaggio intentionally so he could pitch to Gehrig. The strategy worked. He grounded into a double play.

The 1939 Yankees had a focused dedication to winning. Their goal for the coming season was to do something that had not been done before in the twentieth century—win a fourth consecutive World Series. Game after game, the Bronx Bombers saw Gehrig leave men on bases and boot ground balls. At first, they teased Gehrig about getting old, but soon that stopped. The defending world champions could then only watch Gehrig fail and fall in silence, knowing Gehrig's pride would refuse any offer of help.

By the eighth game—a Yankees loss to the Senators by one run—Gehrig's failure to deliver at the plate was noticeably hurting the team. His average stood at .143 with no extra-base hits, and one run batted in. Eleanor Gehrig noted in her biography that after the Senators game, as he approached the clubhouse, Gehrig overheard a Yankees teammate complaining, "Why doesn't he quit? He's through. We can't win with him in there." All conversation stopped when he entered the locker room.

Besides going hitless, something else happened during the eighth game which affected the Yankees first baseman. In Washington's last at bat, with two outs, the hitter chopped a ground ball between Yankees pitcher Johnny Murphy and first base. Murphy got the ball and flipped it to the wheezing Gehrig, who barely got to the bag in time to take the throw.

In the old days, it was a routine play. For a shuffling man barely able to tie his shoes, it was a sensational play. As they walked off the field, the kindly Murphy stopped and told his captain, "Nice play, Lou." Kindness can kill. Murphy's well-intentioned compliment killed the streak.

May 2, 1939: Dahlgren Starts at First Base

Eleanor Gehrig recognized a change in her husband after the loss to the Senators in the season's eighth game. Murphy's praise and the overheard locker room criticism followed by deafening silence made the Iron Horse acknowledge the obvious to his wife. His presence in the lineup hurt his team. As Gehrig's most adoring fan and best friend, Eleanor delivered the direct message:

> "I finally reminded him that he'd always said he would step down as soon as he felt he could no longer help the Yankees on the field. Then gently, probably devastatingly, I told him the heartbreaking words: "Maybe the time's come."

After the Washington loss on April 30, the Yankees had an off day, giving Gehrig more time to reflect. Before the May 2, 1939 Yankees-Tigers game, he met Joe McCarthy to talk about the situation. The famous conversation which followed has been told and retold as much as any other conversation in baseball history.

The many accounts of the Gehrig-McCarthy conversation are replete with inconsistencies. Paul Gallico said in his 1942 biography of Gehrig that Gehrig and McCarthy talked in the dugout; Frank Graham said in his book the conversation occurred in McCarthy's hotel room; and Richard Hubler said Gehrig and McCarthy spoke in a hotel hallway. Donald Honig described it happening on the evening of May 1, while Gallico and Hubler reported it on the morning of May 2. When the story broke in the late morning of May 2, virtually all reports reflected Gehrig's having made up his own mind about stopping the streak and communicating that decision to his skipper. Donald Honig, in his 1985 book *Baseball America*, wrote it was McCarthy who dealt affirmatively with his captain's indecision. Honig quoted McCarthy: "He asked me how much longer I thought he should stay in. I told him he should get out right now. He agreed with me."

By all accounts, the essence of the conversation involved a mutual acknowledgment that Gehrig's play was hurting the Yankees. Gehrig related the Johnny Murphy ground ball incident. Both player and manager expressed hope his departure from the lineup would only be temporary, and that warmer weather might bring the first baseman around to his old form.

Regardless of the conversation's details, the net result was the same. Prior to the start of the May 2 game against the Tigers, the Yankees called a press conference to announce the end of the streak. Long-suffering, three-year bench warmer Babe Dahlgren would start at first base for the Yankees in the ninth game of the 1939 season. Gehrig told reporters, "I can't hit and I can't field."

In the locker room before the game, Dahlgren remembered a silent reverence:

> "As we put on our baseball uniforms that day, there was a strange desire to stay in the clubhouse. What it was, nobody knew, but there was a

silence even too quiet for a Yankees dressing room. Usually, the fellows talked out loud, but this day they weren't talking; when they spoke it was in whispers."

Once in the dugout, photographers took countless pictures of Gehrig and Dahlgren. The Yankees captain took the lineup card out to home-plate umpire Steve Basil, who was incredulous. The crew chief thought there was a mistake until he looked in Gehrig's eyes and saw tears. The crowd stood and roared. Gehrig tipped his cap, disappeared into the sanctuary of the dugout, and cried privately at the water fountain.

The Yankees team focused on the task at hand. They destroyed the Tigers 22-2. By the seventh inning, the rout was so severe, Dahlgren encouraged Gehrig to come into the game and keep his streak alive. He responded, "They don't need me out there at all; you're doing just fine." The Iron Horse stayed on the dugout steps. Kieran of *The New York Times* reported, "So ended an epic."

Lou Gehrig was right. These 1939 Yankees didn't need him. They won 24 of their next 28 games, and the Iron Horse became a cheerleader.

The Mayo Clinic Diagnosis: Terminal

FOLLOWING THE MAY 2 REMOVAL FROM THE LINEUP, Gehrig's physical decline continued. He lacked the strength to open a ketchup bottle. Eleanor Gehrig took matters into her own hands. Dissatisfied with the New Rochelle doctor's gall bladder diagnosis, she called the Mayo Clinic, regarded at that time as the greatest hospital with the most talented doctors in the world. Eleanor obtained Dr. Mayo's personal commitment to test and diagnose her husband. Surprisingly, her "Luke" (as she called him) readily agreed to the examination.

When Gehrig entered the Mayo Clinic's main doors, a team of doctors greeted him. Dr. Harold Habein, the clinic's chief diagnostician, led the team. At once, Habein witnessed Gehrig's shuffle as Lou crossed the hospital lobby. The doctor had seen such a shuffle before, as his own mother degenerated and died with amyotrophic lateral sclerosis. Dr. Habein advised Dr. Mayo of his "eyeball" diagnosis.

For the next six days, the skilled physicians at the Mayo Clinic took Gehrig through a battery of tests. At the conclusion of the testing, the doctors agreed that Dr. Habein's initial hunch had been accurate.

Normally, the clinic's policy was to communicate its findings directly and specifically to the patient. The staff refused to follow their standard procedure with Lou Gehrig for two reasons. First, Eleanor Gehrig told the doctors not to tell her husband—she wanted to shield her "man-child." Secondly, the Mayo Clinic medical team had become so enamored of the humble celebrity they could not bring themselves to tell Gehrig that no ALS patient had ever lived more than two years.

As Lou Gehrig left the Mayo Clinic, he knew he had ALS, whatever that was. He did not know that the doctors held no hope for a recovery. He did not know that a patient with the disease had never lived more than two years after its being diagnosed. Eleanor Gehrig knew everything.

On June 21, 1939, the Yankees held a press conference to advise the public of the Mayo Clinic's findings. Ed Barrow distributed Dr. Habein's report to the reporters:

> This is to certify that Mr. Lou Gehrig has been under examination at the Mayo Clinic from June 13 to June 19, 1939, inclusive.
>
> After a careful and complete examination, it was found that he is suffering from amyotrophic lateral sclerosis. This type of illness involves the motor pathways and cells of the central nervous system and, in lay terms, is known as a form of chronic poliomyelitis (infantile paralysis).
>
> The nature of this trouble makes it such that Mr. Gehrig will be unable to continue his active participation as a baseball player, inasmuch as it is advisable that he conserve his muscular energy. He could, however, continue in some executive capacity.

Joe Williams of the *New York Telegram* attended the press conference. As Williams reflected on Dr. Habein's diagnosis in the context of what he had observed in Lou Gehrig since spring training, he concluded his

June 22 column: "Bad as it is, we should think Gehrig would feel relieved. At least he knows now where to start from. The lingering oppressive uncertainty, which kept him in a continuous mental stew, has been lifted."

Eleanor Gehrig confirmed Williams's hypothesis. In her autobiography, she commented:

> In a way, I think, Lou was relieved by the findings, though he was given no idea of the full consequences. For one thing, it proved to him that he was not just an aging player slowed by time, but the innocent victim of a disease that disintegrated his muscles and destroyed his speed and power. It was no bargain, except in those narrow terms that spare any performer his pride even if he is spared nothing else.

Gehrig returned to the Yankees to perform one ceremonial function. The Yankees captain carried the lineup card to the umpires before the start of every game. Even that sinecure soon became a burden. As a precaution, the Yankees started sending a man to follow Gehrig to home plate before each game to provide support and avoid a public fall.

The Yankees organization realized their All-American hero was failing before their very eyes. While Gehrig could still walk, they quickly arranged for a day of tribute to their first baseman. America would wedge in Lou Gehrig Appreciation Day amongst Mom, apple pie, and baseball on July 4, 1939.

"The Luckiest Man on the Face of the Earth"

WHEN LOU GEHRIG LEARNED the Yankees wanted to honor him with an Appreciation Day, the Iron Horse knew he would have to make a speech as part of the ceremony. As one of baseball's biggest stars for over a decade, he had given many speeches before in connection with receiving awards. Although Gehrig lacked eloquence and wit, he had always impressed audiences through his capacity to speak from the heart.

Eleanor Gehrig tried to help her husband prepare the speech, but Gehrig refused. "No thanks, Eleanor. This must be my speech and I must say these things my way."

The Yankees brought back members of the 1927 Murderer's Row team for Gehrig's Day. New York City Mayor Fiorello LaGuardia and Postmaster General James Farley paid public tribute to the model citizen honoree. The Yankees captain received many gifts, the most meaningful coming from his teammates. The 1939 Yankees presented Gehrig with a silver cup engraved with a poem by sportswriter John Kieran, a man Eleanor said "knew Shakespeare the way other people know the alphabet." Kieran's verse on the cup moved Gehrig and his teammates to tears:

We've been to the wars together;
And we took our foes as they came;
And always you were the leader,
And ever you played the game.

Idol of cheering millions,
Records are yours by the sheaves;
Iron of frame they hailed you,
Decked you with laurel leaves.

But higher than that we hold you,
We who have known you best,
Knowing the way you came through
Every human test.

Let this be a silent token
Of friendship's lasting gleam
And all that we've left unspoken—
Your pals of the Yankees team.

Finally, the moment came for Lou Gehrig to speak. Overcome with emotion because of the gifts, the poem, the politicians' kind words, the presence of his former and current teammates, and the cheering crowd,

Lou Gehrig, the "luckiest man on the face of the earth," pauses to wipe away tears. (UPI/Bettman)

Gehrig could not go to the microphone. After an awkward, extended delay in the proceedings, Joe McCarthy walked over to his favorite player. "Talk to them, Lou. That's an order. They're all your friends and you can't disappoint them. You wouldn't want to disappoint them, Lou."

The fans' affection had eluded the Iron Horse during his entire career. Until July 4, 1939, Gehrig suffered first in Ruth's shadow and then DiMaggio's. Hearing the roaring crowd there to participate in his "Day," Gehrig finally felt appreciated. At last, he responded to McCarthy's command. The Pride of the Yankees walked to the microphone and delivered his remarks from memory:

> Fans, for the past two weeks you have been reading about a bad break I got. Yet today I consider myself the luckiest man on the face of the earth. I have been in ballparks for seventeen years and I have never received anything but kindness and encouragement from you fans.
>
> Look at these grand men. Which of you wouldn't consider it the highlight of his career just to associate with them for even one day? Sure, I'm lucky. Who wouldn't consider it an honor to have known Jacob Ruppert? Also, the builder of baseball's greatest empire, Ed Barrow? To have spent six years with that wonderful little fellow, Miller Huggins? Then to have spent the next nine years with that outstanding leader, that smart student of psychology, the best manager in baseball today, Joe McCarthy? Sure, I'm lucky. When the New York Giants, a team you would give your right arm to beat, and vice versa, sends you a gift, that's something. When everybody down to the groundskeepers and those boys in white coats remember you with trophies, that's something. When you have a wonderful mother-in-law who takes sides with you in squabbles with her own daughter, that's something. When you have a father and mother who work all their lives so that you can have an education and build your body, it's a blessing. When you have a wife who has been a tower of strength and shown more courage than you dreamed existed, that's the finest I know.
>
> So I close in saying that I might have had a bad break, but I have an awful lot to live for. Thank you.

Joe Williams reported, "No Barrymore could have touched the hearts of listeners more deeply than Gehrig." Babe Ruth, estranged from Gehrig for years, walked over and hugged the man who had delivered baseball's most memorable speech. In the Yankees Stadium grandstands and at home glued to the radio, America wept.

Until July 4, 1939, Lou Gehrig had led a storybook life. By talent and perseverance, he had lifted himself and his parents from poverty, played a key role on many championship teams, found a woman to love who reciprocated his tenderness, and, finally, received an outpouring of affection from the American people. The happy storybook soon became a cruel tragedy.

The Rest of the Season: More Honors, Less Control

ONE WEEK AFTER HIS APPRECIATION DAY, Lou Gehrig served as honorary captain for the American League in the 1939 All-Star Game held at Yankees Stadium. The Yankees first baseman had played in each of the previous six All-Star Games. Joe DiMaggio observed the other American League players follow the lead of the six Yankees on the team. They allowed him to stumble and fall in the locker room while suiting up, knowing Gehrig could tolerate a bruised body better than bruised pride.

For the remainder of 1939, Gehrig's capacity to accomplish the routine diminished rapidly. No longer could he shoot pool. No longer could he shuffle or even deal his cards in the Yankees' bridge games on the train. His legs buckled. His fingers shook. Despite the daily ravages of ALS, however, he held on to the hope that somehow he could come back.

Many baseball historians regard the 1939 Yankees, which Gehrig watched from the dugout, as baseball's greatest team in this century. Led by Most Valuable Player and batting champion DiMaggio, the Bronx Bombers never lost the league lead after May 11, and ended the season 17 games ahead of the second-place Boston Red Sox. The men in pin stripes then met Cincinnati in the World Series. Gehrig's former Yankees teammates (he had officially retired at the July 4 ceremonies) acknowledged their comrade's courageous contribution to the year by voting him a full share of their Series money.

The cover of the 1939 World Series opening game program pictured only Gehrig. It featured an article titled "History of the Yankees Ball Club," which captured the time's prevalent feelings of reverence and sadness:

> In relating the story of the New York club it is eminently fitting to pay a tribute to Henry Louis Gehrig. In his fifteenth season with the team, after he had played in 2,130 consecutive league contests, he was forced to take to the sidelines, his career finished.
>
> No man gave more to the Yankees as a team. No great player ever was more self-effacing for the interests of his club. His retirement is one of the most tragic losses suffered by baseball.

Following the Yankees' four-game sweep of the Reds in the Series, on the train ride home from Cincinnati, manager Joe McCarthy snapped at his celebrating players. "Cut that kid stuff out! I thought I was managing professionals!" DiMaggio surmised the skipper's moodiness could have come only from being depressed over knowing his favorite player would never again enter the Yankees dugout.

Yankees president Ed Barrow arranged for the ball club to commemorate Gehrig's contributions. For the first time, a major-league team retired a uniform number. Furthermore, Barrow decided no one in the future could use Gehrig's locker.

After the season, the Baseball Writers of America decided to accelerate the inevitable. They voted to waive the Hall of Fame rule requiring a player to be out of the game for at least one year before becoming eligible for induction. In December 1939, the Iron Horse entered baseball's place of immortality, with a lifetime .340 batting average and 493 career home runs.

The Final Eighteen Months

LOU GEHRIG LEFT BASEBALL FOR GOOD AT THE END OF 1939, since the Yankees inexplicably made no offer of an executive position. Impressed by Gehrig's strength of character, Mayor LaGuardia hired Gehrig to work as a New York City Parole Commissioner after the World Series.

By all accounts, baseball's Iron Horse served admirably in his position with the city during 1940 until he could no longer walk to his office. While Gehrig served on the job, Eleanor accompanied him to provide much-needed assistance. He soon lacked the dexterity to light a cigarette or even hold it in his mouth. Though his weight and strength declined rapidly, the proud Gehrig refused to use a wheelchair.

In retirement, Lou Gehrig's spirits remained remarkably high, but as his agony and helplessness grew, he no longer called himself "lucky." He received thirty thousand fan letters. Friends came by his home often to show their support. Finally, baseball's "Quiet Hero" died in his sleep on June 2, 1941, the former 200-pounder weighing 125 at the end.

His memory endured. The release of the box office smash *Pride of the Yankees* in 1942 preserved the simple poignancy of Lou Gehrig's life and death. Movie fans begged superstar Gary Cooper wherever he went for the rest of his life to recite the "luckiest man on the face of the earth" speech, and he graciously obliged.

In his biography of Gehrig, Richard Hubler described an incident involving celebrated war correspondent Quentin Reynolds. When the journalist returned to the United States in the early 1940s after witnessing Nazi bombing raids throughout Europe, he met an Englishman with a story to tell. The Brit told Reynolds of the bomb removal squad leader who had transported a ticking time bomb from the middle of a crowded city to a rural dumping ground where the bomb finally exploded without injuring anyone. The Englishman gushed, "It was magnificent. You, I'll wager, have never seen anything approaching such courage."

Reynolds replied, "Yes, I have. I knew Lou Gehrig."

By the end of 1939, America knew Lou Gehrig.

The Kid. (Copyright: Mark Rucker, Transcendental Graphics)

CHAPTER TWO

The Kid Arrives at the Show

As Gehrig Exits, Ted Williams Enters

After two days of rain, Lou Gehrig and the New York Yankees finally opened the 1939 season at Yankees Stadium on April 20 against the Boston Red Sox. As the disease-ravaged Gehrig struggled in the field (one error) and at the plate (0-4), a frisky twenty-year-old stringbean kid saw his first official major league game that day. Six-foot-four, 175-pound Theodore Samuel Williams was not in the bleachers to see his first game, but witnessed it as the Red Sox starting right fielder. During their one and only meeting on the baseball field, Gehrig and Williams had two encounters. Williams ran past the Yankees first baseman in legging out a double off the wall, and then caught Gehrig's only solid blow of the day, drilled directly at the rookie outfielder.

Before 1939, sportswriters often ignored Gehrig, dubbing him "the Quiet Hero." Gehrig gave dull interviews. No tape measures were needed for his home runs. His private life made no headlines. Gehrig measured up to the public's expectation that a sports hero should be modest and polite, but his colorlessness sold no copy.

After 1939, Ted Williams became too colorful. "Terrible Ted" spewed four-letter words, saliva, and anything else at critics he perceived as unjust. Williams became sport's first anti-hero, and his antics sold newspapers. Longtime newspaper columnist Harold Kaese noted: "In Boston, you're not a sportswriter until you've psychoanalyzed Ted Williams."

Gehrig's colorlessness and Williams's overabundance of color caused them to share the dubious distinction of being two of only three men in baseball history to have the Baseball Writers of America reject them as league Most Valuable Players in years when they won the triple crown.[1]

In 1934, the sportswriters chose as American League Most Valuable Player the league champion Tigers' fiery catcher Mickey Cochrane (with stats of .320, two homers, and 76 runs batted in), overlooking the quiet Gehrig's .363, 49 homers, and 165 runs batted in. Two-time triple-crown winner Williams failed to attain MVP status in 1942 and 1947, losing out first to steady Yankees second baseman Joe Gordon and then Joe DiMaggio, despite averaging 31 points higher in the batting title race, pounding out 15 more home runs, and driving in 25 more runs than the Yankees teammates in their MVP years. The oversight was particularly egregious in 1947, when the somber DiMaggio edged out the abrasive Williams by one vote because *Boston Globe* writer Melville Webb failed to vote for Williams at all, thinking his unfavorite son not worthy of even tenth-place consideration in a triple-crown season.

In addition to their one common game and triple-crown/MVP oversight, Gehrig and Williams shared something else. During his final season in 1939, for the first time in his career, Lou felt a genuine kinship with writers and fans. The Iron Horse had been underappreciated through 2,122 consecutive games, playing in the sizable shadows of Babe Ruth and then Joe DiMaggio. Noted *New York World* columnist Franklin P. Adams accurately described Gehrig's relative anonymity: "Lou Gehrig, Lou Gehrig. Wasn't he the guy who hit all those home runs the year Ruth broke the record?" Amyotrophic lateral sclerosis brought the "Quiet Hero" out of the shadows in 1939, allowing Gehrig for the first time in his career to enjoy the public adulation which had eluded him before being attacked by the crippling disease.

---

[1]The other was the Phillies' Chuck Klein, who lost out to pitcher Carl Hubbell (23-12 record, 1.66 earned-run average) as the National League's MVP in 1933. Klein had won the award the previous year.

Like Gehrig, Ted Williams felt that same kinship with the press and crowd during most of 1939. Boston's Splendid Splinter enjoyed a rookie season honeymoon before beginning a twenty-year war with Boston writers and fans that lasted until 1960. The man best known for refusing to tip his cap to the crowd throughout his career tipped it repeatedly during 1939. Young Williams went so far as to make a spectacle of acknowledging crowd approval that year, lifting his cap by the button on top, dropping it on his head, and then laughing with the fans.

Baseball's most renowned necktie-avoider actually rented a tuxedo and wore a bow tie to the Boston Writers Dinner when he received the 1939 Tim Murnane Award, given annually to the Red Sox MVP. Thirty years later, Williams would reflect, "I can't imagine anyone having a better, happier first year in the big leagues."

Throughout his rookie season, Ted Williams referred to himself as "the Kid." The nickname stuck because it fit. Whether he was a twenty-year-old rookie, a forty-year-old veteran, or a fifty-year-old manager, when the subject turned to hitting, Williams became enthusiastic in a manner befitting the most animated child. Ted Williams had a year of achievement and fun in 1939. He received praise, respect, and precious little criticism. It was the Kid's year to smile.

Before the Show: The Kid Learns from the Masters

AS A TEENAGER PASSING THROUGH THE MINOR LEAGUES, Williams seized on the opportunity to question baseball's great hitters about what he already referred to as "the art of hitting." While a minor leaguer with the San Diego Padres in 1936 and 1937, the Kid learned the most from opposing San Francisco Seals manager Lefty O'Doul, owner of a .349 lifetime major league batting average. After telling the press Williams was the greatest hitter in the Pacific Coast League since Paul Waner and that he expected Williams to become one of the greatest left-handed hitters ever, O'Doul relieved any self-doubts Williams might have had by instructing the young slugger never to let anyone tamper with his swing.[2]

[2]Twenty-five years later, Williams would pass on the same advice to an insecure twenty-one-year-old named Carl Yastrzemski.

As a Minneapolis Miller in 1938, Williams latched on to batting coach Rogers Hornsby, a lifetime .358 hitter and baseball's only other two-time triple-crown winner. Hornsby emphasized one central point to his inquisitive pupil: "Get a good pitch to hit." One year after Williams accepted Hornsby's advice, Yankees pitcher Spud Chandler described the staff meeting in early 1939 aimed at going over the best way to pitch to the Red Sox hitters. The pitchers agreed that the best way to pitch to Ted Williams was first high and tight, and then low and away. After the game Chandler told reporters, "I'll tell you what we found out. We found out that high and tight is 'Ball One' and low and away is 'Ball Two,' and then you have to throw the ball over the plate."

Rogers Hornsby became Williams's father-figure *on and off* the field. Growing up in San Diego, Williams had rarely seen his own father (a drifter who worked odd hours as a cut-rate photographer) and had idolized Hornsby, baseball's only three-time .400 hitter. In 1938, far from home and having no family or friends in Minneapolis, the young player attached himself to his batting hero. Williams acknowledged the special relationship in his autobiography, *My Turn at Bat*:

> I thought Hornsby was great. He wasn't a very diplomatic guy. If he had a dislike about anything, he came out with it. He wasn't big for criticism, I don't mean that, but he didn't mind laying a blast now and again... If the owner of the club said something he disagreed with, Hornsby would say, "What the hell do you know about it?" He was all the time getting into wringers for what he said.
>
> I liked Hornsby because he talked to me, a kid of nineteen, and, boy, I picked his brain for everything I could. We'd talk hitting, and I'd ask personal questions I had no business asking. "How much money did you lose at the track? How much did you bet?"...
>
> Every day I'd stay out after practice with Hornsby...He was like any of the really great players I have known—he just couldn't get enough of it. He was pushing fifty then, I guess, but we'd have hitting contests and he'd be right in there, hitting one line drive after another....

Ted Williams's description of Rogers Hornsby could have been used to describe the Kid himself at age fifty—tactless, helpful, and still a great hitter. A more accurate title for Williams's autobiography would have been *My War With Baseball*, but Hornsby had already used it for his book. No other significant acquaintance of Williams's youth had an ornery, outspoken, cocky nature like the Rajah. The Kid's daily exposure to his hard-boiled mentor surely accelerated the evolution of Ted Williams's own ornery, outspoken, and cocky personality. Using understandable but imprudent judgment, Williams figured that if petulance seemed to work for his hero, then surely it would work for the hero's disciple.

The First Big League Exposure: 1938 Spring Training

BEFORE JOINING HORNSBY AT MINNEAPOLIS IN 1938, Williams got his first taste of big league life during the Red Sox spring training in Sarasota. Boston had a veteran team led by future Hall of Famers Jimmy Foxx, Lefty Grove, and player-manager Joe Cronin. Williams immediately distinguished himself at the plate. After only a few days in camp, all conversations stopped when young Ted Williams entered the batting cage. Clearly, the Kid had a big league stroke.

Williams also immediately distinguished himself by demonstrating he lacked a big league temperament. A year away from making the team, Williams became the first Red Sox pre-rookie to nickname veterans, calling manager Cronin and everyone else in camp "Scout." The young outfielder further aggravated his manager by expressing disappointment over having to ride buses to games, saying he thought big leaguers were above such bush league transportation.

The Kid's teenage arrogance was unprecedented. Former San Diego teammate Bobby Doerr excitedly told Williams upon his arrival at spring training, "Wait till you see Jimmy Foxx hit." Williams reportedly replied, "Wait till Foxx sees me hit." The Kid's first impression of baseball legend Lefty Grove was anything but respectful. "Sure is a funny-looking old geezer, isn't he?" As his final act of brashness, Williams tried to soothe the concerns of young Red Sox owner Tom Yawkey. "Don't look so worried, Tom. Foxx and me will take care of everything."

Besides alienating the Red Sox with his impudent mouth, Williams further estranged himself from Boston's brass by exhibiting a totally indifferent attitude toward fielding. Williams would stand in the outfield and take practice swings during preseason games, bewildering his coaches, who had somehow assumed Williams understood he had defensive responsibilities. As inquisitive and practice-oriented as the Kid was about hitting, he utilized little practice time learning the nuances of charging ground balls or playing caroms off the wall. Clearly, Ted Williams had no aspiration to be baseball's greatest player. From the outset of his career, Boston's Splendid Splinter limited his professional goal solely to baseball's offensive dimension.

Williams's mouth, his careless defense, and the 1938 Red Sox's projected capable outfield of Ben Chapman, Doc Cramer, and Joe Vosmik (who had hit .307, .305, and .325, respectively, in 1937) led manager Cronin to send Williams to Minneapolis at the close of spring training. The Bosox skipper expressed relief at seeing the problem child leave the team: "I don't think I can stand much more of this kid."

The teenage slugger took his demotion hard. As he departed from Sarasota, Williams pointed to the Red Sox's outfielders and told Boston equipment manager Johnny Orlando, "Tell those baboons I'll be back and that I'll make more money in a year than the three of them combined."

The Kid's cocky attitude aggravated leading Boston sportswriter Bill Cunningham into making one remarkably unprophetic prediction on Williams as training camp broke up. Despite O'Doul's well-publicized evaluation of Williams and Red Sox general manager (and lifetime .333 hitter) Eddie Collins publicly comparing Williams's swing to that of a fair country hitter named Joe Jackson, Cunningham wrote in his column: "Me? I don't like the way he stands at the plate. He bends his front knee inward and moves his foot just before he takes a swing... I don't believe this kid will ever hit half a midget's weight in a bathing suit."

Minneapolis—Williams's Ship Arrives

THE 1938 RED SOX OUTFIELD FULFILLED CRONIN'S EXPECTATIONS. Right fielder Ben Chapman had his greatest season hitting .340 and finishing third in the batting race. Doc Cramer played a great defensive center field, hit lead-off and averaged .301 with 198 hits, and scored 116 runs. Left fielder Joe Vosmick batted second, and led the league with 201 hits while averaging .324. All this production kept Ted Williams in the outfield at Minneapolis for the entire 1938 season.

Before Minneapolis, Williams's minor-league numbers had been decent but not spectacular. In San Diego, Williams had hit .271, with no homers, and 11 runs batted in, in only 42 games in 1936; followed by .291, 23 homers, and 98 runs batted in in 1937. At Minneapolis in 1938, under Hornsby's guidance, the Kid exploded with a .366 average, 43 homers, 142 runs batted in, and 114 walks. He even stole 15 bases. Williams's antics on the field (waving to kids in the stands and taking more practice swings as pitchers delivered) and off the field (punching out a glass water cooler) so aggravated manager Donie Bush that the skipper went to Minneapolis owner Tom Kelly and said "It's Williams or me." Kelly gave his manager no relief.

The strained relationship between Williams and Bush peaked during a late-season game after Williams hit a double. While coaching third base, Bush screamed at his teenage star leading off second, "... Not too far... Watch the pitcher... Be alert..." Williams acted as if he heard nothing. Finally, fed up with the base-running clichés, the Kid snapped back at his skipper, "I got here by myself. I'll get home by myself."

Besides learning patience from Hornsby, Ted Williams gained another important batting lesson at Minneapolis by accident. Fatigued by the season's rigors, Williams decided to use a teammate's lighter bat during a late-summer night game against Columbus. The increased bat speed helped Williams hit a grand slam in his first at bat. He would use lighter bats for the remainder of his career, becoming the first player in the big leagues to understand the importance of bat speed in generating power.

Despite his fielding and personality deficiencies, Ted Williams had hit his way to the major league show by the close of the 1938 season. The Red Sox knew they could not keep the Kid down on the farm any longer, and traded right fielder Chapman (with his .340 average) to Cleveland after the 1938 season to open up a spot in the Bosox starting lineup for Williams. The Kid reacted to the Chapman trade, saying, "I guess that shows what they think of me." The baseball world waited to see whether Ted Williams's hitting could speak louder than his mouth.

1939 Spring Training: Hitter, Interrogator, and Prophet

RECOVERING FROM THE FLU and not interested in getting off on the right foot with manager Cronin, Williams arrived a day late to Sarasota on March 7, 1939. Cronin verbally blasted his right fielder: "You're in a great city working for the best man (owner Tom Yawkey) in baseball. You've got a lot of ability and have had enough schooling. This is serious and there's no place in the game for clowning. I hope you take advantage of the chance you've got."

Cronin and the Red Sox knew Ted Williams would be a great hitter in the big leagues. The manager-shortstop had been a part of the awed bystanders watching Williams take batting practice in 1938, and the tradition continued in 1939. The Red Sox promoted Williams to the press as the league's best-projected rookie at a time when there was no official Rookie of the Year award. *The Sporting News* reported:

> The Boston Red Sox have already nominated Ted Williams [for rookie of the year], the kid outfielder who, in addition to being a great hitter, has the allure that goes with screwball tendencies.

Williams walked around spring training knowing he had a starting position in right field on Opening Day, but realizing he had a lot to learn about hitting American League pitchers. In his autobiography, Williams described himself at Sarasota in 1939 as "a nuisance to everybody, asking questions about hitting, asking about this pitcher or that one, quizzing every player on the team."

One of the Kid's favorite targets for questioning was seventy-three-year-old Bosox first base coach Hugh Duffy, whose lifetime batting average in the major leagues was .324. In 1894, Duffy had won the triple crown by hitting .438, with 236 hits, 18 homers, and 145 runs batted in during the "dead ball" era. Williams wanted to learn everything that

Ted Williams, the self-proclaimed "greatest hitter who ever lived." (National Baseball Library and Archive, Cooperstown, New York)

a .400 hitter could teach, so he interrogated Duffy in 1939, as he had done with Hornsby during 1938.

As training camp wore on, Williams was able to put his circumstances in perspective for *Baseball Magazine*:

> It may take me a year or two to get going very well in the majors, but I can afford that. I'm only twenty years old. I've seen players come up with lots lower averages than I ever made in the minors and make good up here so I don't see why I can't. As I go along, I figure to get bigger and stronger, and I know I'll get smarter with experience.

The 175-pound "human clothespin" at training camp began the process of achieving his goal of getting bigger and stronger. Malnourished as a youth, the six-foot-four Kid weighed 145 pounds during his first minor league season at San Diego. One big league scout reported to his team that Williams was "too frail for the majors." Receiving meal money on the road at San Diego, the Kid ate everything he could as if he were starved, and maybe he was. When San Diego sold Williams to the Red Sox after his second season, the club president told his enraged mother (who didn't want her favorite son to leave home) that Williams's constantly exceeding the two-dollar-a-day meal stipend made the young outfielder unaffordable. His appetite did not subside. By the end of the 1939 season, he weighed 185 pounds.[3]

After the Red Sox broke camp, but before going north for the season opener, the team went to Atlanta for an exhibition game with the minor league Atlanta Crackers. Late in the game, after going hitless in five trips to the plate and being booed for slamming down his bat, Williams failed to catch a foul pop fly. The petulant rookie outfielder picked up the ball in foul territory and threw it over the right-field grandstand. Cronin benched his young star on the spot, fined him fifty dollars,[4] and barked, "I don't understand you. You have all the

---

[3]Williams's appetite kept expanding after his rookie season. By 1950, he weighed two hundred pounds; by 1956, 224 pounds; and he grew to well over 250 pounds in retirement until his stroke in 1994.

[4]Not an insignificant amount of money in a year when Williams's salary was $4,500. An equivalent fine to today's $3-million-a-year ballplayer would exceed $33,000.

natural ability in the world... It seems to me you're intent on throwing away your big opportunity." The young right fielder snapped back, "I'll pay you fifty dollars for everyone I throw out if you'll pay me fifty dollars for every one I hit out." The Atlanta heave made every newspaper, and, clearly, Ted Williams's lack of self-control was going to give sportswriters plenty of material in the coming season.

Before the 1939 season started, the Kid told sportswriters of his simple career goal. It became the most important sentence in Ted Williams's life. "All I want out of life is that when I walk down the street, folks will say, 'There goes the greatest hitter who ever lived.' " The snickering sports world now waited to see whether the fresh rookie with the Joe Jackson swing could achieve his seemingly preposterous ambition.

The Rookie Season—1939

Opening Day arrived and the Yankees started 20-game winner Red Ruffing against Red Sox veteran Lefty Grove.

Waiting in the clubhouse for the game, Williams was approached by sportswriter Bob Considine. The UPI correspondent wanted to know the young slugger's perspective on whom he tried to imitate when he entered the batter's box. Following a thoughtful pause, the twenty-year-old Kid replied, "I hit like Ted Williams."

After leaving the locker room, Williams got his first view of Yankee Stadium. The rookie looked at the outfield and asked his teammates whether any hitter had ever hit a ball over the third deck. Williams was immediately setting his sights on achieving what no one had accomplished before. The incredulous Boston players winced.

Williams's first at bat against future Hall of Famer Ruffing resulted in a quick strikeout. The Red Sox veterans smiled and hoped the whiffing would produce a little humility. Pitcher Jack Wilson found Williams in the dugout and asked him, "Whataya think of this league now, Bush?" Williams snapped back, "That is one guy I know I'm going to hit and if he puts it in the same place again, I'm riding it out of here." The prophet fulfilled his prediction. Later in the game, Williams hit a double off Ruffing for his first major league hit. Later in the year, on Memorial Day, he hit his longest home run of 1939 off Ruffing, a 500-foot tape measure blast.

Ted Williams's first great major league game came on Sunday, April 23, 1939, at Fenway Park, against Connie Mack's hapless Philadelphia Athletics. Boston's phenom went four-for-five, knocking in three runs with a home run, double, and two singles. Following the game, the *Boston Herald* reported "thousands of fans lined up outside the park to wait for the appearance of their new hero." Connie Mack reflected on Williams's hitting display from the perspective of watching baseball's greatest players during his forty-five years as a manager in the big leagues. "I've never seen such a good-looking young boy." The *Boston Globe* headlined that after Williams's playing a grand total of four major league games, the rookie already provoked comparisons with none other than Babe Ruth. Wheaties put the Kid in their newspaper ads. A star was rising.

Williams's next monster game came on May 4, 1939, against the Tigers at Briggs Stadium. *The Sporting News* reported in its May 11 edition that "the highlight of the week was an exhibition of hitting by young Ted Williams that will not be forgotten for years to come." All Williams did that day was hit a two-run homer on top of the right field roof in the fourth inning. Later, accepting Tigers catcher Rudy York's dare by swinging away on a 3-0 pitch in the fifth inning, he smashed a three-run shot which traveled *over* the stadium roof. The bruised baseball landed in a taxi garage.

Ted Williams had become the first hitter to crush a ball out of Briggs Stadium. As Williams rounded third base after his second homer of the day, veteran Tigers third baseman Billy Rogell asked the Kid, "What the hell you been eating?" After the game, Detroit's Hank Greenberg (coming off a 1938 season when he had hit a mere 58 home runs) sent a message to the Red Sox locker room asking if the Kid would be so kind as to give the league's 1935 MVP a few batting tips the next day. After less than two weeks in the major leagues, Ted Williams was no longer a rookie. He had become a legend.

Between his May 4 power display against the Tigers and the July 11 All-Star Game, Williams continued to destroy American League pitching. Over a period of five consecutive games in late May, Boston's rookie outfielder hit four home runs which each measured over four hundred feet. During the last three weeks in June, the Kid hit .458. By July 3, longtime Boston sportswriter Hy Hurwitz had renamed Fenway Park "Williamsburg."

To better accommodate Williams's power, Yawkey started developing plans to bring in the right-field fence in time for the 1940 season. All these circumstances manifested constant comparisons to Babe Ruth, as the press labeled Fenway "the House that Ted Rebuilt."

Williams's defensive lapses remained part of his repertoire. Red Sox relief pitcher Joe Heving spoke for the staff about the mixed blessing of having Ted Williams as Boston's starting right fielder: "Williams is killing the ball at the plate and leaving it alone in the outfield." Cronin groaned and screamed as his rookie free spirit continued to ignore his defensive responsibilities by taking practice swings in the outfield with an imaginary bat or shooting pigeons with an imaginary rifle bearing a remarkable resemblance to a baseball glove. By season's end, Williams led major league outfielders in errors with 19, seven more than Enos Slaughter, the second most error-prone outfielder.

Despite hitting .306 and leading the league with 67 runs batted in at the All-Star break, Ted Williams was left off the American League All-Star team for the only time in his career. Leadoff .331 hitter Bosox teammate Doc Cramer, Yankees' .300 hitter and defensive whiz George "Twinkletoes" Selkirk, and Joe DiMaggio (hitting a cool .420 at the break) played outfield for the American League that year. The trio then led the league to victory,[5] making Williams's absence from the team more palatable and leaving the Splinter's considerable Mid-Summer Classic heroics for future years.[6]

In mid-July, as the Red Sox briefly challenged the defending world champion Yankees by winning 12 consecutive games (to come within five-and-a-half games of the league lead), commentators observed a phenomenon. Fans at Red Sox games, whether home or away, stayed

---

[5]Selkirk and DiMaggio each drove in runs in the American League's 3-1 victory.

[6]In the 1941 All-Star Game, Williams's homer with two outs in the bottom of the ninth off Clyde Passeau won the game for the American League. In the 1946 classic, Williams's second homer of the game off Rip Sewell's "eephus," blooper pitch provided arguably the most celebrated moment in All-Star Game history.

in their seats no matter how lopsided the score, until satisfied that Ted Williams had had his last time at bat.

The respect from the players around the batting cage and the fans sitting through blowouts registered one unambiguous point to baseball people everywhere. Red Sox teammate Doc Cramer verbalized it during a quiet car ride with his young outfield teammate in 1939. "You know who the best hitter in the league is right now? You are, Ted. You're the best." Williams's impossible dream to be recognized as baseball's best hitter had come true in his rookie season.

Being the "best" hitter didn't make Williams everyone's friend. He and manager Cronin tangled on August 8 in Philadelphia. The Kid's mind was simply not on the game that day. Perhaps Williams had received a letter from his mother telling him of family problems at home in San Diego.[7] Perhaps the weary, twenty-year-old right fielder hit the August wall that hot day, facing Connie Mack's perennial last-place deadheads and knowing the Red Sox's mediocre pitching simply could not keep them in the race against the Yankees. Whatever the reason, Ted Williams could only go through the motions on August 8.

In his first at bat, Williams jogged to first base on an infield ground out. At his next turn in the box, after slamming a line drive off the left field wall, Williams trotted to second base. At the end of the inning, Cronin confronted Williams about the rookie's lack of hustle, but the Kid insisted that he wanted to play. Finally, in the sixth inning, with two out and the bases loaded, Williams popped up to center field. Angered by his failure to deliver in the clutch, Williams shuffled toward first base. A strong wind caught the ball and blew it beyond the center fielder's grasp. A hustling base runner would have ended up on second, but Williams barely beat the throw to first. Cronin jerked his young star from the game immediately, and somehow managed not to blow his stack. The next day, manager and rookie star talked before the game. Cronin tried to give Williams some fatherly advice:

> "Ted, you're a boy playing a man's game, but if you're gonna stay in baseball, you gotta be a man. You must learn there are other things

[7]That summer, his parents had finally decided to separate after an extended estrangement, and Williams's brother Danny became a certified juvenile delinquent.

besides base hits in the game. You must learn to accept the bitter with the sweet. You cannot get sulky because things don't go exactly as you wish."

Satisfied his young star had heard the message, Cronin had Williams in right field that afternoon on August 9. In his next eight games, the Kid rapped out 15 hits. By early September, *The Sporting News* featured an article on rookie Ted Williams who "may or may not be another Babe Ruth… At the rate he is slugging the ball, and learning how to improve his play, he may achieve what has been considered impossible to those who have chanted 'There will never be another Babe Ruth.' "

As the 1939 season ended, Williams's twenty-year battle with the fans and press began. In a meaningless September game, when it was clear the Yankees had locked up the pennant, Williams let a ground ball go through his legs. As he chased it, the Fenway right-field fans screamed their disapproval. Williams responded by spewing profanity at the crowd, causing them to retaliate in kind. Hornsby's protégé determined then and there how he would win this war. There would be no more tips of the cap to Boston's fickle fans for the rest of Ted Williams's career.

At the same time, the Kid's relationship with the press also soured. Williams's recent biographer John Holway tells the story of veteran *Boston Post* sportswriter, purported hitting critic, and noted boozer Bill Cunningham approaching Williams for an interview late in the 1939 season. Cunningham had covered the Red Sox since the time of Williams's birth. As the dean of Boston's sports scribes started the conversation with the Kid, Williams interrupted and said, "I'd rather wait until you sober up." Rogers Hornsby would have been pleased. Williams's "war with baseball" had started.

By season's end, Ted Williams had put up staggering numbers—a .327 batting average with a .609 slugging percentage, 44 doubles, 11 triples, 31 homers, 131 runs scored, 145 runs batted in, and 107 walks with only 64 strikeouts. These numbers put the Kid first in the American League in runs batted in,[8] second in doubles and runs scored, third in homers, and fourth in Most Valuable Player

[8]Williams thus became the only rookie in baseball history to lead the major leagues in runs batted in.

balloting.[9] Despite Jimmie Foxx's hitting .360 with 36 homers and 105 runs batted in, the Boston sportswriters named Williams team Most Valuable Player and *The Sporting News* chose him as one of the top three outfielders in the major leagues. No one argued with the frequent comparisons to Ruth, and Williams made a special effort to satisfy his legions of child admirers. With the right-field fence coming in at Fenway in preparation for the coming 1940 season, Ted Williams had the world by the tail.

After the Honeymoon—1940

PLAYERS APPROACHING THEIR SECOND YEAR in the major leagues try to avoid "the sophomore jinx." In 1940, despite hitting .344 with 23 homers and 113 runs batted in, the jinx hit Ted Williams.

Cronin moved Williams to left field giving the Kid less territory to cover and allowing him to avoid the horrible Fenway Park right-field glare. Boston's left-field fans seemed louder and more antagonistic to the rabbit-eared outfielder. The sore spot with the fans involved Williams's declining home-run production despite the shortened Fenway right-field power alley.

An easy explanation existed for the Kid's diminished home-run total. By 1940, American League pitchers had learned prudence that dictated they pitch *around* Williams. *The Sporting News* of June 13, 1940, reported pitchers were "throwing him 'nothing stuff' constantly. He never sees a fast ball." Hornsby's strategy was frustrated as Williams could not "get a good pitch to hit." This Ted-avoidance became an acceptable defensive strategy for the rest of the league as Williams's supporting Red Sox cast slipped significantly from 1939 to 1940—Foxx dropped 63 points in average, Doerr 27 points, and Cronin 23 points.

By August 1940, Williams's complaints about his $10,000 salary, the sportswriters who blasted him, and the fickle Boston fans led to the young star demanding a trade, and publicly wishing he could quit

[9]DiMaggio won his first MVP award that year after spending most of the season above .400. He also won his first batting title with a .381 mark, hit 30 home runs, and knocked in 126. He did all this in only 120 games.

baseball and lead the quiet life of a fireman. Hornsby was gone, and Williams was a twenty-one-year-old Kid afloat, with no significant ties to family or friends. His publicity-shy girlfriend (soon, first wife) chose to spend the year in secluded Minnesota. Williams decided to deal with his loneliness as his mentor Hornsby surely would have done, by lashing out at a baseball world seemingly focused only on his mistakes. Ted Williams's outspoken, victimized perspective never changed for the rest of his major league career.

The Legacy: What About the Kid and His 1939 Ambition?

DESPITE THE TANTRUMS AND TRIBULATIONS WITH FANS and writers during the last twenty years of his career, positive aspects of Ted Williams's career and character endured. As a hitter, Williams's only challenger to achieving his 1939 "greatest ever" ambition was Babe Ruth, and their stats were close. His lifetime batting average was two points higher than Babe's, although Ruth's slugging average was significantly higher.[10] Williams won more batting titles, Ruth more home-run crowns. Williams lost four-and-a-half years to military service,[11] played night games, faced stronger relief pitchers, and did not have a Lou Gehrig following him in the lineup. Whether those circumstances overcome the home run (714 to 521) and runs batted in (2,211 to 1,839) differential between Williams and Ruth obviously cannot be answered with certainty.

Off the field, Williams's lifetime commitment to supporting Boston's Jimmy Fund and children's hospitals, his courageous military record covering two wars, and his leadership in getting Negro league players inducted into the Hall of Fame will hopefully be as much a part of his legacy as his four-letter words, expectorations, and divorces. On the field, in addition to his incredible hitting records,

---

[10]Ruth ranks first all-time in career slugging percentage with a .690 mark, followed by Williams at .634.

[11]Three years of his baseball career were lost to military service during World War II, when Williams was between the ages of twenty-four and twenty-six. Those are regarded by baseball historian John Holway as typically the most productive years in a hitter's career.

Ted Williams's positive relationship with his fellow ballplayers and umpires (who *never* ejected him from a game during his entire career) should diminish the public's disappointment in his fielding deficiencies, batting slump during the 1946 World Series, and refusal to tip his cap during the last twenty years of his career.

John Updike's *New Yorker* magazine essay, "Hub Fans Bid Kid Adieu," now part of every respectable baseball anthology, has immortalized Ted Williams's final major league game on September 28, 1960. On that day, Boston's Splendid Splinter faced two young Baltimore pitchers, Steve Barber and Jack Fisher, both born in 1939 during Williams's rookie year.

Ted Williams delivered a home run off Fisher in his final career at bat to fulfill the baseball world's impossible expectations, just as he had done on the last day of the 1941 season when he stared down a .400 batting average and made .400 blink.[12] If all that really counted to Boston's Splendid Splinter was what he accomplished in the batter's box, then his 1939 stated ambition became baseball's most miraculous prophecy. No fictional "called shot" myth for Williams. Williams's career walk measured up to his rookie talk.

In 1980, two full decades after Williams's retirement as a player, and forty-one years after Williams expressed his goal to be recognized for his hitting by people on the street, Joe Falls of the *Detroit News* randomly interviewed one hundred people on a street in Deerfield Beach, Florida. The Detroit sportswriter asked the subjects of his poll if they had an awareness of someone named "Ted Williams." As they walked the street that day, the people of Deerfield Beach batted 1.000.

---

[12]Williams entered the last day of the 1941 season with a .3995 batting average, which statisticians would have rounded up to .400. Cronin invited Williams to sit out the doubleheader against Philadelphia, but the Kid refused, saying he didn't deserve .400 if he failed to play the final two games. Williams proceeded to get six hits in the doubleheader to finish the year at .406. However, Williams still didn't win the MVP, because DiMaggio's 56 consecutive-game hitting streak impressed voting sportswriters more than did Williams's .406 average.

Rookie manager Leo Durocher (on right, standing) witnesses a neat hook slide. (Copyright: Mark Rucker, Transcendental Graphics)

CHAPTER THREE

THE LIP AT THE HELM

Leo Durocher Begins His Managerial Career under Larry MacPhail at Brooklyn

As TWENTY-YEAR-OLD TED WILLIAMS began the 1939 season as a rookie outfielder in Boston, thirty-three-year-old Dodgers shortstop Leo Durocher became a major league manager for the first time.

In terms of baseball, the Kid and the Lip had many things in common. Both had brash mouths. Williams aimed his four-letter words at sportswriters and jeering fans, while Durocher shot his expletives at umpires and opposing teams. Both possessed magnificent talent—Williams as a hitter, Durocher as a field strategist. Most importantly, both compiled impressive records. Williams has the sixth-highest career batting average in baseball history, while Durocher's managerial stats place him seventh on the all-time list for both games managed and games won.

Off the field, Williams and Durocher had very different priorities. While Williams spent his winters fishing in remote waters to remove himself from the limelight, Durocher preferred to stay in the gossip columns year-round with high-profile running buddies Frank Sinatra, George Raft, Bugsy Siegel, and a host of starlets. Where Williams's career was interrupted for more than four years by distinguished military service in two wars, Durocher's years as manager were broken up by his 1947 suspension resulting from "unpleasant incidents detrimental to baseball," per the ambiguous and still unexplained pronouncement of Commissioner "Happy" Chandler. While Williams gave of his time to the Jimmy Fund and other Boston children's charities, Durocher had time away from the ballpark only for playing cards, shooting pool, and chasing women.

These on-the-field similarities and off-the-field differences led to one result. Ted Williams entered the Hall of Fame in 1966 as a first-ballot, slam-dunk choice. In 1991, Leo Durocher died an embittered man, passed over for more than a decade by Cooperstown's Veterans Committee.[1]

Durocher Comes to Brooklyn—1938

DUROCHER'S ACHIEVEMENTS AS A MAJOR LEAGUE MANAGER began at Brooklyn in 1939. He had come to Brooklyn from St. Louis as baseball's best defensive shortstop in exchange for four marginal players[2] after the close of the 1937 season. Infielder Durocher had captained the "Gas House Gang" Cardinals to perennial pennant contention since 1933, including a 1934 World Series championship over the Detroit Tigers.

In typical Leo Durocher fashion, when the Lip learned of his trade to the second-division Dodgers, he exploded at Cardinals executive Branch Rickey for sending him from the St. Louis penthouse to the Brooklyn basement. Rickey responded first with a subtle jab: "I have heard, Leo, that you don't make friends easily. Now I understand why. The St. Louis general manager then silenced his departing captain by explaining the big picture. "Just go there and keep your nose clean, Leo. You have ambitions beyond being just a player, don't you?"

In his 1948 book, *The Dodgers and Me,* Durocher recognized Rickey's contribution to his managerial career. "Branch Rickey had

---

[1]In 1994 the Veterans Committee finally, posthumously elected Durocher to the Hall of Fame.

[2]The four players sent to St. Louis in the trade for Durocher were utility infielder Joe Stripp, who had batted .243 in 1937; outfielder Johnny Cooney, who had all of two home runs over a twenty-year career; pitcher Roy Henshaw, coming off a 5-12 season; and infielder Jim Bucher, a .253 hitter in 1937.

ideas about my managing and really wanted to give me a break. I wasn't through [as a player]; he could have made a better deal for me elsewhere. But he picked my spot."

Durocher arrived in Brooklyn for the 1938 season along with "Roaring Redhead" Larry MacPhail, whom the Dodgers had hired for the dual positions of executive vice president and general manager out of economic necessity. National League president Ford Frick had labored to keep the league alive through the Great Depression. To rescue the floundering Brooklyn franchise, Frick (with an assist from Branch Rickey) recommended former Cincinnati general manager MacPhail to Brooklyn owner Stephen McKeever, whose team faced insolvency entering the 1938 season. At Cincinnati from 1934-1936, innovative Larry MacPhail had introduced airplane travel (in 1934) and night baseball (in 1935) to the major leagues. More importantly to Frick, MacPhail had shown a remarkable capacity to increase attendance and generate revenues with a second-division ball club.

After withdrawing from the game before the 1937 campaign for an admitted fear of having a nervous breakdown, MacPhail again heard baseball's siren song. So he returned to Brooklyn in 1938 for what would be his greatest professional challenge—to raise attendance, pay off debts, improve a dull, losing team, and somehow coexist with Leo Durocher. The Roaring Redhead agreed to come to the Dodgers on the condition that his contract have provisions which (1) gave him "full and complete authority over the operations of the club," and (2) adjusted his compensation based on attendance at Ebbets Field.

The 1938 Brooklyn Dodgers found themselves coming off a sixth-place, 62-91 season. The 1937 season had ended with the Dodgers losing 16 of their last 17 games. The team's only All-Star player, Van Lingle Mungo, had finished 1937 with a record of 9-11. No player hit over eight home runs. Attendance for the year was below five hundred thousand.

During the Great Depression, Dodgers owner McKeever had allowed Ebbets Field to decay. Paint peeled, seats broke, weeds grew, and McKeever did nothing about it. Thugs employed as ushers made life dangerous for the few die-hard fans willing to sit through an inevitable home-team loss. Lead Dodgers lender, the Brooklyn

Trust Company, placed a representative on the ball club's board of directors. The Dodgers' condition paralleled the country's depressed times.

Enter MacPhail as executive for the Dodgers in 1938. To get the rehabilitation process started, the new GM fast-talked the Brooklyn Trust Company to advance another $200,000 to the team's existing $1.2 million indebtedness. With the infusion of money, Ebbets Field began to shine for the first time since its construction. Fences got painted, chairs were fixed, dugouts and clubhouses got refurbished, the playing field was manicured, civil Brooklynites happy to have a job replaced thug-ushers, and established alcoholic MacPhail installed a lounge behind the press box.

The 1938 team improved slightly to 69-80 under Hall of Fame spitball-pitcher-turned-manager Burleigh Grimes. Before the season, MacPhail had obtained slick-fielding, slugging first baseman Dolf Camilli[3] from the financially strapped Phillies for $50,000. Camilli proceeded to prove his worth by hitting 24 homers and knocking in 100 runs. Although second baseman Johnny Hudson and third baseman Cookie Lavagetto led the league in errors at their positions in 1938, Leo Durocher picked up part of the slack by leading all other shortstops in fielding. His infield wizardry and leadership led to his selection as the National League's starting shortstop in the 1938 All-Star Game, despite hitting .219 for the year.

In addition to the greatly improved ballpark facility and slightly improved team, Brooklyn attendance in 1938 jumped by almost a quarter-million for two other reasons. On June 15, 1938, after obtaining a $72,000 extension of credit from General Electric, MacPhail brought lights to Ebbets Field for night baseball, just as he had done in 1935 at Crosley Field in Cincinnati.[4] The 38,748 fans who came to the ballpark that night witnessed not only Brooklyn's first night game, but also saw Cincinnati's Johnny Vander Meer pitch his second consecutive no-hitter.

---

[3]In 1937 Camilli had batted .339 with 27 home runs, and had led the league's first basemen with a .994 fielding average.

[4]And as he would do on May 28, 1946, at Yankee Stadium upon becoming a Yankees executive.

On June 18, 1938, three days after turning on the Ebbets Field lights, MacPhail then tried to jack up attendance by signing Babe Ruth to coach first base for the Dodgers. Under his Dodgers contract, Ruth, who had played his last major league game in 1935, was required to take batting practice before each home game. If MacPhail could not obtain a superstar hitter to play for the Dodgers during National League games, he could at least try to raise attendance by getting baseball's highest-profile star to hit tape-measure blasts off practice pitchers before the games.

The Babe had aspired to a managerial position since his retirement, and signed on expecting to become Grimes's successor. Ever tactful Leo the Lip told the Bambino in no uncertain terms: "Listen, you big slob. I've got a brain. All you've got is a strong back. We'll see who stays in the big leagues the longest... The line for aspiring Dodgers managers forms over on the right behind me."

The strained relationship between Ruth and Durocher[5] finally resulted in a fistfight in the Dodgers clubhouse late in the 1938 season arising from Durocher's calling a successful hit-and-run play while at bat—with Lavagetto on first—for which first-base coach Ruth wanted to take credit. By the end of the 1938 season, home-run king, man-child Ruth was the man no major league team wanted to hire, while slick-fielding shortstop Durocher had become a rising leadership star.

As the 1938 season approached its end, the Dodgers were well on their way toward fulfilling manager Grimes's preseason prediction of a seventh-place finish. In early September, MacPhail broke the news to Burleigh Grimes that his contract would not be renewed. The discouraged Brooklyn skipper, with three weeks left in the season, told Durocher of his plan to leave the team immediately. Durocher counseled and finally convinced Grimes to stick it out. Burleigh showed his appreciation by encouraging MacPhail to hire Durocher as Brooklyn's next manager.

MacPhail had a negative knee-jerk reaction to Grimes's suggestion. Leo Durocher had no prior managerial experience. Furthermore, the

---

[5]As Yankees teammates in the 1920s, they had battled at the poker table, and Ruth once accused Durocher of stealing his watch.

Lip's frequent spats on and off the field reflected a lack of self-control. Considering all the baseball people in the country, why choose an inexperienced loose cannon?

By the time the 1938 World Series started, MacPhail reconsidered. He decided that what the 1939 Dodgers team needed most was spark, an alien concept to the 1938 Dodgers. If Leo Durocher could be counted on for anything on the baseball field, it was his intense, take-no-prisoners style of play. Durocher told anyone who would listen, "I ain't playing this game for fun. I'm playing it for keeps."

Finances probably also played a part in MacPhail's reconsideration of Durocher. The Great Depression spawned the era of the player-manager. During the 1930s, the New York Giants had been managed by first baseman Bill Terry, the Cardinals by second baseman Frank Frisch, and the Cubs by catcher Gabby Hartnett. All were ultimately Hall of Fame players and all won National League pennants during the Great Depression as player-managers. In the American League, the only chinks in the Yankees' armor since 1931 had come from the 1933 Senators led by manager-shortstop Joe Cronin; and the 1934 and 1935 Tigers managed by catcher Mickey Cochrane.

In the days of daytime depression baseball, few could afford to attend weekday games during working hours. Those out of work obviously could not afford to attend any games. Attendance and, therefore, revenues declined everywhere throughout the major leagues. Prudence dictated paying one salary for a manager who could also play, rather than absorb the luxury of two paychecks. The success of the player-managers made the economical decision that much easier for MacPhail. The Dodgers GM had paid Durocher $12,500 to play shortstop in 1938, and MacPhail knew it wouldn't take much more to get Durocher to play shortstop and manage in 1939.[6]

Needing 1938 All-Star Durocher at shortstop, and seeking ways to reduce his payroll, MacPhail surprised Durocher in a Chicago hotel during the 1938 World Series. As Durocher sat in his boss's suite wondering why he had been summoned, Brooklyn's boss screamed to brother Herman "Max" MacPhail, "Max, come in here and meet the new manager of the Dodgers."

[6]As usual, MacPhail was right. Durocher's 1939 salary as manager/shortstop was $15,000.

Durocher Becomes the Dodgers Manager

FOUR DAYS AFTER THE COMPLETION OF THE 1938 SERIES, Larry MacPhail called a press conference at the Hotel New Yorker to announce his choice of Durocher as manager of the Dodgers for the 1939 season. MacPhail explained his decision to the media: "It seemed to me that Durocher could better supply the thing that our club lacked the most during the past season. Call it morale. Call it anything you want. Whatever you call it, our club didn't have it. I think it's important. You can laugh at me for trying to put the old college spirit into a team of professional ballplayers—but show me a big league team that ever got by without it. I think that's the spirit that Durocher can promote better than anybody else I know. Look at his record. He's never been a manager, but he's been a hustling, standout guy on every team he ever played with."

Durocher told the press that day of his intention to manage like his mentor Miller Huggins, the Yankees manager of the twenties who died suddenly from blood poisoning in 1929 at the age of forty-nine. Durocher and Huggins, as men, could not have been more different. Huggins had a law degree; Durocher was a grade-school dropout. Huggins's self-controlled personality internalized his burning desire to win; Durocher inhibited nothing. Miller Huggins acted "gentlemanly" on and off the field; Leo Durocher spent his adult years living by the creed "Nice guys finish last."

The only similarity between Huggins and Durocher came in sharing the same basic baseball strategy—play aggressively. As the Lip said in his autobiography, "I come to play! I come to beat you! I come to kill you! That's the way Miller Huggins, my first-year manager, brought me up, and that's the way it's always been with me." MacPhail believed Durocher would surely pound that message into the underachieving Dodgers.

Pre-Preseason at Hot Springs

AFTER THE 1938 SERIES, besides hiring Durocher to manage, MacPhail engineered an agreement with the world champion Yankees to play two games at Ebbets Field in April 1939 before Opening Day.

If big crowds filled the Brooklyn grandstands for the games against the Bronx Bombers, the Dodgers would make enough profit to pay for all of their spring-training expenses.

To make fans believe the games between the powerhouse Yankees and perennial second-division Dodgers might be worth watching, MacPhail knew Brooklyn had to have a strong 1939 preseason record. With that in mind, MacPhail sent manager Leo Durocher and all Dodgers pitchers to Hot Springs, Arkansas, for February conditioning and mineral baths to achieve the spring training goal, before joining the rest of the team in March at Clearwater.

The main social activity during Hot Springs evenings in early 1939 took place in the ballroom of the Belvedere Hotel. There, people could play bingo for money. Durocher, already a compulsive gambler at cards and pool, picked up on the local action. At the end of a Belvedere bingo evening came the big jackpot game, with the winner getting more than six hundred dollars. Not surprisingly, Durocher won the jackpot in his first night, and the Brooklyn press was there to report it. A few days before Durocher's hitting the jackpot, the press had also covered his fistfight with a caddy on the hotel's golf course.

MacPhail had read enough. His worst nightmares about his rookie manager were coming to pass before the Dodgers even got to Florida. Brooklyn's general manager telephoned Durocher and roared, "Gambling! Fighting! You're fired! Turn the club over to Andy High right now!" MacPhail slammed down the receiver, and Durocher started packing his bags to catch the next train home to St. Louis.

Shortly before Durocher left Hot Springs, he got another phone call from MacPhail. He wanted to know Durocher's thoughts on a minor league player. MacPhail made no mention of the firing and talked as if Durocher was still the manager. Durocher went along with the Dodgers boss, and conversed as if he still held the reins. He did. The hiring-firing-rehiring, love-hate charade-dance of Larry MacPhail and Leo Durocher had begun. According to Durocher, they performed this unique tango at least sixty different times during the next four years.[7]

---

[7]Perhaps it inspired George Steinbrenner and Billy Martin to try a variation forty years later.

In reflecting on MacPhail, Durocher later said, "Larry was a genius. There is that thin line between genius and insanity, and in Larry's case it was sometimes so thin that you could see him drifting back and forth." The line between genius and insanity became thinnest in the context of MacPhail's handling of manager Leo Durocher.

The Pete Reiser Dispute

Once the Dodgers arrived at Clearwater, Leo Durocher got to see for the first time a nineteen-year-old unknown who had spent the 1938 season buried in the low minors at Class D. Durocher would later say: "Pete Reiser just might have been the best baseball player I ever saw," with the possible exception of a center fielder named Willie Mays.

In an early spring-training game, Durocher decided to give himself a rest from his infield duties. The Lip asked Reiser if he could play shortstop, and the teenager answered in the negative. Durocher retorted, "Well, you're the shortstop today."

Pete Reiser responded to opportunity. In the next three preseason games, he got on base eleven consecutive times, with seven hits, four of which were homers. At a time when baseball had never before had a switch-hitting superstar, Reiser hit two of his home runs right-handed and two left-handed. No one could get him out. He ran the bases faster than anyone in the league. He had a rifle arm in the outfield. Most important to his manager, Pete Reiser would do anything to win. From out of nowhere had come "the Natural."

And from out of nowhere, Leo Durocher got a telegram from Larry MacPhail saying, "*Do not play Reiser again.*" What? Was MacPhail drunk? The 1939 Dodgers team in Clearwater had no stars—particularly in the outfield. Here in the form of Pete Reiser was the player to help Durocher get the jump-start needed to lift the Dodgers from submediocrity. Without any explanation, MacPhail was trying to take the trump card from Durocher's deck. The Lip would not allow it. Reiser played the next game.

MacPhail caught the next plane south to confront his insubordinate rookie manager before a preseason game at Camp Wheeler, Georgia. Dodgers press secretary John McDonald found Durocher dressing for the game in the clubhouse and summoned him to his hotel room. Upon Durocher's arrival, the Brooklyn boss roared, "You're through, retired, suspended without pay, out of my organization!" Expletives flew as MacPhail exploded at his unmanageable manager.

Finally, Durocher had had enough. Durocher grabbed MacPhail by his lapels and threw him over a twin bed onto the floor. "You don't want a manager, you want a rubber stamp! You're not gonna write out my lineups for me. I'm glad I played Reiser yesterday and found you out in time!"

Surprisingly, MacPhail reacted meekly to the unceremonious dump. He quietly told Durocher of his perception that Reiser needed one more year of minor league seasoning. If the young star continued to play every day for the Dodgers in the spring, neither Reiser nor the Brooklyn fans would accept a demotion. More surprisingly, Durocher then proceeded to agree with his boss, and they left the Georgia hotel room arm in arm.

Although Larry MacPhail's explanation to Durocher for Reiser's benching seemed plausible, if not genuinely shrewd, it was a lie. Pete Reiser had to get out of the 1939 New York headlines to allow MacPhail to be in a position to honor an agreement he had made in 1938 with his old boss, St. Louis Cardinals general manager Branch Rickey.[8]

By 1938, Branch Rickey had approached achieving a monopoly on minor league baseball talent. To break up the monopoly, Commissioner Kenesaw Mountain Landis ordered the Cardinals to divest themselves of many young players in their vast farm system.

The player Rickey hated to lose most was Pete Reiser, perceived by the Cardinal chief as a combination Babe Ruth-Ty Cobb. As Rickey had helped MacPhail get major league executive baseball positions first at Cincinnati and then at Brooklyn, the Cardinals general manager knew Larry owed him a favor.

After Landis's ruling in 1938, Rickey and MacPhail agreed secretly that the Dodgers would buy Pete Reiser from the Cardinals for one

---

[8]MacPhail's first position in professional baseball had been as president of the Cardinals' farm team at Columbus from 1931 to 1933. Larry MacPhail had once said about self-confident and religious Branch Rickey, "There, but for the grace of God, goes God."

hundred dollars and keep him obscured in the low minors for two years. Then, in 1940, when it became possible under Landis's edict for the Cardinals to re-obtain players they had been required to turn loose in 1938, the Dodgers would send Reiser back to St. Louis.

Thus, MacPhail's real reason for ordering the teenage phenom's benching was to position himself with the Dodgers fans to fulfill his 1940 obligation to Rickey without fear of a Brooklyn reprisal over the loss of the franchise's best player, which surely would have resulted had Reiser lit up the Dodgers as he appeared capable of doing at Clearwater in 1939.[9]

1939: The Rest of the Story

LEO DUROCHER HAD RUN-INS WITH OTHERS besides MacPhail during spring training. Gabby Hartnett, manager and catcher for the 1938 National League champion Cubs, publicly predicted in a Florida interview that the 1939 Dodgers would finish last. To bottom out in the National League would mean Brooklyn's being worse than the hopeless Phillies, who had finished the 1938 season with a 45-105 record, some 24 games behind the seventh-place Dodgers. Durocher retaliated in a radio broadcast: "If we should happen to get into the World Series, I'll promise that we won't fold up against the Yankees and also that I won't bench myself after losing three games." In 1938, the Yankees had swept the Cubs in the Series, and Hartnett, after going one-for-11 (.091) in the first three games, started backup catcher Ken O'Dea in Game Four. With his public slam of Hartnett, Durocher had made a new lifelong enemy.

When the 1939 season started, the Brooklyn Dodgers moved closer to New York's center stage than they had ever been. MacPhail ended a five-year ban of all major league baseball on the radio in New York, and brought over from Cincinnati a young Floridian named

[9]The Reiser swap back to the Cardinals never came through. In 1939, MacPhail hired Branch Rickey, Jr., into Brooklyn's front office. Presumably, Branch, Sr., looked into his crystal ball and saw himself following his son to the Dodgers. Rickey, Sr., never insisted that MacPhail fulfill the Reiser buy-back obligation. After the 1942 season, Rickey, Sr., replaced MacPhail as Dodgers president, where he could enjoy the performance of 1941 National League batting champion Pete Reiser.

Shortstop/manager Durocher (No.2) ponders the situation at the mound. (Copyright: Mark Rucker, Transcendental Graphics)

Red Barber to call the games. Night baseball continued at Ebbets Field in 1939, and the eight weeknight games averaged well over thirty thousand in attendance. Above all, Durocher's pushing the team to a higher level of play brought forth a new fan base.

Durocher decided early in the 1939 season he liked his position as shortstop *and* manager. He told why in his autobiography:

> Christ, I was into everything; my wheels were spinning all the time. The two things a manager does when his team is on the field are move players and decide when to take the pitcher out. It's much easier to move a player when you're right in the middle of it, and you also have a far better sense of when your pitcher is beginning to lose it. The only other thing I like to do is call a pitch, one pitch, in a clutch situation, maybe ten or twelve times over a season. The hitter fouls it off or takes it for a ball, that's it. Now you're on your own, buddy. When you're on the bench you have to call to the catcher to look over. When I was playing shortstop, he was looking right at me. If I left my glove open, I wanted a certain pitch. Direct communication. Otherwise, in a jam, I'd just make a fist. What that meant was: You call it, buddy, go on. You're catching, you know him better than I do, you're my captain, you run the show, I've got all the faith in the world in you. When the team is at bat, you're in the dugout anyway. Except when you're on base, leading the club by example.

On an early season road trip, as the team struggled to play at the .500 mark, the young manager cut loose at his underachieving players. "I'm fighting out there every day because I love the big leagues. I love this life, these good hotels, these good trains, this good dough. You should, too. Do you want to go back to the tanks, to those blue-plate specials, to the buses and the starvation wages? Well, that's where every one of you is going—unless you get in there and fight!"

Fighting is what Leo Durocher did best. His most notable fight of the 1939 season came on July 2, in a game against the cross-town rival

New York Giants led by their despised manager Bill Terry.[10] Dodgers pitcher Whitlow Wyatt had pitched inside to Giants hitters a little too often, causing Giants hurler "Prince Hal" Schumacher to retaliate against player-manager Durocher. After barely ducking away from Schumacher's brush-back, on the next pitch, Durocher hit a double-play ground ball. As Durocher reached first base running full tilt, he deliberately jumped on the heel of stocky first baseman Zeke Bonura. Zeke turned and threw the ball at Durocher. The Lip kept running down the first-base line into right field as Bonura chased him down. A slugfest ensued involving a total of forty-five players. All of this resulted in Durocher's receiving his first ever major league fine (twenty-five dollars) from league president Ford Frick.

Despite Durocher's motivational talks and fierce play, the 1939 Dodgers managed to have a few underachievers—most notably, a "short-armed curveball" pitcher (per Durocher's description) named "Boots" Poffenberger. MacPhail had obtained the twenty-two-year-old Boots from Detroit, where he had been 16-12 during the 1937-1938 seasons, with more than twice as many walks as strikeouts. The young right-hander was even wilder off the pitcher's mound than on it.

Boots Poffenberger's dictionary left out the word "discipline." He missed curfew as a matter of habit. The young pitcher calmly told MacPhail one night when he staggered in to the Philadelphia hotel several hours after midnight that he had arrived on time—Honolulu time. Boots covered his suitcases with blankets on the sleeper train bunk to make it appear he was sleeping, while the wild man prowled and drank elsewhere.

For the final straw, Boots failed to come to the ballpark one day, resentful of the many fines he had collected. Poffenberger sent first baseman Camilli as his messenger to management. "Tell Durocher that I am tired of the way he is keeping me like a bird in a gilded cage." The Dodgers sent Boots down to Montreal the next day. The

---

[10]Terry had earned his reputation with Dodgers fans during the 1934 preseason, when the Giants manager was asked by a Brooklyn reporter to give his opinion of the Dodgers. Terry smiled and said, "Brooklyn? Is Brooklyn still in the league?" Flatbush saw red. The Dodgers players got the last laugh, however, beating Terry's Giants in the last game of the 1934 season, thereby allowing the St. Louis "Gas House Gang" Cardinals (led by a fiery, weak-hitting shortstop named Leo Durocher) to win the National League pennant.

"short-armed curveballer" failed to report, and never surfaced again in professional baseball.

In spite of screwballs like Poffenberger, Leo Durocher's aggressive style of managing captured the national limelight. Two of the nation's leading magazines profiled the Dodgers manager during the summer of 1939. The *Saturday Evening Post* commissioned veteran journalist Arthur Mann to write on "Baseball's Ugly Duckling—Durable Durocher," and *Collier's* asked Quentin Reynolds to do a story on "The Pop-Off Kid." Making national press helped sell tickets and, with the attendance bonus clause in his contract, MacPhail profited by it.

When Brooklynites went to Ebbets Field in 1939, they saw good baseball but few good players. Only "Cookie" Lavagetto hit as high as .300, and he finished with an even .300. No outfielder hit more than eight home runs or drove in more than 67 runs. Unspectacular Luke Hamlin had a career-best 20-13 year on the mound[11] with a 3.64 earned-run average. The team's only slugger, first baseman Camilli, essentially matched his 1938 production by hitting 26 homers and driving in 104 runs.

How, then, did the 1939 Dodgers go from seventh to third place, ending up at 84-69, after finishing the 1938 season at 69-80? First, led by Hamlin and newcomers Hugh Casey (15-10) and Whitlow Wyatt (8-3), the overall pitching was much better. The staff's earned-run average dropped in one year from 4.17 to 3.64. The Dodgers pitchers led the league in issuing only 399 free passes in 1939, 24 fewer than the second-best Pirate staff. Shortstop-manager Leo Durocher could see better from his on-the-field perspective as his pitchers tired. Baseball historian Lee Allen noted that when arms went dead in the late innings, Durocher "changed pitchers frantically and usually was right."

More than the improvement he made to the Dodgers pitching staff, Durocher's main accomplishment with the 1939 Dodgers came in his refusal to allow the team to coast at the end of the season. Cincinnati had held first place securely for the entire 1939 season. Second-place St. Louis—led by Hall of Famers Johnny Mize, Enos Slaughter, Ducky Medwick, and Pepper Martin—were head and shoulders above the rest

---

[11]In his nine-year, major league career, Hamlin never had another year in which he won more than 12 games.

of the pack. Finishing in third place in 1939 meant gaining a little extra bonus money from the league at season's end. Recognizing what was possible for his cast of ordinaries, Leo Durocher drove the Dodgers furiously down the stretch, and they responded to his whip by winning 21 of their final 30 games.

To clinch third place required beating the Phillies at Ebbets Field on the last day of the season. With the Dodgers leading by one run in the top of the ninth, the Phillies had runners on first and third with one out. Warming up in the bull pen, Durocher had two pitchers: 20-game winner Hamlin and a late-season call-up from the minors named Carl "Billy" Doyle, who had previously appeared in a grand total of four National League games. Durocher summoned Doyle to pitch, and the inebriated MacPhail started screaming from his box loud enough for all of Brooklyn to hear: "Hamlin, you dummy! Hamlin!"

Durocher described his response to MacPhail's second-guessing in his book *Nice Guys Finish Last*: "So I did what I had been wanting to do all year. I put my thumb to my nose and waggled my fingers at him!" As usual, Durocher's choice of relief pitchers worked. The Phillies batter hit Doyle's first pitch back to the mound, and a Doyle-to-Durocher-to-Camilli double play ended the inning, won the game, and clinched third place for the 1939 Brooklyn Dodgers.

Durocher's players responded to his late-season whip because they liked his style. When players made mental mistakes, Durocher corrected them quickly but privately, and physical errors went unpenalized. He also protected his players. When an inebriated MacPhail had invaded the players' sacred clubhouse after a disappointing Dodgers loss to Cincinnati, Durocher ordered his boss out. "Now you! Get out! Get the hell out of here and don't you ever come in here again! You don't belong here. You want to talk to one of my players, you send for him up in your office. This is our clubhouse, our home. Don't you come in here and start ranting and raving. If there's any ranting and raving to be done in this room, I will do it."

Attendance at Ebbets Field for 1939 soared over one million. In the brief time executive-vice-president-turned-president[12] Larry MacPhail

---

[12]As of April 4, 1939.

and shortstop-turned-manager Leo Durocher had served the Dodgers, attendance in Brooklyn more than doubled. A renovated Ebbets Field, the public's radio-addiction to the mesmerizing voice of Red Barber, night games allowing the working man to attend, the creation of "Ladies Nights" (opening up interest for half the population who had previously been ignored), and, above all, the hard-nosed play of a hustling bunch of journeyman led by baseball's most entertaining field leader all contributed to bring a level of interest in the national pastime never experienced before in Flatbush. That new level of fan enthusiasm set the table for the great Brooklyn Dodgers teams of the next eighteen years.

At year's end, *The Sporting News* selected Leo Durocher as National League Manager of the Year. In announcing its selection, the *News* explained its choice of Durocher over St. Louis skipper Ray Blades, who had improved the Cardinals from sixth place in 1938 to second place in 1939, only four-and-one-half games behind the pennant-winning Reds:

> Durocher had no Mizes, Medwicks, or Slaughters to drive in runs as did Blades. In fact, Leo possessed only one .300 hitter... and the team, as a whole, had a batting average of .265, one point ahead of Boston, which topped the [last place] Phillies by three...
>
> Leo patched here, plugged a hole there and played in more than one hundred games at shortstop himself to keep the infield from falling to pieces. That he could elevate such a team, lacking both resources and material, into a position right behind the Cardinals and Reds is a tribute to his sagacity and courage and Leo earns the No. 1 tabbing for the managers.

After 1939—If Nice Guys Finish Last, Where Was Durocher?

The Brooklyn stage was set for further improvement in 1940. In Durocher's second year at the helm, the Dodgers moved up a notch to second place, thanks to both the midseason acquisition of Ducky Medwick in a blockbuster trade with the Cardinals,[13] and the promotion

[13]Medwick and pitcher Curt Davis (12-8 in 1938) came to the Dodgers in exchange for $125,000 cash, outfielder Ernie Koy, relief pitcher Carl Doyle, submarine pitcher Sam Nahen, and utility player Bert Haas.

of a young shortstop from Louisville named Harold "Pee Wee" Reese. By 1941, Leo Durocher continued the Dodgers' improvement, winning one hundred games along with the National League pennant.

After his first three years managing in the major leagues, Leo Durocher had achieved a winning percentage of .591. Had he maintained that pace over the course of his career, he surely would have been elected sooner to Baseball's Hall of Fame. As it was, he finished his twenty-four-year managerial career with a .540 winning percentage, and a record of 2,010 wins and 1,710 losses.

After 1939, Durocher won National League Manager of the Year honors again in 1951 (the Bobby Thomson "Shot Heard Round the World" season) and 1954 (as Willie Mays made "the Catch" leading to a Giants' sweep over the favored Indians in the Series). Victory in the 1954 Series would be Leo Durocher's only world championship out of his three World Series appearances.

Throughout his life, on the field and off, Durocher's abrasive voice acted as an agent for antagonism, never for harmony. Sportswriter Jimmy Powers said in his book *Baseball Personalities*, "If Leo Durocher is to be remembered at all, it will be for his swaggering braggadocio, his vile temper, his arguments, fights, and scandals." Durocher's own players described their manager as a "pathological liar." Durocher took great pride in his lone contribution to *Bartlett's Famous Quotations*: "Nice guys finish last," a saying created not by Durocher, but by the New York press after Durocher mentioned that "Nice guys like Mel Ott (then manager of the Giants) find themselves in seventh place."[14]

As for Durocher's positive contributions, in addition to his deserved reputation as one of baseball's greatest all-time field strategists,[15] Durocher occasionally demonstrated flashes of short-term kindness away from the ballpark—whether in the form of treating a child to a special favor or loaning money to a former player.

---

[14]Branch Rickey once said, "Leo Durocher is the kind of man who if he saw a painter standing in front of a completed painting, he would get rid of the painter, grab the brush and palette, and stand in front of the mural in such a pose as to give you the impression he had done the thing!"

[15]Baseball guru Rickey also said, "If I had a ballclub with a chance to win, there is no one I would prefer as manager more than Leo Durocher."

What the record ultimately showed upon Leo Durocher's death was a man lacking support from friends and family, living alone in a small Palm Springs condominium, completely alienated from the sport he had participated in for fifty years to the point of instructing a friend to turn down Cooperstown if the Hall of Fame called after his death.[16]

In his recent book *The Man in the Dugout*, noted baseball writer Leonard Koppett made this final evaluation of Leo the Lip:

> His disciples admired his ability, imitated his methods, appreciated his help, learned lessons from him, and understood what made him exceptional; but no one ever spoke of him in awesome terms or seemed to love him. They could be deeply grateful and feel perpetually indebted to his guidance and teaching, but few felt any sense of personal loss when he moved on.

Gerald Eskenazi closed his biography *The Lip* with mention of Durocher's lifestyle about-face during his final years. Durocher became an usher at the Palm Springs Catholic Church. He stopped drinking and cursing. His priest became Durocher's most trusted friend.

Leo Durocher's sad story perhaps could have had a happy Hall of Fame ending before he died if the Lip had not attacked life with a "Nice Guys Finish Last" mentality, but rather lived and played in accordance with the constitution and by-laws of the Brooklyn Excelsior Baseball Club in 1860.

Anthologist Charles Einstein recently located the pertinent Brooklyn team rules in 1860:

> 9. Members, when assembled for field exercise, or for any meeting of the club, who shall use profane and improper language, shall be fined ten cents for each offense.
> 10. A member disputing the decisions of the umpire shall be fined twenty-five cents for each offense.
> 11. A member who shall audibly express his opinion on a doubtful play before the decision of the umpire (unless called upon to do so) shall be fined twenty-five cents for each offense.

---

[16]On July 31, 1994, Durocher's family proudly accepted his plaque at Cooperstown.

14. All fines incurred for violation of Sections 9, 10, and 11 must be paid to the umpire, before leaving the field.

When octogenarian Leo the Lip finally chose to follow the *Brooklyn Excelsior Club Rules*, it was too late. His lifetime race toward the Hall of Fame was over, and Mel Ott had already proven that nice guys with lifetime achievements don't finish last at Cooperstown.

Hall of Fame Manager Bill McKechnie. (National Baseball Library and Archive, Cooperstown, New York)

CHAPTER FOUR

THE DEACON OF CINCINNATI

Hall of Fame Manager Bill McKechnie
Leads the Reds to the National League Pennant

AS LEO DUROCHER DROVE, agitated, and pushed the Dodgers to a surprising, first-division finish in 1939, a more serene managerial approach guided Cincinnati to the National League pennant. "Deacon" Bill McKechnie led the Reds to the flag in baseball's centennial year and thereby became the first manager in history to take three different teams to the World Series.[1]

McKechnie's Team

FOR MANY YEARS, the 1939-1940 Cincinnati Reds stood as the only back-to-back league champion without a Hall of Famer in the lineup.[2] The Reds won their pre-war pennants on tight defense, outstanding pitching, and good hitting. During those seasons, McKechnie cemented his reputation as the dean of defensive baseball. Baseball historian Edwin Pope observed that during the McKechnie era, Cincinnati "guarded home plate as though it was the

[1]Prior to 1939, McKechnie had piloted the 1925 Pirates and the 1928 Cardinals to the World Series. Only Dick Williams has accomplished this nomadic hat trick since McKechnie.

[2]This unique achievement stood until 1986, when catcher Ernie Lombardi was elected to the Hall of Fame almost nine years after his death.

last penny in Fort Knox." Author Harvey Frommer described McKechnie's maximizing the Reds' defense in 1939 by keeping his "infield in, the diamond damp, and the grass high."

The year's statistics demonstrated why Cincinnati won the pennant. The 1939 Reds allowed the fewest runs per game (3.87), had the lowest team earned-run average (3.27), and pitched the most complete games (86). The team finished second in the league that year in fielding average, double plays, batting average, and slugging average. They accomplished this with players whose names are now largely forgotten.

In the infield were first baseman Frank McCormick, second baseman Lonny Frey, shortstop Billy Myers, and third baseman Billy Werber. All of them ended up with solid but unspectacular careers.[3] Led by Werber, the 1939 infield (sans first baseman McCormick, perceived by the rest as an underachieving fielder) referred to themselves as "the Jungle Club"—the quick Frey (who had birthmark spots on his skin) was called "the Leopard," the fast Myers became "the Jaguar," and the aggressive Werber answered to "the Tiger." They would psyche up before each game by screaming, "Bounce on the balls of your feet like a jungle cat." The Cincinnati infielders did the little things well—covered territory, made the double-play pivot, stole signs, and rarely struck out. Reds pitcher Bucky Walters summed up their talent: "They were all good, fast, and smart."

McCormick was by far the best hitter, and in 1939 he hit .332, struck out 16 times in 630 at bats, and led the league in runs batted in (128) and fielding average among first basemen (.996). Frey hit .291, played second base in the All-Star Game, and combined with Myers (who hit .281) to form the league's best double-play combination. McCormick, Frey, and Myers all had career-high batting averages in 1939. Leadoff batter Werber led the league in runs scored (115) while batting .289, and also led the league's third basemen in the defensive areas of assists, double plays, and chances per game.

In the outfield, the Reds had 1935 National League home-run king Wally Berger in left, speedster Harry Craft in center, and Ival

[3]McCormick played thirteen years and hit .299; Frey—fourteen years at .269; Myers—seven years at .257; and Werber—eleven years at .271.

Goodman in right. By 1939, Berger was in the twilight of his eleven-year career, hitting .258 and driving in 44 runs in 85 games while covering little ground in left field. McKechnie searched all season for Berger's replacement without much luck. Craft covered so much territory in center he made up for the deficiencies of the left-field cast, but was a mediocre hitter (.257, 13 homers, and 67 runs batted in in 1939). Goodman played in the 1938 and 1939 All-Star Game, led the Reds in extra-base hits both years, and had his career best batting average in 1939 at .323. "Goody" would end his ten-year career in 1944, with a lifetime .281 batting average.

On the mound, the 1939 Reds had the finest one-two punch in the major leagues. Reformed infielder Bucky Walters (who had spent his first four major league seasons as a third baseman before switching to the mound in 1935) was chosen the major leagues' best all-around player by *The Sporting News* for the 1939 campaign, based on a record of 27-11, with an earned-run average of 2.29, and 31 complete games in 36 starts. Paul Derringer posted a 25-7 record with a 2.93 earned-run average, completed 28 of his 35 starts, and walked only 35 batters in 301 innings. At one point, Derringer went 49 2/3 consecutive innings without giving up a walk, throwing a wild pitch, or hitting a batter.[4]

Only senior citizens and historians now remember Walters and Derringer, two great pitchers who never made the Hall of Fame. Walters won 20 games three different years, and finished his career with a 3.30 earned-run average, and record of 198-160. Derringer won 20 games four times, lost 20 games twice (including going 7-27 with a 3.30 earned-run average for the 1933 Reds), and finished his career at 223-212 with a 3.46 earned-run average. Had Walters not lost the first four years of his major league pitching career because of playing third base, and had Derringer pitched early in his career on teams which gave him better run support, both would have been strong contenders for Cooperstown.[5]

---

[4]Excluding intentional walks, the streak lasted 60 2/3 innings.

[5]Per Bill James's "Black Ink Test" (reflecting league leadership in performance categories) described in his recent book *The Politics of Glory*, Walters has "the highest Black Ink Point score of any eligible non-Hall of Fame pitcher."

The 1939 Reds did have one pitcher who is not forgotten. On June 11 and 15, 1938, "Dutch Master" Johnny Vander Meer became the only man in baseball history to pitch consecutive no-hitters. By 1939, Vandy had sunk to 5-9, with a 4.67 earned-run average. Fortunately, McKechnie helped the young left-hander get his career back on track, allowing Vander Meer to pitch through the 1951 season. Though his career 119-121 record will never earn him a plaque at Cooperstown, Vandy's 1938 moment in the sun remains one of baseball's most memorable achievements.

The starting catcher for the 1939 Reds was Ernie Lombardi. Big Ernie (six-foot-three, 230 pounds) was coming off his greatest season in 1938, when he had led the league in hitting (.342). Lombardi's bat dipped to .287 in 1939, but he still caught for the National League in the All-Star Game, and for the season knocked in 85 runs.

Big Ernie's unflattering claim to fame in baseball history is being the slowest baserunner ever to wear a major league uniform. Lombardi took seven seconds to get from home to first, allowing opposing teams to station seven defensive players in the outfield. If Lombardi had had even a little more speed to go with his powerful bat,[6] his average might well have approached .400 during the two years he won National League batting titles.

Backing up Lombardi behind the plate was Willard Hershberger, who in 1939 hit .345 in 63 games. Fifty-one years after his gruesome death (he slit his wrists in a hotel bathtub) in 1940, "Hershy" was immortalized in a May 1991 *Sports Illustrated* article entitled "The Razor's Edge" by William Knack, which described baseball's only in-season suicide by an active player. A July 1939 *Sporting News* write-up on Hershberger as baseball's best second-string catcher described him as a "fidgety chap," perhaps foreshadowing the tragic events of a year later.

This group of *Baseball Encyclopedia* (but not household) names took a down-and-out Cincinnati franchise, which had finished in the 1937 cellar with a record of 56-98, and improved the team to an

---

[6]Lombardi hit .330 or more five different times during his seventeen-year career, and finished with a lifetime .306 average and almost 500 extra-base hits.

Suicidal catcher Willard Hershberger (National Baseball Library and Archive, Cooperstown, New York)

82-68, fourth-place finish in 1938, a 97-57 National League pennant in 1939, and a World Series championship in 1940. One man made this good team great. That man was Bill McKechnie.

McKechnie: Pre-Reds

MCKECHNIE ACQUIRED THE NICKNAME "Deacon" from his lifetime service to the hometown Methodist church in Wilkinsburg, Pennsylvania. McKechnie had met his wife there. As a young ballplayer he sang in the church choir during the offseason. He remained an active member until leaving the area for his retirement years in Bradenton, Florida.

Had he been taller than five-foot-ten, McKechnie's nickname might well have been "Honest Abe," for his lifetime obsession with Abraham Lincoln. No treatise on our sixteenth president was too obscure for the manager's voracious historical appetite. Inspired by the Great Emancipator, McKechnie became among the first to speak out on the need to bring black ballplayers into the major leagues.

As a big league player from 1907-1920, McKechnie had been a marginal "good-field, no-hit" infielder. Like many successful managers, the utility player learned his future trade while gathering splinters on the bench. During McKechnie's playing days, his New York Yankees manager Frank Chance recognized the future manager's field leadership and smarts. He played him steadily during part of the 1913 season, despite a .158 batting average. Chance told sportswriter Fred Lieb he kept McKechnie in the lineup "because he has more brains than the rest of this dumb club put together."

McKechnie got his first major league managerial opportunity at Pittsburgh in the middle of the 1922 season. Pittsburgh owner Barney Dreyfuss had hired him back into baseball as a player-coach in 1920, after McKechnie had given up the game for a job at an Ohio industrial plant during 1918-1919. With Pittsburgh in 1922, the Deacon took over a floundering 32-36 team in July and led them to a third-place finish with a 53-36 record for the balance of the 1922 season. As Pirates manager that season, McKechnie made the decision to play Pie Traynor at third base every day. Traynor proceeded to have a Hall of Fame career and establish himself as one of baseball's masters at the hot corner.

Under McKechnie, the Pirates improved slightly to 87-67 in 1923, good enough for third place, but not good enough to catch John McGraw's Giants. Pittsburgh's record improved to 90-63 during the 1924 campaign, but they remained in third.

In 1925, McKechnie won his first pennant with a record of 95-58, and then led the Pirates back from a 3-1 deficit to a come-from-behind World Series crown over Walter Johnson and the Washington Senators. The next year brought another third-place finish for Pittsburgh. Throwing his prior managerial-experienced weight around,[7] Pirates coach Fred Clarke engineered a feud between the Deacon and his players during the 1926 season, leading to an insurrection against

[7]From 1897 to 1915, Clarke managed nineteen years for the Pirates, and won two World Series for them.

McKechnie. Owner Dreyfuss decided to fire his manager as a means of calming the storm, despite McKechnie's four-and-a-half-year record (409-293), his winning a pennant and a World Series, and the Pirates never finishing lower than third during his regime.

The Deacon's next stop was at St. Louis, where history repeated itself. McKechnie took over the Cardinals' reins in 1928, led them to the National League pennant with a record of 95-59, and then got run over in a four-game World Series sweep by the New York Yankees freight train. Incredibly, St. Louis president Sam Breadon fired his pennant-winning manager after the Series.

Through 1928, McKechnie's five-and-a-half-year career as a big league skipper reflected a .589 winning percentage, two pennants with two different teams, a World Series triumph, and no finish lower than third place. Despite those achievements, the Deacon felt the sting of termination twice in a space of two years.

Normally, winning does not provide a big league manager with job insecurity, and McKechnie's dismissals seemed a paradox. Unlike a Leo Durocher or, later, a Billy Martin firing, the Deacon getting canned could not be attributed to an obnoxious personality. Writer Leonard Koppett described McKechnie's personality as "cerebral... not a talker, but a listener." Opposing player Dick Bartell called him "an owlish little guy, almost dry." *Sporting News* columnist Dan Daniel labeled McKechnie as a "softspoken, back-patting, detail-watching manager who never shouted."

Despite lacking the credentials to win a personality contest, McKechnie's record demonstrated that the quiet manager had the characteristics necessary to win ballgames at the major league level. The Deacon's countenance was self-confident but never arrogant. He treated his players fairly and always took time to explain lineup changes and roster moves to those involved. When the weather got cold, sportswriter Joe Williams observed that the paternal skipper "fussed over his players like a mother hen," making them coffee and distributing neck warmers.

Above all, per author Al Hirshberg, as one of the game's great strategists, teachers, and psychologists, Bill McKechnie could "squeeze more baseball out of less talent than any man alive." The

Deacon's unselfishness and constant dedication to his players accounted for the manager's getting "so much out of so little," concluded Joe Williams in a *Saturday Evening Post* profile.

McKechnie's "problem" as a manager, which caused his job insecurity, was his colorlessness. Cincinnati reporter Harry Grayson described McKechnie as being "as drab as a coat of paint." McKechnie cared nothing about reading his name in the newspapers. He managed by "the book," playing percentages rather than hunches. McKechnie's teams specialized in defense and winning one-run, low-scoring games—the kind of games which bored the casual fan. The "Great Unwashed"[8] wanted the excitement and charisma of bulldog John McGraw, not the solemnity of bespectacled Bill McKechnie.

Distressed by the post-pennant firings at Pittsburgh and St. Louis, the Deacon justifiably began to wonder about his future in baseball. In the fall of 1929, McKechnie tried his hand at politics, and ran for the position of Wilkinsburg tax collector. Presumably, his hometown friends knew of the Deacon's Scottish thrift, and feared that it would lead McKechnie to do too good a job in collecting their tax money. McKechnie lost the election, but got a call from Judge Emil Fuchs, owner of the Boston Braves.

When Judge Fuchs originally considered hiring the two-time pennant-winning skipper, he was understandably concerned about McKechnie's prior dismissals. To evaluate his reservations, Fuchs called McKechnie's former boss at St. Louis, Branch Rickey, regarded by most as the smartest man in baseball. Rickey eliminated Fuchs's worries: "Don't pay any attention to any rumors you hear about why we fired him. They're all wrong. We like Bill and we think he's a great manager, but we have to fire managers out in St. Louis to furnish divertissement for the fans. We had to do this in McKechnie's case and will have to do it with more managers until the fans change their attitude."

Judge Fuchs knew the Braves needed immediate help—the kind of help only winning could provide. To save money in 1929, Fuchs had even managed the insolvent team himself, and proceeded to finish in last place, a performance consistent with his previous salaried man-

[8]To borrow a phrase from Dallas sportswriter Blackie Sherrod.

agers. Between 1920 and 1929, the Braves finished higher than seventh place only twice[9] and won only 603 games while losing 928.

Based on Branch Rickey's recommendation, drab winner McKechnie took the Braves' helm in 1930. Not including the disastrous 1935 season (when the hapless Braves suffered the major league's second all-time worst record of the twentieth century of 38-115[10] with the season disrupted in part by the 28-game appearance of .181-hitting Babe Ruth), the Deacon's record while managing Boston through 1937, stood at 522-551, a respectable .487 winning percentage for the league's pre-McKechnie perennial doormat.

As Bill McKechnie achieved respectability for the Boston Braves from 1930-1937, Cincinnati became the league's worst team. During those eight years, the Reds never finished in the first division or even above .500, and stumbled to a 485-741 record. Could the Deacon do for the Reds after 1937 what he had done for the Braves after 1929? Cincinnati general manager Warren Giles decided to let McKechnie try.

True to Bill McKechnie's underappreciated past, when Giles announced the Deacon's hiring in the fall of 1937 for the upcoming 1938 campaign, the Cincinnati fans revolted. They wanted popular but aging outfield hero Kiki Cuyler to take over the team, and had no grasp of McKechnie's accomplishments at Boston.[11] Giles boldly defended his choice, and prophesied to the Cincy fans: "You just wait and see. This fella's the best manager in baseball. He'll bring us a championship in two years at least. Maybe even this year." Giles made his seemingly unrealistic prediction in the unstated context of the Reds (1) not having had a .500 team since 1928, and (2) having suffered the worst record (56-98) in the National League in 1937.

---

[9]They finished in fourth place in 1921 and fifth place in 1925.

[10]The 1935 Braves had a worse winning percentage (.248) than the 1962 Mets (.250), but were better than the 1916 Philadelphia A's, who had a record of 36-117.

[11]After the 1937 campaign, *The Sporting News* recognized McKechnie as National League Manager of the Year for taking the 38-115 Braves of 1935, and, in two years, turning them into a respectable 79-73 team.

How the Reds Took off Under McKechnie

A team doesn't go from last place to first in two seasons by accident. The last-place 1937 Reds became the first-place 1939 Reds (and the World Champion 1940 Reds) for several reasons. First, after the 1937 season, Giles moved home plate twenty feet closer to the outfield fence at Crosley Field. The new dimensions caused a surge in the Reds' power production. The combined home-run total by holdovers Goodman, Lombardi, and Myers went from 28 in 1937 to 61 in 1938.

Secondly, the addition and development of new players made the team better. McCormick and Craft became starters for the first time in 1938. Frey was acquired by trade from the Cubs before the start of the 1938 season. Walters and Berger were picked up in midseason trades during 1938. Werber was obtained in a trade with the A's before the start of the 1939 season over a $1,500 salary dispute with Connie Mack. Pitcher Junior Thompson was a rookie on the 1939 league champions. Thus, only catcher Lombardi, rightfielder Goodman, shortstop Myers, and pitcher Derringer served on the 1937 losers and made contributions to the 1939 winners. Lombardi had always been a star. Goodman and Myers blossomed after 1937 because Crosley Field got smaller. Derringer became an All-Star pitcher after 1937 because of McKechnie.

In 1937, Paul Derringer went 10-14 with a 4.04 earned-run average under manager Charlie Dressen for the last-place Reds. After hiring McKechnie in the fall of 1937, Giles wrote his new manager a letter giving his impression of the various Cincinnati players. The Cincy GM's comment on Derringer was: "Lacks guts. Should try to trade him." Fortunately, while managing the Braves, Bill McKechnie had seen enough of Derringer to reject Giles's advice. In his first three years under the Deacon, the tall, hot-tempered right-hander went 66-33 with a combined earned-run average under 3.00.

McKechnie's special gift with pitchers turned Bucky Walters's career around as well. Pre-Deacon, Walters's four-year pitching career record was 38-53 with an earned-run average of 4.40. With McKechnie at Cincinnati for eight-and-a-half years, Walters went 152-96 with an earned-run average well under 3.00.

Bucky Walters and Joe DiMaggio talk before the 1939 All-Star Game. (National Baseball Library and Archive, Cooperstown, New York)

Derringer and Walters were not the first pitchers made over by Bill McKechnie. Most notably, before the start of the 1937 season at Boston, the Deacon found a thirty-year-old career minor leaguer named Lou Fette, put a Braves uniform on him, and then guided Fette to a 20-10 record with a 2.88 earned-run average. McKechnie did the same that season with thirty-three-year-old Jim Turner, who went 20-11 with a 2.38 earned-run average for the Braves in 1937. Never before or since have two journeymen bush leaguers, without any prior major league experience, gotten the call from the same big league team in the same year, and then each proceeded to win 20 games.

What did McKechnie do to turn pitching junk into All-Star hurlers? He insisted on starting with physically strong raw material. "Rowdy Richard" Bartell played against McKechnie teams during most of his eighteen-year, major league career, and observed that the

Deacon "liked big strong pitchers." Derringer was six-foot-three and weighed 205 pounds. Walters, Thompson, and Vander Meer all stood six-foot-one and weighed 185. Whitey Moore (13-12 in 1939) was six-foot-one and 195, while Lee Grissom (9-7 in 1939) was six-foot-three and weighed in at 200 pounds. Bartell was right. No pipsqueaks took the mound for the Deacon.

Once McKechnie had the coal, he had the wherewithal to polish it. The word around the National League during the pre-war years was "If you can't pitch for McKechnie, you can't pitch for anybody." Bill McKechnie started the process of building a staff with calculated conditioning. At spring training, the skipper would have the pitchers warm up with men standing in the batter's box without bats, to prevent overthrowing before their arms were ready. The Deacon then taught his hurlers the proper mechanics of using the entire body (heel, leg, backbone, and shoulders) as one coordinated pitching unit. With his knowledge of mechanics, McKechnie added at least ten years to Vander Meer's career by changing his sidearm delivery to straight overhand.

Once the pitchers had conditioned their arms and mastered their mechanics, McKechnie worked on repertoire. He forced his staff to throw curveballs in jams until they gained confidence in the pitch. "You're not a big league pitcher until you can throw a curve on command. I'm not going to get beat with my pitchers throwing fastballs." To avoid injuries, McKechnie refused to allow his pitchers to throw a slider, calling it "a sore-armed pitch."

After developing each pitcher's repertoire, the manager's next step came in motivating his pitchers to develop control over their temperament. McKechnie simply refused to allow an angry pitcher to stay in a game, no matter how he was doing. "If you're angry, you can't think, and if you can't think, you can't pitch for me." Bartel remembered a game when McKechnie took out pitcher Whitey Moore while pitching a shutout because Moore was overly disturbed by an umpire's call.

McKechnie further gained and improved his pitchers' confidence in themselves and in their manager by sticking with his starting rotation no matter what, and rarely upsetting their rhythm by using relievers as starters, or vice versa. In fact, the Deacon was reluctant to use relief pitchers at all. The 1939 pennant-winning staff totaled just nine saves on the year.

Finally, beyond the conditioning, mechanics, repertoire, self-control, and rotation rhythm, McKechnie proved throughout his manager-psychologist career that he could motivate and handle any pitching temperament, whether it be the proud, high-spirited Derringer or the cool, quiet Walters.

Beyond his special talents with pitchers, manager Bill McKechnie made business-like, high-percentage decisions for the good of his whole team. He knew how to pick talent, how to make talent fulfill its potential, and how to "catch more flies with sugar than with vinegar." He firmly enforced team rules,[12] and moved on the field with consistent integrity, intelligence, and self-control. All of this produced remarkable results, and the Reds' statistics tell the tale.

	Manager	Team ERA	Complete Games	Team Errors	Opponents' Runs
1937	Dressen	3.94	64	208	707
1938	McKechnie	3.62	72	172	634
1939	McKechnie	3.27	86	162	595
1940	McKechnie	3.05	91	117	528

In a period of three years at the Reds' helm, defensive master Bill McKechnie masterminded a pitching staff which completed an amazing 60 percent of its games, assembled a defense which committed 44 percent fewer errors, with the pitching and defense reducing opponents' runs by 25 percent.

In his book on the Reds, Lee Allen accurately said of McKechnie and his amazing Cincinnati results: "There is an air about him that makes others want to appear at their best. He is the sort of man that other decent men would want their sons to play for... Nothing escapes him on the field. He knows which players to flatter and which ones to edge with his acid tongue. He is a master of psychology who

[12]Midnight curfew, no whiskey, no poker, beer in the clubhouse only after wins, and no singing or laughing in the clubhouse after losses.

never went to college... He has infused the team with the morale necessary for winning."

Reds' pitchers and players confirmed Allen's description of McKechnie. Vander Meer said the Deacon "was one of the greatest individuals I ever met in my life either on the field or off." Junior Thompson reflected, "I couldn't have had a better manager than McKechnie. He and his wife were like parents to me." Outfielder Harry Craft praised his manager, saying, "You always knew where you stood with him. He called a spade a spade." First baseman Frank McCormick described McKechnie as "real fatherly. Very understanding, sympathetic, and tough." Third baseman Bill Werber wrote in his autobiography that McKechnie was "the type of man who inspired players, won their confidence and affection, and built high team morale."

Regardless of Crosley Field's changed dimensions, and the addition and improvement of players on the Reds' roster after 1937, Cincinnati went from last place to first in two years because Warren Giles had the guts to stand up to the Reds' fans by making the unpopular decision to hire boring, beloved, and baseball brilliant Bill McKechnie to manage the team.

The 1939 Season

AFTER THE REDS HAD STAYED IN THE RACE through most of the 1938 season, the experts knew Cincinnati would be a contender in 1939. In spring training, Giant manager Bill Terry predicted the Reds were "the team to beat." *The Sporting News* ran a feature story in March stating why Cincinnati could win the pennant. *Cincinnati Post* sportswriter Tom Swope saw the home team as having "fewer 'ifs' than any of the other pennant-contending clubs." With the addition of third baseman Werber in March, the April 20, 1939 issue of *The Sporting News* acknowledged that the Reds "went into the championship season as the winter book favorite."

After an underwhelming 11-10 start, with Walters and Derringer getting nine of the victories, the team took off from May 16-27, winning 12 straight. During the streak, left-hander Lee Grissom won four, and Walters and Derringer took three victories each; leadoff batter Werber got on base almost half the time; and McCormick suddenly became a power hitter, with six home runs. The streak moved Cincinnati into first place, where they would stay for the rest of the season. Pennant handwriting found its way to the wall and by June 1, long-suffering Cincinnati fans (who had not seen post-season action in twenty years since the Black Sox Scandal) were already figuring out how to obtain tickets for the World Series.

St. Louis manager Ray Blades reached the same conclusion as the Cincinnati fans after his team finally stopped the Reds' streak in late May. "Cincinnati's team looks like the one to beat in the National League this year. It has everything a winning team needs, including spirit, pitching, fielding ability, speed on the bases, plenty of the old sock, intelligent direction, and reserve strength."

After the May streak, the team played competent but unexceptional baseball (23-19) through the All-Star break. The American public was taking notice of McKechnie's team. Sellouts on the road became the rule. No issue of *The Sporting News* would dare omit a featured update on Cincinnati's season. McCormick, Goodman, and Lombardi gained notoriety as a slugging trio to match any in the league. When Lombardi went down with a foot injury on June 11, Hershberger actually outperformed him. By June 15, with the season only one-third gone, Walters had won nine games and Derringer eight. McKechnie publicly declared his expectation that his first-place team would improve after the July 10-12 All-Star break. The Reds fulfilled their skipper's prophecy, winning fourteen out of fifteen from July 17-30. As important to Giles and McKechnie,[13] by July 19 the Reds had drawn 450,000 in attendance through only 36 home games.

As the Reds left the National League behind, McKechnie's star finally started to rise. Cincinnati sportswriter Swope dubbed the Deacon as "the most self-effacing, least boastful and most revered man among the eight men managing National League teams... Players do not look upon him as their boss, rather they regard him as their father... He doesn't curb any player's enthusiasm for baseball, or for harmless

[13]McKechnie had an attendance incentive bonus in his contract. When the Reds drew 450,000 fans in a season, (being the attendance level for the entire 1937 season before the Deacon took over), the manager received an extra $5,000.

jokes. But he does, without any iron discipline, curb their taste for improper actions on or off the field."

As the 1939 season wore on, one of McKechnie's greatest gifts as a manager became more apparent in his handling of umpires. The Deacon treated the men in blue like he did his players. If possible, he patted them on the back and let them do their job. When necessary, McKechnie would vent his paternal wrath. Above all, Bill McKechnie tried to be fair with umpires without jeopardizing his team.

Two examples from 1939 establish the way the Deacon handled umpires. On July 15, 1939, while manager McKechnie coached third base, Harry Craft hit a ball into the left-field bleachers off the Giants' "Prince Hal" Schumacher. Everyone in the park except third-base umpire Ziggy Sears and senior crew chief umpire George Magerkurth (at first base) saw the ball's being at least ten feet foul. Sears declared the ball "Fair," giving Craft a home run. Magerkurth affirmed his junior umpire, and all hell broke loose. Giants shortstop Billy Jurges punched Magerkurth, and big George later admitted to League president Ford Frick that the fight was as much his fault as Jurges's. Frick later fined both umpire and player, and suspended them for ten days. Soon after that game, major league parks started putting screens on foul poles to help the umpire determine whether balls hit into the seats on the line were fair or foul.

While Magerkurth and Jurges went at it, McKechnie kept quiet. As third-base coach, he knew the ball was foul. Regardless of his religious principals and admiration for Honest Abe, McKechnie did not see it as his job to correct umpires to the Reds' detriment. Craft anxiously asked his manager where McKechnie saw the ball drop, and he told his young outfielder, "The umpire called it fair."

Later in August, again while coaching third base, McKechnie saw Bill Werber hit a ball down the left field line. Initially, third-base umpire Babe Pinelli called the ball fair, giving Werber a double and driving in a Cincinnati run. Then, home-plate umpire Beans Reardon overruled Pinelli, and called Werber's hit foul, thereby taking away a Reds run.

A manager like Durocher would have exploded, but from his third-base coaching perspective, McKechnie acquiesced to Reardon's ruling without any argument. McKechnie had seen the ball left of the foul line and, therefore, knew that Reardon had ruled correctly. The Deacon could not argue a position he knew to be false, and did not see it as part of his job to do so.

When an umpire made a bad call to the Reds' detriment, however, Bill McKechnie had the capacity to turn on his quiet but forceful anger. Leo Durocher described it in his autobiography: "McKechnie went out to discuss an umpire's call with his arms crossed and walked real slow as if it pained him deeply to have to be doing this. He wore glasses and he had a mild reasonable way about him. The umps allowed him to get away with murder."

When the Deacon had a bone to pick with an umpire, despite his "mild, reasonable way," McKechnie waved his players away and went directly at the man in blue. Reporter Joe Williams observed, "Let an umpire call one against the Reds in a tough game and you will see the Deacon walk out on the field with his hands jammed deep in his pockets and his jaw stuck out. This is when he really takes his hair down..." Bartel remembered a game when McKechnie got into it with Hall of Fame umpire Bill Klem. "Old Arbitrator" Klem ended up throwing the Deacon out of the game, and McKechnie got a letter from National League president Ford Frick: "I cannot believe the terminology you used with Mr. Klem yesterday. If it were anybody else I would have to suspend him three days. I'm fining you two hundred dollars." Outside of the occasional crisis, McKechnie treated umpires as he did his players, supporting them with praise for their good games, and making no unnecessary or unwarranted noise.

As the Deacon guided his players and massaged umpires to keep the Reds in first place through the late summer, Cincinnati fans ignored the depression and focused on the home team. *Chicago Herald* sportswriter Warren Brown observed that the Cincinnati "press and radio do not seem able to serve up enough news and gossip about the heroes to satisfy the demand." Brown recognized the media's difficulty in coming up with stories on the team. "Toughest subject for all the purveyors of words happens to be Deacon Bill McKechnie. There isn't a great deal of color to McKechnie. He doesn't have much to say to his players and less to the purveyor of words... As a matter of fact, there isn't a great deal of 'color' in the entire cast of Reds. They are simply a businesslike lot of young and old men with a view toward winning a pennant, and so far they have attended strictly to business."

By the first of September, McKechnie felt secure enough to predict a pennant for his team on the front page of *The Sporting News*. Cincinnati had suffered through August with a record of 13-15, held first place by at least four games during that slump, and gotten their players rested and healthy for the finish. The Reds' leader could not be shaken from his belief in the team's destiny, and the club responded to its manager's confidence by winning 18 of its last 24 games, finishing four-and-a-half games in front of the Cardinals.

Into the valley of the shadow of Yankee Stadium marched the Reds to take on the Bronx Bombers in the World Series. Having blown out the American League,[14] the Yankees licked their chops to do what no other team had done in the twentieth century—win a fourth consecutive Series.

In a recent interview, Reds pitcher Junior Thompson remembered that World Series: "One of the things about the game of baseball is, when you're overmatched, you've got to admit it. That's the way that 1939 World Series was. I don't believe anyone was more overmatched than we were playing the New York Yankees. Those guys were absolutely awesome!" Werber said, "I think the team going into Yankee Stadium was maybe a little bit awed. The ball club went into a general hitting slump. I don't think it was the Yankees pitching that did it so much as possibly the awe of getting into this World Series."

Though the Yankees swept the intimidated Reds, the first and fourth games were close,[15] and the difference in the team batting averages during the Series was minimal—the Yankees hit .206, while the Reds hit .203. The Series turned on the abundance of Yankees power (seven homers in the four games, while the Reds hit none), causing a 20-8 run differential.

The only publicized story of the short Series was "Lombardi's Snooze." Bucky Walters put the Series and the Snooze in perspective:

---

[14]Second-place Boston finished seventeen games back in 1939.

[15]The Reds lost Game One 2-1 on a misplayed fly ball by Goodman in the ninth inning. In the finale, the Yankees scored two runs in the top of the ninth to tie the game, and then three in the top of the tenth to win it.

Joe DiMaggio slides safely across the plate while catcher Ernie Lombardi "snoozes." (Associated Press/Wide World photo)

"It was a dull series and they had nothing else to write about so they picked on poor old Ernie. It was the big story and it was no story."

Lombardi's snooze in the tenth inning of Game Four started with Crosetti on third, Keller on first, and Joe DiMaggio at bat. The Yankees Clipper singled to right bringing Crosetti home with the go-ahead run. When rightfielder Goodman juggled the ball, "King Kong" Keller broke for home and slammed into catcher Lombardi, inadvertently kneeing Ernie's groin. Down went Lombardi on his back, writhing in pain, as DiMaggio rounded third and kept on coming. Grantland Rice wrote that Joe DiMaggio came home "as Lombardi still lay at rest, a stricken being," and pre-television America read the account and visualized Big Ernie asleep while Joltin' Joe romped home.

Ernie Lombardi had to deal with the humiliation of his groin-damage-induced "snooze" for the rest of his sad life. Authors James

Costello and Michael Santa Maria recently chronicled the post-snooze tragedy of Ernie Lombardi in their book *In the Shadows of the Diamond*. After his retirement from the game in 1947, Big Ernie bounced around the odd-job market as a grease monkey and peanut vendor, battled depression, and even attempted suicide. The quiet catcher with the big nose, 46-ounce warclub bat, huge hands,[16] and heavy feet would die an embittered man in 1977. Like Durocher, he felt the sting of Cooperstown's annual rejection during his final years. When the call of induction finally came from the Hall of Fame, Big Ernie had been "snoozing" permanently for nine years.

After 1939

FOLLOWING THE BRONX BOMBERS' BREAKAWAY from the American League pack throughout the 1939 season, and the lopsided destruction of the Reds in the Series, the call went out all over baseball to "Break up the Yankees." McKechnie would have none of it. "I know how I'd feel if I had players like those fellas and somebody came along and told me I had to get rid of them. There should be more teams like the Yankees, that's all. We'll have to build to their level."

And so McKechnie did. Adding relief pitcher Joe Beggs in a trade with the Yankees and then obtaining Boston Brave gray-haired phenom Jim Turner, the Deacon made his already National League best pitching staff even better in 1940. Despite Hershberger's suicide in early August,[17] McKechnie held his team together. They finished the season prevailing in 41 of the team's 100 wins by one run, blowing out Durocher's second-place Dodgers by 12 games. Cincinnati then beat the Hank Greenberg-led Tigers four games to three in the 1940 World Series with Walters and Derringer accounting for all the wins.

---

[16]Lombardi's hands were each capable of holding seven baseballs, and had sufficient meat on them to absorb catching outside pitches barehanded from time to time when the slow catcher could get to them no other way.

[17]McKechnie counseled Hershberger extensively in the days before the suicide. Hershberger apparently fully disclosed to his paternal skipper the many things on his mind troubling him. Following his catcher's death, McKechnie held the confidence and never told anyone the particulars of Hershberger's concerns during his final days.

Following the 1940 season, McKechnie kept the Reds in the first division until 1945, by which time the war had wiped out the entire Cincinnati lineup. After the 1946 season, with the fair-weather Cincinnati fans clamoring for a change, Giles found himself in the same predicament experienced by Branch Rickey after the 1928 season. The Cincinnati general manager told the sportswriters, "These fans just forced me to fire the best manager in baseball."

Bill McKechnie never managed again in the major leagues after 1946. He served as the Cleveland Indians' pitching coach under Boy Wonder player-manager Lou Boudreau from 1947-1949, and guided the Feller-Lemon-Beardon pitching staff (with a league-leading team earned-run average of 3.22) to the 1948 American League pennant and World Series triumph over the Spahn-Sain Boston Braves.

After leaving Cincinnati in 1946, McKechnie refused four major league managing opportunities. The Deacon saw his role as pitching coach to be a full-time job, and decided that the optimum managerial approach necessarily utilized two team leaders—one to preside over the pitchers, and the other to look after everything else. Boudreau and McKechnie informally had that arrangement with the Indians, and enjoyed obvious success with it. Other than Cleveland's Gabe Paul, however, McKechnie never found a general manager willing to buy off on the two-manager premise.

In 1962, the Deacon entered the Hall of Fame. In his modest induction speech, Bill McKechnie told the crowd, "Anything that I have contributed to baseball I have been repaid seven times seven." Three years later, he died a wealthy man in his retirement community of Bradenton, Florida, having celebrated his fiftieth wedding anniversary. As a final tribute after his death, Bradenton residents named their town baseball facility "McKechnie Field," still used today by the Pittsburgh Pirates during spring training.

These honors served as Bill McKechnie's final earthly rewards for a lifetime of baseball achievement and decency to his fellow man. To Durocher's everlasting ire, the Deacon proved to be another nice guy who finished first.

Leo Durocher (without cap) and broadcaster Red Barber (coat and tie) together making history–the first televised game. (The Sporting News)

CHAPTER FIVE

THE REDHEAD IN THE CATBIRD SEAT

Red Barber Comes to Brooklyn, Television Comes to Baseball

AS THE SUMMER OF 1939 WORE ON, the first game of an August 26 doubleheader between McKechnie's Reds and Durocher's Dodgers turned into the most important baseball game since Doubleday's mythical scrimmage in Cooperstown one hundred years before. The National Broadcasting Company positioned two cameras at Ebbets Field, and beamed baseball from its tower on top of the Empire State Building. Visitors to the television pavilion at the New York World's Fair, as well as those few hundred homeowners with a set in their living room, got to see the Deacon tangle with the Lip on that Saturday afternoon in the first televised major league game. The landmark telecast opened with a voice already familiar to Baseball America: "This is Red Barber speaking. Let me say hello to you all."

Well before August 26, the summer of 1939 had been a historic time for sportscasting. Baseball's centennial year became the first year when all sixteen major league teams carried their games on radio. The last holdouts to the "ether waves" had been the Big Apple teams. From 1934-1938, fearing that radio coverage would cut home attendance, the Yankees, Giants, and Dodgers had signed an agreement banning baseball on the radio in New York. As the pact expired, the Yankees and Giants wanted to extend the radio boycott, but new Brooklyn boss MacPhail refused. Larry signed his Dodgers with 50,000-watt station WOR, and lined up General Mills, Socony Vacuum, and Proctor & Gamble as sponsors. Reluctantly, the Yankees and Giants followed suit and made their own radio deal with WABC.

Dodgers general manager Larry MacPhail had the station and the sponsors he needed to open the 1939 Dodger season. To conclude the radio package, the former Cincinnati Reds vice president hired away from his old team a thirty-one-year-old Southerner who had already become baseball's best sportscaster. His name was Walter Lanier Barber.

Red Barber and Baseball on the Radio—Pre-1939

GROWING UP IN MISSISSIPPI AND FLORIDA, Red Barber aspired to sing, tell jokes, and play trombone in blackface minstrel shows. As it became clear during college that his career choice faced obsolescence, Barber encountered a desperate University of Florida radio announcer about to be forced into reading three agricultural academic papers on a farm report show. For the sake of variety, the announcer asked Barber to read the middle paper on "bovine obstetrics" over the college radio station. The station manager heard Barber's reading and decided that anyone capable of vitalizing cattle procreation tastefully for the radio listener deserved a job. On March 4, 1930, twenty-two-year-old Red Barber signed his first radio contract with University of Florida at Gainesville station WRUF earning a Great Depression starting salary of fifty dollars per month.

By the time Barber signed with WRUF, radio had carried bits and pieces of major league baseball for eight seasons. The first broadcast of a big league game had taken place August 5, 1921, from Pittsburgh's Forbes Field. Harold Arlin of local station KDKA sat in a field-level box seat with his equipment behind the home plate screen. Arlin called the Pirates-Phillies game using a mike he called a "mushophone" which looked "like a tomato can with a felt lining."

The Pittsburgh experiment became an immediate success. Exactly two months after the first broadcast, Arlin's KDKA engineered wiring

Graham "the King" McNamee. (National Baseball Library and Archive, Cooperstown, New York)

from New York's Polo Grounds to Pittsburgh allowing the first live play-by-play coverage of a World Series game. By 1922, World Series radio coverage went to most of the eastern part of the country.

In 1923, baseball's first radio superstar announcer arrived in the form of Graham "the King" McNamee. McNamee's career as baseball's premier early radio voice lasted thirteen years. In his definitive baseball radio history *Voices of the Game*, author Curt Smith quoted Heywood Hale Broun on the impact of McNamee:

> McNamee justified the whole activity of radio broadcasting. A thing may be a marvelous invention and still dull as dishwater. It will be that unless it allows the play of personality. A machine amounts to nothing unless a man can ride it. Graham McNamee has been able to take a new medium of expression and through it transmit himself—to give it vividly a sense of movement and of feeling. Of such is the kingdom of art.

With McNamee popularizing baseball, football, boxing, political conventions, and anything else America seemed interested in hearing, national networks soon formed to capitalize on the country's newest fascination. NBC opened its doors in November 1926 and CBS followed ten months later. In the decade between the early twenties and early thirties, the number of home radios increased from three million to eighteen million, supplemented by the birth of the car radio in 1923.

Most baseball owners were initially concerned that live game broadcasts would cause listeners to follow the game at home rather than attend in person. Such fears initially prevented all the eastern teams except Pittsburgh from going forward with radio baseball. The western cities never feared the ether waves. Before radio aired the national pastime, farmers and residents of small towns in the Midwest largely ignored major league games. As baseball broadcasts started beaming into living rooms in the twenties, rural families began spending their evenings cheering the nearest big-city team, and soon found themselves traveling to the urban green cathedrals where their hardball heroes played. Increased attendance from radio in the Midwest spurred eastern teams to follow suit, except in New York.

With radio baseball growing each year in popularity, and Graham McNamee becoming a national celebrity, Red Barber soon longed for horizons beyond Gainesville. After months of interviewing across the depression-starved country, Barber caught on with the Cincinnati Reds before the start of the 1934 season.

By the time Barber left WRUF, he had worked his salary up to fifty dollars per week. He took a 50-percent pay cut to go to Cincinnati. His father told Barber he was making a mistake. Barber replied, "I want the chance," knowing opportunity at that stage in his career meant more than money.

At the time Barber arrived in Cincinnati, new Reds vice president and general manager Larry MacPhail was the straw stirring the drink. Between arriving in 1934 and departing after the 1936 season, MacPhail's innovations at Cincinnati caused attendance to more than double while the Reds stagnated in the second division. Though the team played poorly during the brief MacPhail era, the Cincinnati fan base expanded for two reasons—Red Barber's Southern charisma enticed radio listeners to follow the Reds closer, and Larry MacPhail's May 24, 1935 commencement of major league night baseball at Crosley Field allowed working people to attend more games.

Twenty-six-year-old Red Barber had never even seen a major league baseball game before calling Opening Day for the 1934 Reds, and he didn't "see" many that first year in Cincinnati. MacPhail's initial media strategy consisted of broadcasting very few home games from Crosley Field (only twenty in 1934), and focusing primarily on having Barber "recreate" road games as Western Union wired the basic facts into his studio. The young broadcaster could then use his substantial imagination and knowledge of the players' mannerisms to transform a telegraph ticker tape into a mental picture of action which Barber succeeded in communicating to the Cincinnati listeners.

In his 1993 book *My Life As a Fan*, author Wilfrid Sheed shared his recollection of listening to a Red Barber recreation with the tick of the telegraph in the background:

> "Raht now, the bases are F.O.B.—fulluv Brooklyns," he would purr. "Whitlow Wyatt seems to be sittin' in the catbird seat, ma friends.

> The flags are barely rifflin' today in Crosley, [tick] which means theah's prob'ly just the merest hint of a breeze blowin' off the Ohio Rivuh—[tick, tick]—meanwahl, Frank McCormick adjusts the bill of his cap and Kubby Higbe looks in long and slow for the sign [tick, pause]—whoops [long pause, and tickety-tick, tick] he jest missed with that one, a fastball hah inside—you know how ol' Kubby lo-oves that pitch."

By 1935, as Barber raised the Reds' profile in Cincinnati, MacPhail decided if a little coverage helped attendance a little, then increasing the number of games broadcast would help a lot. Never one to show restraint about anything, MacPhail so gushed with enthusiasm for his new broadcaster, he compared Barber to an earlier communicator who broadcast his most famous performance at the Sermon on the Mount.

As the 1935 season progressed, Barber's reputation became national. The recently formed Mutual Broadcasting System chose Barber to team with Chicago's Bob Elson and Quin Ryan to broadcast the World Series. Barber would continue to get the October nod each year for the remainder of his tenure at Cincinnati. At the 1935 Series, Graham McNamee covered his last Fall Classic and passed the baton to the voice of the Reds. During the 1936 Series, McNamee sat in the booth as a guest and observed the young craftsman at work. Between innings, "King" McNamee leaned over to Red Barber and said, "Kid, you've got it." Barber knew that with the exposure of a national network and the blessing of radio's most historic figure, there were bigger markets in his future than Cincinnati.

Barber Goes to Brooklyn—1939

WHEN MACPHAIL HIRED RED BARBER TO COME to Brooklyn for the 1939 season, the thirty-one-year-old sportscaster took another pay cut. Brooklyn paid Barber $9,000 his first year, which he accepted in lieu of Cincinnati's $18,000 offer to stay. In explaining his decision, the young broadcaster later told *The Sporting News*: "Cincinnati was good to me, but, like all country boys, I wanted a crack at New York."

What happened in Brooklyn beginning in 1939 became baseball history's most important media story. Respected baseball historian and co-author of Barber's autobiography, Robert Creamer, summarized the significance of Barber's rookie year covering the Dodgers:

> The three of them, MacPhail, Durocher, and Barber, revolutionized baseball in 1939 and Barber's part in the revolution was by no means the least important. Other major league teams had been broadcasting their games, but often on a sporadic now and then schedule. There had been no baseball broadcasts in New York City except at World Series and All-Star time. After Barber and the Dodgers exploded into prominence, baseball broadcasting became as integral a part of a major league club's operation as the third-base dugout.

When Barber signed with Brooklyn, followed by the Yankees and Giants hiring Arch McDonald away from the Senators to broadcast their home games, commentators were initially skeptical about radio baseball in New York. In February 1939, *The Sporting News*'s Dan Daniels warned: "This is very tough territory for radio announcers. It is apparent that a *new technique* in announcing is necessary. That old stuff about 'the pitcher has the ball, he is winding up, there goes the pitch' is not going to work in this neck of the woods."

What Barber brought from Cincinnati into the Ebbets Field press box were two characteristics that helped form his unique style, which satisfied Daniels's perceived New York requirement for a "new technique." The first element in Barber's style was that he regarded himself as a broadcaster, *not* a fan. Before the start of the 1935 World Series, Commissioner Kenesaw Mountain Landis called Barber, McNamee, and the other broadcasters covering the Series into his Detroit hotel suite and gave them unambiguous advice for calling the Fall Classic:

> Gentlemen, I wouldn't presume to tell you how to conduct your business. But I will tell you to let the ballplayers play—they don't need your help. Let the managers manage. And above everything else, you let the umpires umpire... Gentlemen, you report. Report everything you can see. Report what the ballplayers do...

> Report what the managers do... Report what the umpire does... By report, I mean you have the right to say what is going on, no matter what is going on, or where it is going on. But don't voice your opinions. Don't editorialize. Report...

Barber heeded Landis's advice throughout his career. The Redhead was not a baseball fan. When Barber left broadcasting after the 1966 season, he never attended another major league game. Whenever he was asked to name his favorite player, Barber's answer was always, "I don't have one." Hall of Fame sportscaster Vin Scully described Barber's broadcast approach as "Look with your eyes, not with your heart."

The second feature to Barber's technique involved constantly using his expanded vocabulary and Southern metaphors which came to be known as "Barberisms." In his autobiography *Rhubarb in the Catbird Seat*, Red Barber was upfront about his verbal preferences. "I like words. I like colorful language. I think most people do."

From his English-teacher mother, Barber gained an appreciation for a broad word base. When a hitter singled, and got to second because an outfielder misplayed the ball, Barber explained the runner's advancing on the fielder's "concomitant" error. When a player erred on an inopportune play resulting in jeers from the crowd, Barber told his listener the goat of the game stood suffering in "ignominy."

From his raconteur railroad-conductor father, Barber learned to use figures of speech. A team didn't put together a scoring rally; it "tore up the pea patch." A runner didn't knock down an infielder to break up a double play; he "swung the gate on him." A relief pitcher didn't come in for a failed starter; he "assumed the ballistic burden." It wasn't a beautiful day for baseball; the day had a "robin's egg blue sky with very few angels in the form of clouds in it."

In short, as disciple Scully ultimately concluded, Barber's Southern accent and unique descriptions of the game on the field "made broadcasting a conversation with the listener, with Barber chatting on the microphone as if gathered around a pot-bellied stove." This was the technique Red Barber had perfected in Cincinnati for five years, and brought to Brooklyn in 1939.

Unbeknownst to anyone at the time, New York City had a subconscious yearning for a thirty-one-year-old Floridian who already sounded like a favorite grandfather.

MacPhail sent Barber to 1939 spring training in Clearwater. Having already discovered in Cincinnati that the bigger the radio-listening fan base, the better the home-game ticket sales, MacPhail required WOR to broadcast the Dodgers' spring training games.

While at spring training, Barber asked the Dodger president if he had any specific instructions for broadcasting in New York. At first, MacPhail said "No," and walked away. After a pause, the Roaring Redhead walked back to his broadcaster and worked himself into a rage:

> Yes! Yes! I have! When I told the Yankees and Giants that I was not going to be a party to that anti-radio ban anymore and that I was going to broadcast, Eddie Brannick of the Giants said to me, "If you dare broadcast, if you dare break this agreement, we'll get a 50,000-watt radio station and we'll get the best baseball broadcaster in the world and, MacPhail, we'll blast you into the river."
>
> That's what Brannick said to me. He threatened me! Now, yes, I have an instruction for you. I've got a 50,000-watt radio station: WOR. And I've got you. And I don't want to be blasted into the river.

Red Barber understood the MacPhail mandate. And if the boss's Clearwater roar failed to motivate Barber to win the battle for the New York radio listener, *Time* magazine succeeded. The April 17, 1939 issue of *Time* featured an article on baseball radio broadcasts for the coming season. It began with the observation, "This week, radio starts its biggest baseball season in history." Each team now had radio broadcasts and sponsors. Pictured and profiled as "the biggest and best announcer" was the Yankees' and Giants' Arch McDonald. Nowhere in the article was the name "Red Barber" mentioned. In *Rhubarb*, Barber still seethed from the oversight: "*Time* magazine had given me the ultimate insult. It had ignored me."

When the Dodgers opened against the Giants on April 18, 1939, Barber dedicated himself to proving *Time* wrong. Upon his arrival,

Barber recognized that Brooklyn's three million residents had always suffered an inferiority complex in comparison to their Manhattan neighbors. While Manhattan glistened with Wall Street and Broadway, Brooklyn could only claim an old bridge, Coney Island, and Flatbush Avenue. *Time* magazine now made Red Barber feel as underappreciated as Brooklyn and projected Arch McDonald as the Manhattan sportscasting star.

Sensing himself as a metaphor for the borough, Barber acted quickly to become an integral part of Brooklyn. He and his wife Lylah lived there, walked there, and shopped there. He rode the subway to the Dodgers games. Barber expressed his goal as the voice of the Dodgers. "I didn't broadcast with a Brooklyn accent, but I did broadcast with a Brooklyn heart."

Barber's Brooklyn heart took over on Opening Day. Not content to just arrive at the ballpark and call the game, Barber got to work early and induced WOR to give him an extra fifteen minutes for a pre-game show. He persuaded Giants manager Bill Terry and new Dodgers skipper Leo Durocher to share their game plans with the radio audience. The man with a front-row ticket didn't have access to this kind of inside information. Soon fans started taking portable radios to the games to have the best of all worlds.

When baseball began on the radio in New York in 1939, many media experts predicted the national pastime would lose in competition with the already popular soap operas. Red Barber quickly proved the experts wrong. The July 27, 1939 issue of *The Sporting News* reported that 60 percent of the radios in New York were turned to baseball on weekdays, and most favored Barber and Brooklyn over Arch McDonald and the Yankees and Giants. Native New Yorker Vin Scully recalled Barber's "play-by-play blanketing the entire New York metropolitan area. You could drive with your car window down and never miss a pitch."

Poet Donald Hall remembered for author Peter Golenbock how his family spent Sunday afternoons in the summer of 1939 in a Studebaker listening to Dodgers games, and the effect Red Barber had on his mother. "At first my mother was totally disinterested in baseball, but more and more she began to listen, the three of us sitting in the front seat, and finally she got into it."

Red Barber's main contribution to MacPhail's surging Dodgers attendance was his capacity to inspire women to attend games. The February 2, 1939 issue of *The Sporting News* reflected doubts that radio broadcasts would boost baseball attendance in New York, and compared it to Ladies Days there. "In other cities,[1] Ladies Day is a big institution. In New York, it has no vogue or standing at all." After Barber landed in the Ebbets Field broadcast booth, women like Donald Hall's mother couldn't get enough of the Dodgers. In a 1942 profile of Barber in the *Saturday Evening Post*, journalist Richard Hubler observed:

> He is a lady's favorite. Before he came to Ebbets Field, the games generally resembled a for-men-only preview, but last year fifteen thousand women stormed the gates for one game. His favorite fan letter concerns a woman fan. "My wife was a semi-invalid. She enjoyed your broadcasts. Yesterday she began to sink, but she heard the last out. She died happy."

Throughout the 1939 season, Barber demonstrated uncompromising professionalism and self-confidence in his work. After leaving spring training in Clearwater, the Dodgers headed north to play exhibitions along the Atlantic seaboard. Barber went straight home to Brooklyn from Florida to do recreations of the games. In South Carolina, a telegraph operator who didn't understand baseball and its terminology sent the account of the Dodgers game to Barber at the WOR studio in New York. He began the broadcast of the Carolina game with imaginative commentary to amplify that the Dodgers had gotten a "hit to short," followed by a "hit to center," and then a "hit to third." Barber reported for the listener that Brooklyn appeared to be heading for a big inning with the bases loaded and nobody out. The next signal telegraphed into WOR announced the Carolina team coming to bat.

Knowing that recreating a game with a baseball-ignorant wire operator was impossible, Barber immediately told the WOR listening audience that technical problems had arisen preventing any further account of the game, called off the broadcast, and walked out of the

---

[1]All other cities except New York had baseball on the radio in 1939.

studio. WOR and Western Union weren't happy with the Brooklyn rookie sportscaster's unilateral decision to cancel the game recreation, but Barber's rage exceeded his employer's. Barber was not going to be humiliated into putting men on base without being able to explain what happened to them. Within a day, WOR located a telegrapher with a thorough knowledge of baseball and got him to South Carolina.

After standing up to his radio station, Barber's next confrontation came with MacPhail shortly after the 1939 season commenced. WOR wanted to delay the broadcast of a Dodgers doubleheader until the completion of former President Hoover's radio speech, meaning Barber would likely begin calling the first game at its halfway point.

MacPhail roared at the prospect of partial preemption. The Dodgers boss told his broadcaster that if Barber didn't get to call the game from the first pitch, he was ordered not to call the game at all. Knowing he could not be insubordinate to his station, Barber told MacPhail that when WOR told him to begin calling the game, he would comply with the instruction. MacPhail screamed back that if Barber picked up the broadcast at midgame, then the strongest Ebbets Field employees would physically evict the broadcaster from the booth. Barber refused to buckle, causing MacPhail to send two burly electricians into the booth to have the announcer removed.

Fortunately, a station engineer overheard the argument, and recognized the very real possibility that a Dodgers broadcast would be cut short by MacPhail having Red Barber thrown out of the booth—on the air. A WOR executive decided that such live confrontations could not be in anyone's best interest, and canceled the broadcast for the entire first game of the doubleheader.

In *Rhubarb*, Barber led into his account of the Hoover speech incident in describing his lifelong friendship with MacPhail by saying:

> I don't believe two people can have a deep friendship unless it's based on respect, and I don't believe two people can have real respect for one another until they test each other—get on the opposite sides of the line and look each other in the face, nose to nose.... You don't find out who a man is if he's always agreeable.

MacPhail had tested Barber, the broadcaster had responded with steely conviction about his professional responsibility, and the friendship took off.

After standing up to his radio station on the preseason recreations and to MacPhail on the delayed broadcast, Barber had his final confrontation in the summer of 1939 with General Mills, lead sponsor for the Dodgers broadcasts. Throughout the season, the sponsor's executives had required the celebrity broadcaster to come to the corporate office before and after each game to discuss business incidentals. Barber went along for a while, but soon realized the sessions served no purpose except to waste his time.

After a few months, Barber told General Mills' executives he was not going to come to their offices anymore unless he knew there was a specific business reason for meeting. The sponsor recognized that they could not afford to lose Barber, who had already become one of New York's biggest stars. Backed into a corner, General Mills reluctantly gave Barber permission to skip the meetings on the condition he not tell the other broadcasters. In *Rhubarb*, Barber cited the importance of the incident:

> If I needed pinpoint documentation that the broadcasts in Brooklyn were on the main line and breezing along, that did it. That's when I knew. I walked out and went down the elevator and got on the subway, and while the subway was taking me out to Ebbets Field, I knew I was on the way—and to something more than just a ballgame that day.

By late August 1939, less than ten years since describing "bovine obstetrics," Red Barber had arrived in the world of radio. He had broadcast four World Series for a national network. He had been anointed heir apparent by "King" McNamee. He had come to the Big Apple and stood his professional ground with his station, team, and sponsor. Clearly, the man in Brooklyn's Catbird Seat needed a new horizon. He found it in a brown box.

The First Televised Game

THE MARCH 30, 1939 ISSUE OF *THE SPORTING NEWS* carried a picture of minor league players being interviewed on television. In the caption beneath the picture, baseball's bible reported: "The time may be *rather distant* when the fan can sit at home and not only hear an account of the games but witness the players in action as well." *The News's* prediction of a "rather distant" timetable did not anticipate the effect of a World's Fair.

The 1939 New York World's Fair gave most of its visitors their first opportunity to see live television. As with all preliminary technology, the quality of the product was unrefined. Yet because it was the first visual live outside entertainment for the home, the small black-and-white image at Flushing Meadows quickly became the talk of the country.

NBC vice president "Doc" Morton sensed that baseball on television might enhance the public's appetite for his company's newest product, and knew Red Barber was the right man to sell Larry MacPhail on the Dodgers hosting the first televised game. In *Rhubarb*, Barber explained his analysis of the assignment:

> In being around Larry MacPhail, it became rapidly apparent to me that one of the things he dearly loved was to be first. He particularly loved to be first in something new and constructive, the way he was first with a season-ticket plan, first with night ball, first with a radio broadcast in New York... So it was obvious to me that if you wanted to get him to do something, all you had to do was show him how he could be first in it.

After Barber determined the proper psychology for handling MacPhail, he went to the Dodgers' president's office. The meeting was brief. Barber asked MacPhail if he wanted to be the first man in history to put a major league game on television, MacPhail said "Yes," and the meeting ended.

After MacPhail and Morton quickly negotiated a rights fee with the sole consideration being the network agreeing to install a television in the Ebbets Field press room, the cameras were ready to roll.[2] Burke Crotty, NBC's director of the telecast, decided two cameras behind home plate were sufficient—one at ground level and the other in the upper deck. After losing communication with Crotty early in the game, Barber broadcast from an upper deck seat behind third base, without the benefit of a monitor, hoping the action he called coincided with where the cameras pointed.

Overflow crowds at the World's Fair watching the game saw what Harold Parrott described for *The Sporting News* in the August 31, 1939 issue:

> The players were clearly distinguishable, but it was not possible to pick out the ball. The close-up images left a much better impression than did the general view of the field.

During the course of the game, Barber ad-libbed three commercials in front of the camera, one for each Dodgers' sponsor. For Proctor and Gamble, Barber held up a bar of Ivory Soap and talked about what a great soap it was. For General Mills, he poured Wheaties into a bowl, sliced a banana, poured milk on top, and told the viewers, "Now, that's the breakfast of champions." For Socony, Barber put on a Mobil gas station cap and raised up a can of oil. As Barber said later, "There was not a cue card in sight."

After the game, Barber went on the field and got Reds' pitching star Bucky Walters to show the viewers how a major league pitcher holds his pitches. Next, rival managers McKechnie and Durocher talked about their teams' pennant chances. Finally, Barber persuaded Dodger Dolf Camilli to show how he held his hand in his first baseman's glove. The broadcaster had always had a fascination for Camilli's large, strong, and graceful hands. Barber thought the television camera could capture Dolf's manual charisma better than any radio account, no matter how good the broadcaster's vocabulary.

MacPhail was pleased with the telecast, and wanted more. Beginning with Opening Day of the 1940 season, the Dodgers

---

[2]Three months before the Dodgers and the Reds played their August 26 televised game, a trial balloon had gone up. Columbia and Princeton had battled before NBC's cameras on May 17, proving that televising the national pastime was possible.

Red Barber and Bob Elson at the mike, broadcasting the 1939 World Series for the Mutual Broadcasting System. (University of Florida Archives)

president arranged for the showing of at least one Dodgers game each week until the start of World War II.

After the 1939 Season: A Lifetime of Achievement

WHEN THE REGULAR SEASON CLOSED, Gillette contracted with Major League Baseball to have exclusive radio rights to broadcast the 1939 World Series. The razor company selected the Mutual Broadcasting Network to call the games, thus giving Red Barber the chance to do his fifth consecutive Fall Classic. Following the Series, *The Sporting News* presented Barber with its Outstanding Baseball Announcer award, and its editor J. G. Taylor Spink dubbed him "the number-one man of the air."

Barber's greatest satisfaction came in proving *Time* magazine wrong. Arch McDonald knew the competition with Barber was futile and that he had met his match. After the 1939 season, McDonald retreated to Washington, where he could be the most important radio voice in town, preferring top broadcast billing of the lowly Senators over second-tier New York recognition calling games for the world-champion Yankees. Replacing McDonald was his backup during 1939, a gregarious Alabaman named Melvin Israel who preferred to be called "Mel Allen."

Early in World War II, Barber got MacPhail's permission to be the first American broadcaster to use the word "blood" on the air, allowing Barber to rally the borough for donations to the Brooklyn Red Cross Blood Bank during every Dodgers broadcast. There never was a shortage of blood at the Brooklyn facility during the war, and Barber's constant inspirational encouragement received well-deserved credit for the steady stream of donors.

Following the war, Larry MacPhail moved uptown to run the Yankees, and former Cardinal General Manager Branch Rickey took over the Dodgers' reins. With Rickey's prodding, Barber faced and, of course, prevailed in what he ultimately regarded as his greatest professional challenge. Rickey came to him in 1945 to advise the broadcaster of his agenda for integrating major league baseball. As a born and bred Southerner, Barber went home to his wife Lylah and told her of the Dodgers' plans. His first reaction was to resign, thinking Rickey's "Great Experiment" would likely turn into a social circus, and Barber wanted no part of it.

Lylah calmed down her husband, and with almost two years to prepare, Red Barber was ready in 1947 to follow Landis's advice from 1935. When Jackie Robinson broke in as the Dodgers' first baseman on Opening Day 1947, Barber reported the ballgame as an athletic contest without offering any social commentary. He recalled his two years preparing for integration in a 1988 interview with David Halberstam:

> The more I thought, the more I saw myself clearly, and the more I realized that I had no more control over being white than he [Jackie Robinson] had over being black. And I thought to myself: Why am I so proud of something over which I have no control and was in no way a matter of achievement? It was all a matter of chance. Do you know that I never said he was black? Never once. He was a baseball player, and I reported on him as a baseball player, which was my job.

From 1947 until his premature death in 1972, Jackie Robinson gave Red Barber much of the credit for Brooklyn's early and constant acceptance of him as player and man. Barber would later write *1947: When All Hell Broke Loose in Baseball,* detailing Robinson's rookie year.

Barber opened *1947* by explaining the importance of the Trailblazer's first season. "Baseball that year became a force, not only in sports but also in the overall history of this country." Barber felt it inappropriate to broadcast a social commentary in the context of Dodgers play-by-play, but saw writing a book with the benefit of three decades' worth of reflection as his best forum for evaluating baseball's "Great Experiment."

Before the start of the 1953 World Series, Barber told Gillette that his fee would have to be increased from the standard two hundred dollars per game, which the exclusive radio sponsor had browbeaten broadcasters (including Barber) to take in years past. Not interested in being rebuffed, Gillette revoked its offer to allow Barber to broadcast the Series. Walter O'Malley, whose regime in Brooklyn had replaced Rickey's in 1950, refused to back his radio voice in the Gillette fee dispute. Disappointed with O'Malley's decision, Barber resigned from the Dodgers[3] and accepted Larry MacPhail's New York Yankees' offer to

---

[3]Barber's resignation opened the door to his backup of the previous four seasons, Vin Scully, who would proceed to embark on his own Hall of Fame career.

come to the Bronx.[4] Beginning in 1954, Barber teamed with Mel Allen for Yankees radio and television broadcasts, where they worked together until Allen was fired before the 1964 Series.

Although Barber stayed active in television until he left the Yankees' booth in 1966, he never developed the affinity for TV he had for radio. In *Rhubarb*, he explained why:

> On radio, the play-by-play announcer is the show. He is the artist... He sees the game for his listeners, he interprets it, and it is his skill, his preparation, and his approach that are important... On TV, it's the director's show and the broadcaster is an instrument of his like a camera... On radio, you're an artist. On TV, you're a servant.

After Yankees president Mike Burke fired Barber late in the 1966 season for Red's insisting on telling the television audience about the small attendance in Yankee Stadium during the season's final home game, the broadcaster never looked back. Between 1966 and 1981, he wrote three books in addition to *Rhubarb* and *1947*, covering topics as diverse as the history of broadcasting, the strength of the human spirit, and spiritual preparation for death. During those years, Barber also narrated films, wrote newspaper columns, and preached frequently as a lay minister in the Episcopal Church. In 1978, Barber and Mel Allen became the first Cooperstown recipients of the Ford C. Frick Award for their outstanding broadcasting contributions to baseball.

Beginning in 1981 until shortly before his death in October 1992, Barber returned to the radio, teaming with Bob Edwards of National Public Radio's "Morning Edition" show. Every Friday morning, Edwards presented four minutes with Barber in his spontaneous glory, endearing the Ol' Redhead to a new audience for whom he became America's grandfather figure on the air.

In his book *Walk in the Spirit*, Barber closed with words from his father he had heard as a child:

> "I can't know, son, when you grow up and go out into the world what you will do for a living, who you will know and be around

[4]MacPhail had joined the Yankees front office following World War II.

> with, where you will go. Son, I can't know these things. But I do know this: No matter where you go in life, whatever you do, whoever you are with, when you wind up each day… and finally go to sleep—you have to sleep with yourself."

Red Barber could always "sleep with himself." He pursued career opportunity over money. He adhered to the highest broadcasting and personal standards regardless of the wishes of those with the power to fire him. He pleaded for blood to support the war effort. He played a key role in baseball's Great Experiment. He committed his knowledge and wisdom to five books. He ended his life sharing his insights for a new generation of radio listeners.

Although Brooklyn's radio voice viewed 1947 as the most important year in baseball, 1939 proved to be the turning point in Barber's life. In baseball's centennial year, Barber got his chance in the nation's biggest market and established himself for *Time* magazine and everyone else as baseball's greatest radio and television sportscaster.

Joe DiMaggio and bride-to-be Dorothy Arnold.

CHAPTER SIX

The Greatest Player in His Greatest Year on the Greatest Team

Joe DiMaggio and the Yankees Peak

As Red Barber dominated baseball on the radio in 1939, so the New York Yankees dominated baseball on the field. The Bronx Bombers triumphed in 106 games and lost 45 against American League colleagues appropriately nicknamed "the Seven Dwarfs" by sportswriters. Second-place Boston came in 17 games off the pace and last-place St. Louis finished 64 1/2 games out. The Yanks then swept McKechnie's Reds, thereby doing what no major league team had ever done—winning a fourth consecutive World Series.

Many respected analysts (Dan Daniel and Charles Alexander to name two) regard the 1939 Yankees as the greatest baseball team of all time. Most recently, in January 1994, *Baseball Weekly* concluded its computer-programmed tournament to determine the "best ever," declaring the 1939 Yankees winners in the semifinals over the 1927 Yanks and in the finals over the 1953 Dodgers.

How could a baseball team get better after losing Lou Gehrig eight games into the season? Well, position players Red Rolfe, George Selkirk, Joe DiMaggio, and Charlie Keller[1] had career years, while pitchers Red Ruffing, Johnny Murphy, Oral Hildebrand, Steve Sundra,

[1]Some might argue whether 1939 was right fielder Keller's greatest year. He hit .334 that year as a rookie, by far (36 points) the best average of his career, though he generated more power in subsequent seasons.

and Marius Russo did the same. Second baseman Joe Gordon (.284, 28 homers, 111 runs batted in) and catcher Bill Dickey (.302, 24 homers, 105 runs batted in) merely had great (but not career) years. The only weak links weren't so weak. Light-hitting Frank Crosetti led the league's shortstop in put-outs, double plays, and fielding average, while driving in 56 runs, and Gehrig's replacement Babe Dahlgren knocked in 89 runs, while playing a great defensive first base.

The Sporting News acknowledged the Yankees' dominance when its January 11, 1940 issue named Gordon, Rolfe, Dickey, DiMaggio, and Ruffing as the best players *in the game* (not just in the American League) at their respective positions for the 1939 season.

The 1939 Yankees were men among boys, and the statistics proved it. Over the course of the season, they scored 77 more runs, allowed 144 fewer runs, hit 42 more home runs, and committed 41 fewer errors than any other team in the league. Their pitchers threw 87 complete games, including 12 shutouts, while fireman Murphy led the league with 19 saves. Their hitters scored 10 or more runs in 31 games, and 15 or more in nine games. The difference between the 1939 Bombers' average runs/game (6.36) and their opponents' average runs/game (3.66) is the largest in major league history.

At the helm was Hall of Fame manager Joe McCarthy who had a simple goal—to win every game by as high a score as possible. In the field, the leader after Gehrig's departure was a Bay Area product christened in November 1914 with the name "Giuseppe Paolo DiMaggio."

DiMaggio—Before the Yankees

JOE DIMAGGIO GREW UP IN A SMALL TWO-BEDROOM San Francisco rent house with his parents, four brothers, and four sisters. Mama and Papa DiMaggio spoke Italian in the home and rebuked young Joe for his weak efforts with their mother tongue. The scolding shaped the boy's inclination toward talking for life—nothing said, nothing to get in trouble over. In his 1993 book *The Era*, Roger Kahn related that Joe DiMaggio's childhood quietude made his sister Maria wonder "if Joe was backward, not quick. I mean I wondered what was the matter with Joe. Then I decided it was mostly that he was so shy."

Though his father made his living as a crab fisherman, DiMaggio learned as a child that his stomach could not handle the sea on a daily basis. What he could handle was playing baseball every possible minute with brothers Vince and Dominic, who would go on to have successful major league careers of their own.[2] DiMaggio later described for St. Louis writer Bob Broeg how the DiMaggio brothers honed their skills:

> We used to play catch out in front of the house after dinner and we were always correcting each other's mistakes. If one of us picked up a new trick, like shading the eyes for a fly ball, we'd pass it along to the other. Like most kids, we always tried to outdo each other. We'd throw high flies to each other and try to make impossible catches, over the shoulder, backhanded, shoestring, etc., or maybe we'd have some kind of contest on throwing like how far or how accurately we could fire the ball. And we used to hit by the hour."

Before playing his first minor league game for the San Francisco Seals at the end of the 1932 season, young Joe DiMaggio had flopped as a fisherman, a student,[3] a newsboy, and an orange peeler at a juice factory. Biographer Jack Moore described the adolescent DiMaggio as a "recalcitrant, lazy, and wrong-headed boy." But he could play baseball.

DiMaggio's minor league career in San Francisco set the tone for his Yankees stardom. In 1933, at the age of eighteen, he hit .340, with 28 homers, 45 doubles, 13 triples, 169 runs batted in, and ended the year hitting in 61 consecutive games. *The Sporting News* of May 25, 1933, noted: "This hard-hitting kid seems to have no weakness at the plate."

In 1934, hampered by a knee injury, DiMaggio played in only 101 games, but hit .341 with 36 extra-base hits, and 69 runs batted in. All

---

[2]Vince DiMaggio played ten years with five National League teams, hit 125 homers and drove in 584 runs. Dom DiMaggio played eleven years with the Red Sox, averaged .298, had six years where he scored over 100 runs, and was regarded as one of baseball's best defensive outfielders.

[3]DiMaggio dropped out of high school in his sophomore year in protest of having to take ROTC instead of physical education.

major league teams except the Yankees lost interest in DiMaggio because of the injury. After the 1934 season, the Yankees hired a Los Angeles orthopedist to examine DiMaggio's knee. With the diagnosis of full recovery, Yankees executive Ed Barrow made a deal with the Seals to pay them $25,000 and send five players in exchange for DiMaggio. New York Giants manager Bill Terry called Yankees farm director George Weiss and told him "Congratulations! You bought yourself a cripple."

The Seals agreed to the deal on the condition DiMaggio be permitted to play one more year in the financially strapped Pacific Coast League, where the local hero's presence kept turnstiles spinning. DiMaggio's last season at San Francisco proved the soundness of the orthopedist's assessment and the shrewdness of Ed Barrow.[4] A .398 average, 101 extra-base hits, and 24 stolen bases convinced *The Sporting News* to name DiMaggio league Most Valuable Player in 1935.

DiMaggio's Yankees Career Begins: 1936-1938

Joe DiMaggio began his Yankees career by riding from San Francisco to St. Petersburg for 1936 spring training with infielders Frank Crosetti and Tony Lazzeri. Presumably, Crosetti's and Lazzeri's parents also scolded their sons for poor Italian as the DiMaggios had done to Joe, because none of the young ballplayers favored initiating conversation. Somewhere in Texas, the players spoke their only words of the trip when Tony asked DiMaggio to drive. The young star-to-be replied, "I don't know how." The weary Crosetti retorted, "Let's throw the bum out," but the Yankees veterans accepted their roles as the rookie's chauffeurs, and drove in silence the rest of the way to Florida.

Upon arriving at spring training, reporters hounded the much ballyhooed West Coast outfielder, asking for a quote. High school

[4]Barrow's capacity for seeing diamonds in the rough was legendary. In addition to seeing through DiMaggio's leg injury, as Red Sox manager in 1918, Barrow decided that pitcher Babe Ruth should play the outfield so he could hit every day. Before that, as a young Pittsburgh executive before the turn of the century, Barrow saw a young man in suit clothes hitting targets with lumps of coal at a Carnegie, Pennsylvania, railroad station. The Pirates soon had under contract the coal chucker, John Peter Wagner, whose family and friends called him "Honus."

dropout DiMaggio replied, "I don't have one," later admitting he thought a "quote" was a type of soft drink.

Though his mouth did little talking at St. Petersburg,[5] Joe DiMaggio's bat screamed. Three days into training camp, veteran journalist Dan Daniel pronounced the San Francisco phenom as the replacement for Babe Ruth in the Yankees lineup. Every time DiMaggio entered the batting cage, 20-game winner Red Ruffing stopped to watch the young slugger. DiMaggio biographer Maury Allen reported that the Yankees players took an instant liking to him because "he did his job and kept his mouth shut."

The 1936 Yankees were ready for a return to World Series glory, having played in the Fall Classic seven times between 1921 and 1932. McCarthy's troops entered the 1936 season coming off three consecutive second-place finishes, earning the winning-obsessed Yankees manager the despised nickname of "Second-Place Joe." Although Gehrig continued to put up remarkable numbers during the second-place seasons, averaging .342 with 37 homers and 141 runs batted in over 1933-1935, the Iron Horse couldn't drive the Yankees to the pennant with Ruth in decline in 1934 and gone in 1935.

Enter twenty-one-year-old Joe DiMaggio in 1936—quiet, talented, and seemingly the player to take the Yankees back to the top of the hill. As expectations rose at spring training for the coming season, the rookie outfielder squelched the excitement by inadvertently burning his foot in a diathermy machine. The burn kept DiMaggio out of action through Opening Day, ultimately delaying his major league debut by two weeks. Finally recovered on May 3, DiMaggio began his major league career, starting in right field and drilling two singles and a triple.

After his first three games, Joe DiMaggio had eight hits. On June 14, McCarthy traded established .300 hitter Ben Chapman to the Senators, allowing DiMaggio to move to center field. On July 7, DiMaggio became the first rookie ever to start in the All-Star Game. On July 13, having played in a grand total of 70 major league games, he appeared on the cover of *Time* magazine. Yankees front-office manager Barrow became concerned that all the attention might spoil his young star's

---

[5]Even Yankees owner Jake Ruppert observed that his prize rookie was "very hard to get acquainted with."

performance. DiMaggio assured his boss, "Don't worry, Mr. Barrow. I never feel excited."

With Joe DiMaggio's .323 batting average, 88 extra-base hits, 125 runs batted in, and 22 outfield assists inspiring the team, the Yankees blew out the American League, finishing ahead of the second-place Tigers by 19 1/2 games, then beating the Carl Hubbell-led Giants 4-2 in the Fall Classic. Under the glare of national attention, the "unexcited" DiMaggio hit a cool .346 in the subway Series.

The 1937 season was a carbon copy of 1936 for the team and its center-field star. Again, they won 102 games. Again, they ran away from the rest of the league, with second-place Detroit 13 games off the pace. Again, they put away the Giants in the Series, this time in just five games.

Leading the way through this extended instant replay was DiMaggio. He again missed Opening Day (this time because of a tonsillectomy), but hit .346 with 167 runs batted in, and led the league in slugging average (.673), homers (46), runs scored (151), and putouts by an outfielder (413).

By 1938, Joe DiMaggio decided it was time for his paycheck to reflect his performance. In 1936, DiMaggio had made $8,000. In 1937, he had gotten Barrow up to $15,000. Both years' incomes were supplemented by World Series checks of $5,000.

DiMaggio started his 1938 negotiations at $40,000, and the Yankees opened at $25,000. When Barrow informed DiMaggio that he was asking for more money than Lou Gehrig made, Joe coolly replied, "Mr. Barrow, there's only one answer to that—Mr. Gehrig is terribly underpaid." The sportswriters (and, therefore, the fans) sided with the Yankees in the negotiations, and, finally, DiMaggio knuckled under to a $25,000 contract,[6] making him the third-highest-paid player in the game (behind Gehrig and Greenberg) and the highest-paid, third-year player in baseball history.

After missing the first week of the 1938 season because of the salary dispute, DiMaggio's bat roared through the year at .324, with 32 homers and 140 runs batted in. Despite his outstanding perfor-

---

[6]In 1938, President Herbert Hoover earned $25,000 per year.

mance, and a third consecutive pennant and World Series triumph, DiMaggio described the year as "the season I wanted to forget." When the center fielder took the field, the depression-starved fans booed the young holdout for the first (and only) time in his career.

The catcalls traumatized the twenty-three-year-old superstar. "It got so I couldn't sleep at night. I'd wake up with boos ringing in my ears and walk the floor sometimes until dawn. I resolved that I would never be booed again."

Joe DiMaggio brought that attitude into baseball's centennial year. There would never again be an extended holdout. DiMaggio would never again initiate anything that might disappoint his fans.[7]

The Greatest Year—1939

JANUARY 1939 BROUGHT GOOD AND BAD NEWS TO YANKEES FANS. On the positive side, the January 11 issue of *The Sporting News* named five Yankees as the best players in baseball at their positions during the 1938 season—DiMaggio in center field, Rolfe at third, Dickey at catcher, Ruffing the right-handed pitcher, and Gomez the left-handed pitcher. With three World Series championships in a row, dominant players at almost every position, and the major league's best farm system, cries to "break up the Yankees" began and became more constant throughout the year.

■ Ruppert Passes Away

On the negative side of the Yankees ledger, owner Colonel Jake Ruppert died January 13, 1939, after a brief illness. The multimillionaire brewer had bought the Yankees with a partner in 1915 for $400,000. At the time, the team had no home park and perennially finished in the second division. In 1920, they acquired Babe Ruth. In 1922, Ruppert bought out his partner for $1.25 million. In 1923, he opened Yankee Stadium. At the time of the Colonel's death, the lifelong bachelor lived alone in an $800,000 French chateau he had built in Garrison, New York. Ruppert spent his final years alternating his

[7]This attitude surely led to his early retirement after the 1951 season. At his December 1951 press conference, DiMaggio said he was retiring because "I will not embarrass myself on the ball field. I no longer have it. I don't want them to remember me struggling."

attention among show girls, the Yankees, and twenty-four species of monkeys he kept on the chateau's grounds.

Colonel Jake had no interest in league balance. The 1936 team led the league by 17 games late in the season, and Ruppert complained, "I can't stand the suspense. When are we going to clinch it?" As the league begged the Colonel to play on a level field by trading his stars and depleting his stockpile in the vast Yankees farm system, the owner bristled, "Let the other teams build to our level!"

Ruppert made sure Yankees personnel shared his attitude. Upon hiring Joe McCarthy after the 1931 season, the owner told his skipper, "I don't like to finish second." McCarthy looked his new boss in the eye and said, "Neither do I." Ruppert relished an on-field massacre and his manager felt the same. When Yankees players gloated over winning a preseason game 17-0, field marshall McCarthy tore into his troops: "Against those monkeys, you should have won 50-0."

The loss of Ruppert took none of the winning tenacity out of his baseball organization. Ed Barrow still pulled the front-office strings, McCarthy still "pushed the buttons"[8] on the field, and the players aimed to become the first team in history to win a fourth consecutive world championship.

Spring Training

Joe DiMaggio was particularly hungry for the coming season. In February, he told the press 1939 "is going to be my big year." Upon signing his $27,500 contract on March 4, DiMaggio focused on having a year where he could play from Opening Day through the end of the season in good health and without financial disputes.

The rest of the league fully expected DiMaggio to realize his goal. A preseason polling of managers, coaches, and players named him as their first choice if they had their pick of any player in the game. Although they perceived that "DiMaggio has yet to flower," they were particularly impressed by "the timeliness of his hits, his manner on the field, and his assuming responsibility for winning."

Although DiMaggio had followed his career routine by doing no

[8]White Sox manager Jimmy Dykes had labeled the Yankee Skipper as a "push-button" manager for his conservative style of play.

off-season training before arriving at St. Petersburg on March 6, he went to work immediately. *The Sporting News* reported his being the first man on the field in the morning and the last to leave at night. He came into camp weighing over two hundred pounds, and left at 185. Sportswriters observed that they had never seen a man work so hard.

As DiMaggio worked to prepare for Opening Day, only one Yankees worked harder. Lou Gehrig pushed his "useless rag" muscles mercilessly to get them to respond as they had in years past. DiMaggio's spring-time quest for a full healthy season of greatness did not match the St. Petersburg copy devoted to Gehrig's disturbing demise.

During spring training, in addition to playing baseball, DiMaggio made daily long-distance phone calls to actress Dorothy Arnold—calls which the press described as "fifteen dollars a coo." They had met in late 1937 during the filming of DiMaggio's cameo movie appearance in the musical *Manhattan Merry-Go Round*. Dorothy would announce their engagement during the first week of the 1939 season, and they would marry in November.

■ The Start of the 1939 Season: Down Goes DiMaggio, Out Goes Gehrig, and McCarthy Leads the Charge

On April 20—Opening Day—Red Ruffing shut out the Red Sox 2-0 at Yankee Stadium, and DiMaggio finally realized his dream of starting the season ready to play. By the seventh game, he was hitting .435, when along came adversity.

Running in wet grass to retrieve a line drive hit by the Senators' Bobby Estalella, DiMaggio tried to stop and turn when the ball took a funny bounce. His right shoe stuck in the mud while his body tumbled forward. "I felt something tear—it was the muscles of my right leg, torn away from the bone, just above the ankle." Under doctor's orders, the Yankees center fielder spent most of the next month in the hospital missing more than 30 games until his return on June 7.

During his stay at the infirmary, DiMaggio saw himself on the May 1 cover of *Life* magazine. On May 2, he missed being with the team when Gehrig stopped his consecutive-game streak. Missing their two biggest stars, from May 2 until June 7, the Yankees proved their power and balance by winning 28 out of 34 games. The conductor of the runaway freight train was "Marse Joe" McCarthy. The New York skipper told sportswriter Joe Williams in a *Saturday Evening Post* feature that summer, "A manager is supposed to win even if he has fifteen injured men."

McCarthy's Managerial Greatness Defined

The key to McCarthy's success came from his capacity to handle a team made up of very different men, his baseball smarts, and his seemingly ego-less personality. Raised in poverty without a father, McCarthy spent his late teens and twenties knocking around the minor leagues as a mediocre second baseman. After winning two pennants while managing Louisville in the American Association from 1919-1925, he took over the last-place Chicago Cubs in 1926 and moved them up to the first division in his first season. By 1929, he turned them into blow-out, 10 1/2 game pennant winners.

McCarthy took over the Yankees in 1931, and led them to eight pennants and seven World Series championships in the next thirteen years. Marse Joe demanded player compliance with his image for a New York Yankees. Only baseball could be discussed in the clubhouse. No card playing. No celebrities milling around. No arguments.

When the Yankees traveled, they wore coats and ties, pulled no shenanigans, and ate together. Teamwork became a reality off the field, as well as on. McCarthy told *The Sporting News* his rules for handling players:

1. Any ballplayer who cannot go at top speed mentally and physically for two hours at current salaries is not welcome on my club.
2. I am no stickler for prohibition. I do not believe in watching players and enforcing teetotalism. But any player caught drunk is finished with me.
3. I do not believe in watching players with detectives. The joyrider always gives himself away on the field.
4. Riding a player never appealed to me. A slap on the back and a word of encouragement all help.

Hall of Fame Manager Joe McCarthy. (National Baseball Library and Archive, Cooperstown, New York)

5. I do not believe in controlling the game at all times and telling pitchers what to pitch and hitters what to hit unless we reach critical points.
6. The main things are hustle and realization that one run is very important.
7. You must place all players on one level. You cannot play favorites and win a pennant.

In addition to those rules, when it came time to play, the Yankees skipper adhered to his *Ten Commandments of Baseball*, which he had formalized while managing Louisville:

1. Nobody ever became a ballplayer by walking after a ball.
2. You will never become a .300 hitter unless you take the bat off your shoulder.
3. An outfielder who throws back of a runner is locking the barn after the horse is stolen.
4. Keep your head up and you may not have to keep it down.
5. When you start to slide, slide. He who changes his mind may have to change a good leg for a bad one.
6. Do not alibi on bad hops. Anybody can field the good ones.
7. Always run them out. You never can tell.
8. Do not quit.
9. Do not find too much fault with the umpires. You cannot expect them to be as perfect as you are.
10. A pitcher who hasn't control hasn't anything

On top of enforcing his rules and abiding by his commandments, McCarthy succeeded as baseball's winningest manager[9] because of his humble personality. On the back of his Yankees uniform, he wore no number. When his team checked into a hotel, McCarthy waited for all his players and coaches to check in before he did. Arthur Daley of *The New York Times* described the Yankees skipper as leading with

---

[9]His .615 winning percentage during regular seasons and his .698 percentage in World Series play both rank first among all major league baseball managers.

"phlegmatic[10] unobtrusiveness." Writer Joe Williams described McCarthy as a "pleasant, sociable fellow with no pretenses or conceits... who seldom uses an iron hand. Modesty and simplicity are the keys to his character."

For a player to succeed under Joe McCarthy, he had to dedicate himself to teamwork and winning. When the Yankees ran out on the field to open a game, they left the dugout together, with their heads up. When it became clear to McCarthy that star pitcher Johnny Allen thought more of himself than the team, he was banished to Cleveland. Marse Joe maintained the perspective, "If a player isn't doing his best for the team, he's replaced."

McCarthy and DiMaggio—A Good Chemistry

All of Joe McCarthy's characteristics and attitudes meshed perfectly with his star center fielder DiMaggio. Off the field, they both kept their distance from the rest of the team, but were happy to provide support when asked. Both were hard losers, who assumed personal responsibility for winning and losing. Mrs. McCarthy told sportswriter Joe Williams, "Every game to him is life or death, and when he loses it might as well be death." Spud Chandler and Charlie Keller said the same of Joe DiMaggio.

Jack Sher of *Sport* magazine concluded that the attraction of McCarthy and DiMaggio was "the attraction of the lonely for the lonely. DiMaggio patterned himself after McCarthy who was an unreachable, silent, let-me-alone sort of guy." Dan Daniel of *The Sporting News* said of McCarthy, "He is a man whom nobody really knows completely." DiMaggio's biographer Jack Moore said the same of the Yankees center fielder.

Above all, Joe DiMaggio was Joe McCarthy's kind of player. The Yankees skipper described his star as "a perfect player—perfect instincts, perfect judgment, a nice fellow who never made trouble... I've never had to coach him at all... He is the one ballplayer who has never made a mental mistake." When McCarthy was asked by a reporter if his center fielder could bunt, Marse Joe replied, "I'll never

[10]Defined by *Webster's* as "unemotional; impassive."

know." When DiMaggio got hit in the ribs with a fast ball, and trotted down to first, McCarthy told Tommy Henrich and the rest of the Yankees bench, "He won't rub it." And he didn't.

The respect was mutual. DiMaggio reflected on his manager, "If you put out for McCarthy, he never lets you down. I've never heard a player beef about one of Joe's moves. I never saw Joe show up a ballplayer... Never a day went by that you didn't learn something from him... He was like a father to us."

DiMaggio Rejoins the Team

Joe DiMaggio stepped back into the Yankees lineup June 7, and the team kept winning, taking 17 of the next 22 games. On June 28, in a doubleheader against the A's, the team set a major league record by smashing 13 home runs, with DiMaggio, Gordon, and Dahlgren each hitting three. The Yankees entered July with a record of 50-14, a winning percentage of .781 over the Seven Dwarfs.

In early July, the team faltered. En route to the All-Star break, the Bronx Bombers dropped nine out of 12. In the midst of this losing stretch was Lou Gehrig Day on July 4, when the Iron Horse told his teammates and the multitudes that he considered himself "the luckiest man on the face of the earth." On the field, DiMaggio and his teammates wept.[11] McCarthy explained his team's July slide by telling the press that Lou Gehrig's testimonial caused his club "to go through an emotional state." *The Sporting News* commented, "The Yankees must be credited with more romance and sensitivity than usual in ballplayers."

The 1939 All-Star Game gave the team the break it needed to shake off the sadness. Appropriately played at Yankee Stadium, baseball's ninth Mid-Summer Classic featured Yankees Rolfe at third, DiMaggio in center, Dickey behind the plate, Selkirk in left, Gordon at second,[12] Ruffing on the mound, McCarthy calling the shots from the dugout, and Gehrig as the honorary American League captain.

---

[11]DiMaggio did not cry publicly again until he was honored at Yankee Stadium with his day in 1949.

[12]Rolfe, DiMaggio, Dickey, Selkirk, and Gordon all played the entire game.

DiMaggio hit his first All-Star Game homer, Selkirk singled in a run, and Gordon's grounder got by Pirate Arky Vaughan allowing Greenberg to score, accounting for all the runs in the American League's 3-1 win.

After the break, the Yankees resumed their winning ways, taking 13 out of 17 during the rest of July. DiMaggio closed out the month being featured in *Collier's* magazine and crushing a 450-foot home run against the Browns at Sportsman's Park on July 25. DiMaggio entered August with a sizzling .405 average.

DiMaggio Earns a Nickname in His Greatest Month

If ever a man turned into a baseball-playing machine, it was Joe DiMaggio in August 1939. Between August 1 and September 1, while the Yankees won 22 out of 32 games, DiMaggio hit .405, crashed 14 homers, drove in 52 runs, and had 10 games where he knocked in at least three runs. His game had become so dominant and his celebrity status so pronounced that when the Yankees traveled to Cooperstown on August 22 to play an exhibition against the Newark Bears in connection with the centennial, McCarthy had to take his star out in the fourth inning because fans kept running out on the field to get DiMaggio's autograph.

DiMaggio's 1939 celebrity came from his play, the media's fascination with him, his off-the-field style,[13] his movie actress fiancée, and a new nickname. Pan American Airlines introduced to the world in 1939 a big, fast, glamorous, powerful forty-one-ton airplane with pontoons underneath, capable of crossing the Atlantic in twenty-four hours. Because of its grandeur and aquaflight design, Pan Am called its newest contribution to luxury air travel, "The Yankee Clipper," in honor of the tall ships with the same name.

First Lady Eleanor Roosevelt christened the flying ship on March 3 at Anacostia Naval Air Station just outside the nation's capital. Aviation historian R.E.G. Davies concluded that "the magnificent aircraft outstripped all rivals in size, load-carrying ability, and performance… Efficient and elegant, it was in a class of its own."

---

[13]DiMaggio earned a spot on the 1939 list of the nation's ten best-dressed men.

New York Yankees broadcaster Arch McDonald anointed DiMaggio baseball's "Yankee Clipper" late in the 1939 season, and the nickname stuck. He was big (six-foot-two, 190 pounds), he carried the load for his team, he performed efficiently and elegantly, and he was versatile. Just as Pan Am's Yankee Clipper could fly, float, and carry passengers and cargo, so could Joe DiMaggio hit, run, field, and throw as well or better than anyone else in the game.

The accomplishments of baseball's Yankee Clipper exceeded the scope of the mere English language. Historian Charles Alexander resorted to Italian to describe DiMaggio in 1939. He played with "sprezzatura"—making the difficult look easy. Author Michael Seidel had to rely on Greek in expressing DiMaggio's play, observing that he had the capacity to maintain the "aristeia," whereby "great energies are gathered for a day, dispensed, and then regenerated for yet another day in an epic wonder of consistency."

Certainly, the great DiMaggio "gathered, dispensed, and regenerated" his energy throughout 1939. Bill Dickey witnessed the Clipper accelerating faster than anyone thought possible to leg out a double, beating an outfielder's unexpected quick throw. The Yankees catcher turned to his teammates and said, "You know something? That guy can run as fast as he has to." Tommy Henrich observed that when DiMaggio came to bat against Feller, "you could see the veins sticking out of Joe's neck." Writer Wilfred Sheed described his swing as "controlled savagery." Throughout the summer, DiMaggio's hard slides produced massive strawberries on his legs. After each game, the Yankee Clipper sat alone in front of his locker going back over the ballgame in his mind. When asked whether the internal review helped, DiMaggio replied, "Not much." The Yankees center fielder's constant pressure on himself soon caused stomach ulcers.

Donald Honig summarized the Clipper's driven attitude on and off the baseball field. "Every day the trigger of unrelenting compulsion was reset and cocked." No wonder the 1939 Yankees' greatest pitcher Red Ruffing said of DiMaggio, "You saw him standing out there and you knew you had a pretty damned good chance to win the baseball game."

Beyond his capacity to hit timely, slide hard, run down fly balls, and throw hard to the right base, DiMaggio possessed unparalleled self-control. *Never* did he collide with a teammate in the field, get thrown out of a contest by arguing with an umpire, talk to an opposing player during a game, fight, or show emotion in any way.[14] When a Yankees did something to displease the Clipper, he shot the offender a piercing frown. When an opponent stepped over the line against a teammate, DiMaggio retaliated within the rules by making a hard take-out slide.

Two plays at the end of the 1939 season exemplified the greatness of Joe DiMaggio. In mid-August, late in a game at Yankee Stadium, McCarthy's team found themselves getting bombed by Detroit. With one out and Earl Averill on first, Hank Greenberg blasted a ball to deepest center. Playing his customary shallow center field, DiMaggio turned his back to the ball, and took off.

He told Red Smith about his best all-time catch. "I ran at top speed with my back to the infield. I managed to get behind the flagpole, and couldn't have been more than two feet from the bleacher wall (460 feet from home plate). I stuck my glove up at the last moment and there was the ball."

Henrich called it the greatest catch he ever saw. After DiMaggio caught the ball, he crashed into the unpadded wall, and still managed to hang on. The game's lopsided score, and the August reality of his team running away toward another pennant had no effect on DiMaggio's desire to chase down the ball. Yankees pitcher Spud Chandler put the historic catch in perspective. "Nothing was at stake. But that's the way Joe played ball—everything was at stake for him, all the time."

DiMaggio's second landmark play concluded the otherwise forgettable 1939 World Series sweep over Cincinnati. In the tenth inning of Game Four, with Crosetti on third, and Keller on first, DiMaggio singled to right. Reds outfielder Ival Goodman booted the ball, allowing "King Kong" Keller to score after a head-on collision with Cincinnati catcher Ernie Lombardi. Yankees third-base coach Art Fletcher waved DiMaggio home as Lombardi stretched out writhing in pain. As Big Ernie finally lunged, DiMaggio slid over the attempted tag and

[14]DiMaggio's only emotional display during his career came in the 1947 World Series, when Dodgers outfielder Al Gionfriddo robbed him of a home run. Using every bit of emotion in his body, DiMaggio lightly kicked the dirt.

Outfielder Joe DiMaggio was as good with a glove as he was with a bat. (National Baseball Library and Archive, Cooperstown, New York)

touched home safely with his hand. "Lombardi's Snooze" became one of the most famous plays in World Series history, in large part because marquee name DiMaggio had been the opportunist.

THE 1939 SEASON IN PERSPECTIVE

With the season over, and a fourth consecutive World Series ring on each Yankee's finger, the honors rolled in for DiMaggio. *The Sporting News* named him Most Valuable Player in recognition of his batting title and team leadership. His .381 batting average in 1939 turned out to be his career high, and likely would have topped .400 had McCarthy allowed him to rest in late September when an eye allergy caused a severe optical twitch. Without clear vision, DiMaggio hit .233 from September 10-30, after being at .409 as late as September 9. McCarthy told his star that to sit down with an eye twitch would open him up to being labeled a "cheese champion."

Respected baseball historians on the order of Ed Linn, Bob Broeg, Lee Allen, and Tom Meany have called 1939 DiMaggio's greatest year. Not only did he win the batting title and lead his team to a runaway pennant and world championship, but as biographer Jack Moore put it, "In 1939, DiMaggio showed that he was playing at a different level than anyone else." Losing 32 games to injury, DiMaggio still knocked in 126 runs, while striking out only 20 times in 462 at bats.

Over the course of DiMaggio's first four years, the Yankee Clipper had averaged better than one run batted in and almost one-and-a-half hits per game, while appearing in four All-Star Games and four World Series. At the age of twenty-four, Joe DiMaggio was on top of the baseball world and had become an international celebrity. The son of a San Francisco crab fisherman had success, fame, and money. All he needed was love.

On November 19, 1939, with thirty thousand fans clamoring outside from trees and rooftops, Joe DiMaggio married Dorothy Arnold at the Church of Saints Peter and Paul in downtown San Francisco. The twenty-one-year-old bride from Duluth, Minnesota, had already appeared in fifteen movies, but told the press she did not plan to continue with her career, intending to be a "real wife" and have children. As DiMaggio biographer George DeGregorio pointed out, being a beautiful movie actress, and having converted to Catholicism before the wedding, Dorothy Arnold appeared to be the perfect wife for the handsome young Italian-American superstar.[15]

Later, in the spring of 1940, at the New York World's Fair Academy of Sports, DiMaggio received the Golden Laurel Award as the country's best athlete in 1939. On display at the fair was a huge photograph of the Yankee Clipper finishing his majestic swing.

As for the rest of the 1939 Yankees team, their place in history as baseball's greatest team appears secure. Respected historian Robert Creamer gave his perspective of that pin-striped team of the late thirties, saying, "Never before or since has a baseball team been so overwhelmingly dominant. The pitching was deep and excellent—the staff had the lowest earned-run average in the league for four straight years—but it was the Yankees' powerful, unrelenting hitting that awed rival teams and earned them the nickname 'the Bronx Bombers.'"

Dan Daniels picked the 1939 Bombers over the 1927 Murderer's Row in the October 19, 1939 issue of *The Sporting News*. Daniels concluded that the 1939 team was faster on the bases and stronger on defense, had better condition and balance, and won against a better league. In comparing the two teams position by position, the sportswriter picked Gehrig over Dahlgren at first, Lazzeri barely over Gordon at second, Red Rolfe over Joe Dugan at third, Crosetti over Koenig at short, Ruth over Keller in right, DiMaggio over Combs in center, Meusel and Selkirk even in left, with Dickey way ahead of the 1927 catchers. Pitching matchups between the two teams were close with a slight edge going to the 1927 team.

Daniels favored the 1939 New York team because it was "all business, ambition, seriousness and superb condition," and because "McCarthy was in full command." This combination had led the 1939 team to four straight World Series triumphs while the 1927 Yankees could not even three-peat.

At the end of the 1939 season, the Yankees' dominance led Washington owner Clark Griffith to persuade all of the other Seven Dwarf league owners to pass a rule prohibiting teams from making

[15]The marriage resulted in the birth of the Yankee Clipper's only child, Joe DiMaggio, Jr., in 1941, but ended in divorce in 1944.

trades with the previous season's pennant winner. With the unlimited Yankees bank account during depression times, and a vast supply of talent in the New York farm system, the other owners foresaw the Bronx Bombers going into the marketplace to get even better by trading for the likes of Hank Greenberg. The no-trade rule was repealed before the end of the 1940 season.

After 1939

TO THE SURPRISE OF THE BASEBALL WORLD, history's greatest team couldn't make it five in a row. Hank Greenberg led the Tigers to the American League flag in 1940, with the Yankees finishing third, two games off the pace. Dickey, Rolfe, Keller, Selkirk, and Crosetti saw their batting averages disintegrate by over 50 points per man. The team scored 150 fewer runs (thereby averaging one fewer run per game than the 1939 team), while the pitching staff gave up 115 more runs. Ruffing, the heart of the staff, went from 21-7 to 15-12, and Russo (at 14-8) was the only other pitcher with double-figure wins.

Only Joe Gordon and the great DiMaggio maintained their performance level through the 1940 campaign. Gordon stayed at the 30-homer, 100-runs-batted-in level for a third consecutive season, achieving rare offensive production for a second baseman.

Joe DiMaggio won his second consecutive batting title in 1940, and maintained his one-run-batted-in-per-game pace through his fifth full season. The Yankee's Clipper season was clouded by Commissioner Landis's investigation of DiMaggio using boxing manager Joe Gould as his agent. He escaped penalty by establishing to Landis's satisfaction that he had used Gould only for negotiating his endorsements, and not his Yankees contract.

The year 1941 brought the return of glory to Yankee Stadium. The Bronx Bombers blew out the second-place Red Sox by 17 games. Thanks to Mickey Owen's passed ball after Tommy Henrich had seemingly struck out to end Game Four, the Yankees proceeded to take the Dodgers in the 1941 Series.

The 1941 season is best remembered as the year of DiMaggio's 56-game hitting streak. Although DiMaggio won his second

Most Valuable Player award that year, and led the American League with 125 runs batted in, he could no longer maintain his one-run-batted-in-per-game pace, as he had his first five years, leading St. Louis sportswriter Bob Broeg to observe that DiMaggio "was so good he actually was slipping in 1941 when he put together his streak."

DiMaggio and his team finished the pre-war-interruption years with another pennant in 1942, although he tasted his only World Series defeat that year as the St. Louis Cardinals took the defending champs in five games. Redbird rookie left fielder Stan Musial would again lead his team to the Fall Classic in 1943 and 1944.

Three years of military service caused DiMaggio to miss all of the 1943-1945 seasons. Baseball's Yankee Clipper had put up remarkable pre-war numbers in his first seven seasons, averaging .341, 31 homers, and 133 runs batted in from 1936-1942. In his six post-war years with the Yankees, DiMaggio had only two great full seasons, in 1948 and 1950,[16] and a spectacular half season in 1949. In a year immortalized by David Halberstam in his classic *The Summer of 1949*, DiMaggio again made the cover of *Life* by returning from a severe heel injury to hit .346 with 67 runs batted in in 76 games, leading the Yankees to the pennant and a world championship over the Dodgers.

After retiring in December 1951, baseball's Yankee Clipper achieved national recognition again only in the context of marrying, divorcing, burying, and then grieving for Marilyn Monroe, and by advertising Mr. Coffee appliances.

The Legend of Joe DiMaggio

JOE DIMAGGIO'S STATUS AS AN AMERICAN LEGEND is secure not only because of his baseball career and relationship with Marilyn Monroe, but also because his life became celebrated in the works of American legends Rodgers and Hammerstein (in *South Pacific*), Paul Simon (in "Mrs. Robinson"), and Ernest Hemingway (in *The Old Man and the Sea*).

---

[16]In 1948, DiMaggio again made the cover of *Time*, hit .320, and led the league in homers (39) and runs batted in (155). In 1950, he hit only .301, but had good production, with 32 homers fueling 122 runs batted in. DiMaggio won his third league MVP in 1947, though his numbers were, by his standards, underwhelming—.315, 20 homers, 97 runs batted in.

Some sabermetricians have attempted to belittle DiMaggio's career numbers—a lifetime .325 batting average, with 361 home runs. Such oversimplified statistical analysis essentially ignores DiMaggio losing three full years in his prime to military service, while being victimized throughout his career as a right-handed pull hitter to Yankees Stadium's expansive left field.

The compelling statistic of Joe DiMaggio's career, which sets him apart from the rest of the baseball fraternity, led to his being named the game's greatest living player in 1969. DiMaggio's greatness is measured by the only statistic that matters in baseball—ten pennants and nine world championships in thirteen seasons.

As Ted Williams had ultimately fulfilled his 1939 dream to be recognized by the people on the street as baseball's greatest hitter, Joe DiMaggio also achieved his goal. "I'm just a ball player with one ambition, and that is to give all I've got to help my ball club win."

During the thirteen DiMaggio years, the men in pinstripes won 1,272 and lost 724 during the regular seasons for a .637 winning percentage. In winning nine out of ten World Series with DiMaggio in center field, the Yankees went 37-14 in the Fall Classic for a .725 post-season clip.

Bill Terry said it best about baseball's Yankee Clipper. In the aftermath of the DiMaggio-led Bronx Bombers winning another World Series, the Giants manager ate his 1934 words about the Yankees buying "a cripple." Terry reflected, "I've always heard that one player could make the difference between a losing team and a winner and I never believed it. Now I know it's true."

Bob Feller warming up. (Copyright: Mark Rucker, Transcendental Graphics)

CHAPTER SEVEN

Rapid Robert Hits His Stride

Twenty-Year-Old Bob Feller Becomes Baseball's Youngest Twenty-Game Winner

EXCEPT FOR THREE-AND-TWO-THIRDS INNINGS at the All-Star Game on July 11, the players Joe McCarthy needed to win the big games in 1939 all wore pin stripes. Joe's Yankees had essentially become a team of All-Stars, and proved it by having six American League starters in the 1939 Mid-Summer Classic played at Yankee Stadium. In the top of the All-Star Game's fifth inning, with the American League in front 3-1, the Nationals loaded the bases against Tigers pitcher Tommy Bridges, and Pirates shortstop Arky Vaughan came to bat.

The .300-hitting Vaughan already had singled and scored his team's run in the third. With the game on the line, McCarthy pulled Bridges and brought in Cleveland's four-year veteran Bob Feller. The Indians' stopper threw one pitch and extinguished the fire. Vaughan's ground ball became a Gordon-to-Cronin-to-Greenberg double play, preserving the American League's lead.

For the next three innings, Bob Feller overpowered the National League. Future Hall of Famers Ernie Lombardi, Joe Medwick, Mel Ott, Johnny Mize, and Vaughan could manage only one hit and one walk off Cleveland's ace. Feller ended the game by fanning Mize and Stan Hack, providing a fitting climax to his virtuoso performance.

Joe McCarthy would later say it was the greatest exhibition of clutch pitching he ever saw. Journalists and fans now knew twenty-year-old Bob Feller could do more than throw hard. Four months before he could vote, the pride of Van Meter, Iowa, had become the game's best pitcher.

Feller's Road to Glory

IN W. P. KINSELLA'S 1980 NOVEL *SHOELESS JOE*, (on which the movie *Field of Dreams* was based), an Iowa farmer has a dream and then builds a baseball diamond in his corn field. Kinsella had a precedent.

In the early 1930s, Bill Feller had a dream. He wanted his young son to become a major league pitcher. To give himself maximum time to develop his son's skills, Bill raised wheat (which required little maintenance) on his Iowa farm, instead of corn and oats, the area's traditional crops. He then depleted the family's savings by purchasing a $3,500 tractor so he could farm quicker to free up more father-son baseball time.

Bill's plan worked. At age nine, Bobby Feller heaved a baseball 275 feet. At eleven, the boy broke off such a sharp curve Bill couldn't put a glove on the ball, leaving the father with three cracked ribs.

The Fellers lived three miles outside of Van Meter, population four hundred. In that farming community, Bill found it virtually impossible to organize a full baseball game with eighteen players. Bobby's father knew that no matter how much he played catch with his son, no matter how hard or how many different pitches the young boy could throw, he would not become a complete pitcher until he could play regularly in game competition.

One day, as Bill Feller tractored around his wheat field, frustrated with his inability to generate a competitive baseball league in the rural neighborhood, he realized Van Meter needed a well-constructed baseball facility. He had the land. So Bill decided if he built a baseball field on his farm, people would come to play. Bob Feller described Oak View Park on his family's farm in his 1990 autobiography *Now Pitching, Bob Feller:*

> We leveled part of the pasture land and cut down trees for poles to support a chickenwire fence from first to third base to protect the fans. We

> had a temporary fence to protect the infield from the livestock between games... Together we built the bleachers and put up the scoreboard so everything would look first-class... Dad formed a team and scheduled games for every Sunday all summer long. On most Sundays, two or three hundred people came to watch our team of players in their late teens and twenties, and one thirteen-year-old play baseball against good teams from Des Moines and other cities and towns.

That thirteen-year-old pitcher soon became the talk of Iowa. Bobby Feller could strike out almost anyone of any age.[1] By the time the boy reached fifteen, he had struck out 23 batters in one game, and umpires in the Iowa farm league started calling major league scouts.

In the summer of 1935, Cleveland's Cy Slapnicka became the first scout to arrive at Van Meter. Baseball's rules were then such that an amateur player could not sign directly with a big league club, but first had to become the property of a minor league team.

The cagey Slapnicka (who became the Indians' general manager the following year) knew the rules. Rather than sign Bob Feller to a contract with Cleveland, Cy got the teenage fireballer to sign with the Indians' farm club at Fargo-Moorhead in the Northern League, transferred the agreement to the Tribe's farm club in New Orleans, and then had the parent team acquire Feller's rights from its Louisiana affiliate.

In the middle of the Fargo-to-New Orleans-to-Cleveland paper shuffle, fifteen-year-old Bobby Feller "voluntarily retired" to allow himself to keep pitching in the Iowa American Amateur Baseball Congress during the remainder of the 1935 season. Feller's signing bonus for this transaction? A single dollar bill, and a ball autographed by the 1934 third-place Cleveland Indians.

As Feller dominated Iowa schoolboy pitching in the summer of 1935,[2] major league scouts from everywhere came knocking on the

---

[1]Bill and Bob Feller drove to St. Louis in October 1934 to see the World Series. Watching Cardinals pitchers give up ten runs to the Tigers in Game Four, Bob leaned over to his father and said, "I can do better than that."

[2]Feller went 25-4 that summer, averaging more than 19 strikeouts a game, and leading his team to the playoffs of the state championship.

young right-hander's door. Soon they realized what Slapnicka and the Indians had pulled off, but there was no urgency to challenge Cleveland's deal until Feller proved himself at the major league level. The proof came in 1936.

Stocky,[3] seventeen-year-old Bob Feller spent the first half of the 1936 season working out with the Indians at Cleveland's League Park. His chance to pitch against big leaguers came July 6, in an exhibition game during the All-Star break against the St. Louis Cardinals. Redbirds skipper and second baseman Frank Frisch saw the teenager warming up, observed Feller's speed and wildness, and decided that he was "too old to get killed in the line of duty." Frisch asked young Cardinals outfielder Lynn King if he had ever played second base. When King replied in the negative, Frisch bellowed, "Well, you are today."

In three innings against the Cardinals, Feller struck out eight. The first Redbirds batter, Brusie Ogrodowski, begged Indians catcher-manager Steve O'Neill to "let me outta here in one piece." St. Louis shortstop Leo Durocher faced Feller next, and ran to the dugout after a called strike to cower behind the water fountain. When Durocher returned, he became Feller's first major league strikeout victim.

Seasoned umpire "Red" Ormsby told the press that day, "He's the best pitcher I've seen come into the American League. I don't care if he's only seventeen. He showed me more speed than any I've ever seen from any American League pitcher, and I don't make an exception for Walter Johnson."

Clevelands skipper Steve O'Neill had seen enough to know that Feller was ready for prime time. After the Cardinals' exhibition game, he pitched Feller six times in relief before giving the teenager his first start on August 23, 1936, against the weak St. Louis Browns who were battling Philadelphia for last place in the American League. All Feller did that day was pitch a complete-game, 4-1 victory, striking out 15.

On Labor Day, Feller beat St. Louis again, striking out ten. Then, against the hapless A's on September 13, he struck out 17, breaking Rube Waddell's American League record and tying Dizzy Dean's major league record for strikeouts in a single game.

---

[3]Feller had already completed his growth while a teenager, standing five-feet-eleven-and-one-half inches tall and weighing more than 180 pounds.

After the 1936 season, Feller headed home to finish high school.[4] During the offseason, the baseball world challenged the legitimacy of Feller's contract with Cleveland. Slapnicka's 1935 slight-of-hand magic in getting Feller from an Iowa wheat field to Cleveland's League Park without having pitched one minor league inning was disputed until it landed on commissioner Landis's desk.

With other big league teams standing in line to pay a $100,000 bonus to Feller if Landis declared the young pitcher a free agent, Bill Feller felt so strongly about the sanctity of his son's contract with Cleveland he threatened litigation if Landis voided the agreement. The Commissioner went with Cleveland, and Ohio breathed a sigh of relief.

Eighteen-year-old strikeout phenom Bobby Feller made the cover of *Time* magazine at the beginning of the 1937 season. His spotlight dimmed when an arm injury sustained during the season's first week troubled him most of the year. Feller finished the 1937 campaign at 9-7, but managed to strike out 150 batters in 148 2/3.

Fully recovered in 1938, Bob Feller became the Indians' workhorse, going 17-11, completing 20 games in 36 starts, leading the league in strikeouts with 240, and also setting a major league, single-season record for walks with 208.

All the pieces finally came together in Feller's final start of 1938. On October 2, Bob Feller gunned down 18 Detroit Tigers to break the major league, single-game strikeout record. Coming off his magnificent 1938 finale, Feller prepared to take his game to the next level.

Bullet Bob in 1939

GREAT EXPECTATIONS

In February 1939, Cleveland manager Oscar Vitt predicted a 20-win season for twenty-year-old Bob Feller. The Indians' front office seconded Vitt by giving the young hurler a $2,500 raise for the coming season, boosting him to $17,500 annually.

By the start of the 1939 season, Cleveland's best pitcher had become baseball's biggest drawing card. Veteran sportswriter Jimmy

---

[4]That winter, Feller went to Des Moines for a radio interview with a young broadcaster named Ronald "Dutch" Reagan. He, too, would go on to bigger things.

Powers explained why people wanted to see Bob Feller perform. "In 1939, Feller was recognized as the most sensational pitcher since Walter Johnson. He didn't have the flair and color of Dizzy Dean, but his fastball and youth made him a standout. He was a picture of health. He was modest and unassuming, but he knew that he was a great pitcher, and he accepted that talent gracefully."

When Bob Feller took the mound in his fourth season, baseball fans knew exciting things were likely to happen. If Cleveland's ace could strike out 18 in one game in 1938, would he strike out 19 in 1939? Having thrown a one-hitter against the Browns when he was nineteen, would Feller's inevitable first no-hitter come when he was twenty? With the advent of baseball under the lights in the American League in 1939, could any batter see Feller's fastball in a night game? Knowing that Feller had beaned and seriously injured the Giants' Hank Leiber in a 1937 exhibition game, would Feller's high, hard one kill a batter wearing only a cloth cap? Radio wasn't good enough. Fans wanted to see Feller in person.

■ FELLER'S FAVORITE CATCHER

Indians skipper Vitt handed Feller the ball for his first Opening Day start on April 21, 1939. The right-hander proceeded to three-hit Detroit in a 5-1 Cleveland victory, with Feller picking up where he left off at the end of 1938 by striking out ten Tigers. Vitt's selection of second-stringer Frankie Pytlak to catch Feller instead of his regular backstop, Rollie Hemsley, provided the game's only unusual wrinkle.

Feller and Hemsley had first met in exhibition games after the 1936 season. As the young pitcher struggled with his control in a game against Negro league All-Stars, Rollie (then a St. Louis Brown) walked out to the mound and told the teenage phenom, "Listen, Bob. There are just two of us in the ballpark. You and me. And we're playing catch. Forget about everybody else and just toss the ball to me." The veteran's calming assurance settled Feller down and the pitcher quickly retired the side.

Cleveland decided Hemsley was just the man to help Bob Feller control his pitches better. St. Louis manager Rogers Hornsby sensed the Indians' desperation and set Hemsley's price tag at $100,000. The talks stalled. By mid-season in 1937, the Browns' 25-52 last-place record resulted in Hornsby's unemployment. Cleveland finally swung a deal with the Browns' new regime on February 10, 1938, sending catcher Billy Sullivan, second baseman Roy Hughes, and pitcher Ed Cole to St. Louis for Hemsley.

In Feller's first start with his new catcher on April 20, 1938, he fired a one-hitter against the Browns. The right-hander demonstrated enhanced effectiveness throughout the season as Hemsley forced him to rely on his curveball to keep hitters off balance. By the middle of the 1938 season, Feller publicly paid tribute to his catcher: "Rollie gives me confidence just the way he handles himself behind the plate. He's constantly making me pitch to the batter's weakness and to stay away from the spot where the batter likes them. I don't worry now with men on base as I used to, and I give Hemsley credit for improving my control."

When Bob Feller needed him on Opening Day 1939, Rollie Hemsley was in an Akron hospital undergoing alcoholism rehabilitation. Cleveland General Manager Slapnicka had had his fill of the rowdy catcher. On the Indians' trip north after 1939 spring training, Hemsley had gotten drunk, located a trumpet, and blown the horn through every car on the train. Manager Vitt sent his catcher home to dry out. When Rollie returned to Cleveland for Opening Day, Slapnicka had Alcoholics Anonymous representatives meet him at the train station and take the veteran catcher directly to the hospital.

Before Hemsley's involuntary hospitalization in April 1939, *Baseball Magazine* described the saga of "Rollickin' Rollie" in its June 1938 issue:

> Of all the players in the majors, Hemsley is easily the biggest enigma. His violations of training rules and love of fun have cast a dark shadow across his career to say nothing of the dent they've put in his paycheck. He's lost more money in fines than any other active major league ball player. He's been fined and suspended with every club with which he's played.
>
> He broke some sort of record last season when the Browns fined him approximately $5,000—half his salary. But he's never squawked or moaned about his fines. He takes his medicine and goes on his way but at thirty-one "Rollicking Rollie," as he's now

called because of his escapades, is jeopardizing his chances of a blazing windup as Feller's battery mate to a hitherto spotty career.

Fortunately, the counseling from AA changed Hemsley's life. Feller said in his autobiography Hemsley never backslid. By early May 1939, Rollie had stopped being "rollickin," and focused on guiding the Tribe's twenty-year-old flamethrower toward superstardom.

HAPPY MOTHER'S DAY

Mother's Day fell on May 14 in 1939. Bob Feller invited his family to sit on the front row between home and first at Comiskey Park so his mother could see her only son mow down the White Sox. In the bottom of the third, Feller threw a fastball to Marvin Owen. The right-handed-hitting Sox third baseman nicked the pitch, and the foul ball shot into the stands where the Fellers sat. The ball hit bespectacled Mrs. Feller in the face above her left eye, shattering her glasses. Blood poured from her eyelid and forehead, and Cleveland officials rushed her to the hospital.

A visibly shaken Bob Feller stood on the mound, saw what had happened to his mother, but decided to stay in the game. The White Sox proceeded to score three runs. After the third, Feller regained his composure and breezed through the rest of the game, which the Indians won 9-4. The dutiful son got to the hospital shortly after the game, relieved to hear that doctors did not consider Mrs. Feller's mild concussion and six-stitch wound to be serious.

COMMAND IN THE DAY AND NIGHT

On May 25, Feller threw the second one-hitter of his career against the power-hitting Red Sox. Future Hall of Famers Joe Cronin, Jimmy Foxx, Bobby Doerr, and Ted Williams combined for one bloop single (by Doerr) over second base, as Feller gained his first shutout of the season. After the game, he criticized himself to the press for his one bad pitch of the day—*not* the one blooped for the single, but a pitch to Foxx's power zone in the sixth which Boston's first baseman popped up to end the inning. Feller had reached such a level of excellence by May 1939 he expected to pitch perfect baseball every time out.

Unlike previous star fastball pitchers, Bob Feller didn't wait until the end of his career to master a complete pitching repertoire. Tribe skipper Vitt told *The Sporting News* early in the 1939 season, "Feller needs to be told something only once. He has become one of the most capable technicians in the business. He knows when and how to throw to a base. He takes his time between pitches. With a curve and fastball which need no introduction, he has added a change-of-pace which is as effective as any pitch he has."

Feller's one-hitter against Boston came exactly nine days after seeing his teammates win the first American League night game at Philadelphia on May 16. As Connie Mack started American League play under the lights, Cleveland hurried to prepare Municipal Stadium for its night opener against Detroit on June 27, 1939. The June 15 issue of *The Sporting News* reported that General Electric was installing a 124-million-candlepower-lighting system at a cost of $50,000 to the Indians—"enough power to light the homes and operate the electrical appliances in three thousand average American homes." The people of Cleveland turned out for the show, with 55,305 expecting to see Bob Feller throw fastballs so hard no batter could see them under the lights.[5]

Feller went into the June 27 start against the Tigers not expecting miracles. He knew the most difficult pitches for a hitter to see at night were balls low in the strike zone, and Feller's specialty was the high hard one. Still Feller handcuffed Detroit before the huge crowd, allowing one hit (a single to Earl Averill in the sixth) and striking out 13, while shutting out the Tigers 5-0. Future Hall of Famer Averill applauded Feller's performance. "I've never seen him faster. The pitch I struck out on in the first inning was the fastest ball I've seen in eleven years in the major leagues."

The All-Star Game

After the one-hitter against the Tigers, Feller's next heroics came in the July 11 All-Star Game described earlier. Frank Graham of the *New York Sun* said Feller shutting down the Nationals was the most dominant

[5]Night baseball helped American League teams weather the Great Depression just as it had already done for Cincinnati and Brooklyn in the National League. In 1939, during their home day games, the Indians averaged twelve thousand fans. For the seven Cleveland night games in 1939, the Tribe averaged thirty-three thousand.

"Rapid Robert" Feller, probably throwing some real heat. (National Baseball Library and Archive, Cooperstown, New York)

pitching exhibition since Carl Hubbell's legendary performance in the 1934 Mid-Summer Classic when King Carl mowed down Babe Ruth, Lou Gehrig, Jimmy Foxx, Al Simmons, and Joe Cronin in succession. Graham put Feller's day in perspective for his young career. "The Boy Wonder of Van Meter, Iowa, has grown up. He has acquired poise so that he works more deliberately than he used to. His pitching motion is smoother. He doesn't try to strike everybody out. But when he's really fast as he was in the last inning, it's pretty hard for anybody to hit him."

The white-shirted crowd in Yankees Stadium's bleachers aided Feller in his annihilation of National League hitters. Before the game, Feller saw the ushers taking down the screen in center field to provide additional seating for the fans, and confidently said to himself, "I'm going to throw it by these guys."

Home-plate umpire George Magerkurth's expansive strike zone didn't hurt Feller either. Big George liked his games played quickly, and issuing walks didn't facilitate that goal. The All-Star affair in 1939 lasted 155 minutes.

In the victorious clubhouse after the game, shy, likeable All-American boy Bob Feller opened up to the press for the first time in his career with an indiscreet honesty which would become his unfortunate trademark later in life. Rather than follow the traditional interview path of complimenting his opposition and speaking humbly of his great fortune in getting the Nationals out, Feller told *The Sporting News*, "The fellows in our league are tougher. I didn't expect to be called into the game so soon, so I wasn't quite loosened up. I didn't begin to throw them real fast until the ninth inning." Cleveland's ace was telling the National League that not only had he blown them away, he had blown them away before he was even properly warmed up.

THE REST OF THE SEASON

After going into the All-Star break at 14-3, Bob Feller performed as a mere mortal during the second half of the season with a record of 10-6. On August 7, Cleveland called up shortstop Lou Boudreau and second baseman Ray Mack from Buffalo, providing a keystone combination that would serve the Indians well for years. As Boudreau pointed out in his 1993 autobiography, the Tribe barely broke .500

(at 51-47) before he and Mack arrived. With the new infielders in place, the Indians went 36-20.

Feller had two more shutouts in the month of August, whitewashing the White Sox on the thirteenth, and then the Red Sox on the twenty-seventh. Boston's Ted Williams later told reporters about the change in his mental preparation when Cleveland's ace was on the mound. The Kid said he needed only two hours to prepare when facing the league's second-best pitcher. Against Bullet Bob? "I would start thinking about Bob Feller three days before he pitched. I'd sit in my room thinking about him all the time."

Heading into September, Bob Feller had a chance to become the youngest player in baseball history to win 20 games. On September 8, 1939, at St. Louis' Sportsman Park, Feller fulfilled Vitt's preseason prophecy by winning his twentieth game at age twenty, beating the hapless Browns 12-1.[6]

The season closed at Detroit on October 1 with Feller beating the Tigers 8-3 for his 24th win. On the year, Feller beat Detroit six times without a loss despite the Tigers having three future Hall of Famers (Hank Greenberg, Charlie Gehringer, and Earl Averill) in their lineup.

What did Bob Feller do differently in 1939 compared to 1938? His record went from 17-11 to 24-9 while his earned-run average improved from 4.08 to 2.85. Most important, Feller maintained an acceptable level of wildness by reducing his walks from 208 to 142. For a fastball strikeout pitcher to be effective, issuing some walks was a necessary evil. Lou Boudreau explained why in his book *Covering All the Bases*:

> Feller's control problems weren't nearly as bad as he wanted batters to think. He'd knock down guys intentionally although they all thought it was accidental. Nobody ever dug in against Feller including Greenberg who had a habit of playing policeman when he stepped into the batter's box. When Greenberg would finally be ready to hit, Feller would throw his fastball up and then Greenberg would go down. Once I remember he knocked Greenberg down twice in a row and I'm sure that both those pitches were not accidental.

---

[6]The record stood until twenty-year-old Dwight Gooden (younger than Feller was by thirteen days) won 20 games in 1985.

Veteran Cleveland sportswriter Gordon Cobbledick watched Feller every day in 1939, and after the season asked Feller to explain his dramatic improvement. "*I learned not to be in a hurry*. I took time to find things out and I found that the more time I took, the more pressure I transferred from myself to the other fellows." It was a lesson that would stay with Feller until his wartime departure.

After pitching his last game of the season, Cleveland's ace hurried home to Van Meter for the celebration of Bob Feller Day on October 3, 1939. The governor of Iowa and hundreds more were there to celebrate the achievements of the favorite son. Feller joined local ballplayers in an exhibition game, and Iowa's greatest pitcher surprisingly lost a duel to his cousin Harold Manders.

The only thing left to do in 1939 was sign a contract for the coming year. On December 2, Feller agreed to a base salary for the 1940 season of $26,000, making him the highest-paid player in Cleveland history. Cleveland president Alva Bradley promptly insured his crown jewel for $105,000.

In the offseason, Feller spent his time obtaining his pilot's license and watching construction of the new $25,000 ten-room home he was buying for his parents. The house had a state-of-the-art "electric eye" garage door opener and a maid-summoning foot switch under the dining room table. At the close of baseball's centennial year, Bob Feller and his family found themselves living out the American Dream.

Before and During the War: 1940-1945

FELLER STARTED THE 1940 SEASON WITH A FLOURISH, throwing the first no-hitter of his career against the White Sox on Opening Day. It remains baseball's only Opening Day no-hitter. White Sox leadoff hitter Mike Kreevich responded to an unhittable and virtually invisible called strike by telling the umpire, "That sounded a little high." Feller kept up the 20-win habit he had started in 1939 by going 27-11 in 1940 and 25-13 in 1941, leading the league both years in games, innings pitched, strikeouts, and shutouts.

Two days after the bombing of Pearl Harbor in December 1941, Feller became the first professional athlete to sign up for the war effort, joining the Navy to serve under Lieutenant Commander (and former heavyweight boxing champion) Gene Tunney. Feller's pay went from the Indians' $40,000 a year to the Navy's ninety-nine dollars a month, or $1,087 a year.

With father Bill battling the final stages of cancer (which took his life in January 1943), Feller could have gotten an exemption from military service as his family's sole provider. Instead, the star pitcher expressed his immediate desire to get into combat. "I don't care where I'm sent as long as I can get in the middle of the fight soon."

Feller first went to gunnery school at Norfolk, and graduated with highest honors. From there, he served almost two years in the Pacific on the USS Alabama, where he was in charge of an anti-aircraft gun, earning eight battle stars for bravery. Between battles, Feller worked to perfect a slider on board the ship.

During Feller's extended military service in World War II, Cleveland sportswriter Cobbledick noted that there "seems to be sound reason for the supposition that Feller spent much of his time brooding over the loss of those precious earning years from a career that would be short at best—and formulating the determination to make it up as quickly as possible."

When Bob Feller finally got off the USS Alabama in the summer of 1945, he reported to a Navy facility at Great Lakes, Michigan, for rest and relaxation until the war's end. The officer in charge of base athletics was Paul Brown, the founder and head coach of football's Cleveland Browns. Feller attacked calisthenics like a man possessed. Brown, a stickler for conditioning in his football players, watched Feller's compulsive training and said, "I don't think it's wise for any man to work as hard as he does to prepare for an athletic contest."

On August 23, 1945, Bob Feller returned to Cleveland after receiving his honorable discharge from the Navy. On August 25, in his first start, he whipped the Tigers and their back-to-back league Most Valuable Player Hal Newhouser. Feller finished the year at 5-3, with a respectable 2.50 earned-run average.

After the War—A Changed Man

SPORTSWRITER JIMMY CANNON DESCRIBED the pre-war Feller as "a pleasant young man who handled his success with a special grace." The *Washington Times Herald*'s Vincent X. Flattery said in a 1943 article that "more than any figure in baseball, Feller's homespun goodness, his small town naiveté, his wholly unspoiled modesty and down-to-earthiness always impressed me hugely. Feller symbolizes the American boy."

After the war, a new Bob Feller emerged. Anxious to compensate for the loss of four years in his prime, Feller forgot the lesson he expressed to Cobbledick in 1939 about finding success by not hurrying. Beginning in 1946, Rapid Robert became maniacal in his quest to make up for lost time. During the season, when not on the mound, Feller broadcast a radio show, wrote a newspaper column, and pursued endorsements and business deals of every kind. His business activities became so numerous he decided to incorporate himself as "Ro-Fel, Inc." Opposing players soon nicknamed him "Inky"—a derogatory short-hand for "Incorporated." In 1948, Cobbledick observed the transition in Cleveland's former Boy Wonder:

> He has changed. Not only has the boy been taken out of the country, but all trace of the country has been taken out of the boy… There can be little doubt that Feller is the busiest man in baseball… More than any other athlete, Feller identifies himself frankly and openly with the commercial side of baseball. Since returning from the war, this characteristic has been accentuated… His days have become a succession of business conferences, consultations with attorneys, and meetings with an endless procession of people who want something from him, and from whom he hopes to get a profit in return.

Feller's wife Virginia (whom he had met in 1940 and married in 1943),[7] observed the change in a 1952 article about her famous husband:

---

[7]They divorced in 1971.

> It seems to me that there was a big change in Bob after his Navy duty. He seemed unsettled and was constantly using up nervous energy—trying to make up for lost time. He sought out business angles and attached more importance to each game.

When baseball seasons ended after the war, Feller organized and promoted barnstorming trips around the country with players from both leagues sometimes playing each other and sometimes playing Negro league All-Star teams. Feller pitched in virtually every game, slowly but surely wearing out his arm, which had already been damaged in a 1947 fall from a slippery mound. Though he stayed with Cleveland until the early part of the 1956 season, his record during the last five years of his career was a mediocre 36-31.

What should have been the brightest moments in Feller's post-war career turned out to be his biggest disappointments. The Indians finally reached the Fall Classic in 1948, but Feller was tagged with the world champion Tribe's only two losses to the Braves. Cleveland made it back to the World Series in 1954, but manager Al Lopez didn't use Feller at all during the Dusty Rhodes-led Giants' sweep of the Indians.

After Retirement—Honors and Setbacks

IN 1969, THE BASEBALL WRITERS OF AMERICA chose baseball's greatest living players at each position, and Bob Feller was selected as the game's greatest living right-handed pitcher. At the banquet honoring the players, honest but tactless Feller used his opportunity at the microphone to blast Jackie Robinson for suggesting that baseball owed black Americans more than they were getting.

Feller's capacity to offend became almost habitual after his jab at Robinson. In the early seventies, he disparaged Hank Aaron for "not having the wrists and bat control he used to" as Aaron challenged and broke Babe Ruth's home-run record. Feller even denigrated everyone's favorite nice guy, Nolan Ryan, labeling the man who shattered his own records "not a pitcher, but a thrower."

After his retirement from baseball, Bob Feller's personal life and business ventures crashed and burned. In the 1970s, he was sued twice for alienation of affection by the husbands of married women with whom Feller admitted having affairs; was arrested for the alleged theft of an airplane; was charged with passing hot checks; and ended up in litigation with his best friend and benefactor Allen Lowe over the sale of his baseball memorabilia. Feller ultimately resolved the litigations and prosecutions favorably, but the stigma of trouble remained.

Beginning in the 1980s, Bullet Bob finally slowed down and calmed his life. He enjoys a successful second marriage, and found financial salvation by promoters' renewed interest in his attendance at Old-Timers' Games and baseball card shows. Most rewarding for the old hurler, the Indians welcomed him back to their spring training as a pitching instructor. All of these developments allowed him to speak with a regained self-confidence in his 1990 autobiography *Now Pitching, Bob Feller*.

Feller retired with outstanding career statistics—a record of 266-162 for a .621 winning percentage, three no-hitters, 12 one-hitters, 46 shutouts, and over 2,500 strikeouts. His spending almost four years in the armed forces surely cost him at least 100 career wins, 1,000 strikeouts, and probably two no-hitters.[8] By inserting the statistical projections for the four lost war years, Feller's numbers make him one of baseball's five all-time greatest pitchers, if not its greatest, clearly meriting his 1962 first-ballot induction into Cooperstown.

In his fourth major league season, by learning the importance of not hurrying, Bob Feller became baseball's most dominant pitcher and one of the fans' favorite players. As Feller pushed himself after the war to make up for lost time, he lost sight of that 1939 lesson which had enabled him to hit his peak as a player and a person. More significant than any baseball statistical loss, World War II permanently imbalanced the wholesome farm-boy equilibrium of an American hero.

---

[8]He averaged 25 wins and more than 250 strikeouts in his last three years before the war, and roared back in 1946 with 26 wins and a major league record 348 strikeouts. His no-hitters came in 1940, 1946, and 1951.

Hall of Fame Pitcher Satchel Paige (National Baseball Library and Archive, Cooperstown, New York)

CHAPTER EIGHT

MOVING TOWARD THE DAY

Marian Anderson, Satchel Paige, and Wendell Smith Advance the Position of Negro League Baseball

BOB FELLER MAY HAVE BEEN the major leagues' best pitcher in 1939, but he was not necessarily the best pitcher in baseball. Barnstorming through the Pacific Northwest that summer was a tall, thin right-hander considered by many, including Joe DiMaggio, to be the greatest pitcher of 1939 or any other year—the legendary Satchel Paige.

In his recent biography of Paige, *Don't Look Back*, author Mark Ribowsky described Negro league baseball as being, for many years, "an American Atlantis." Since 1970, the research and writings of Robert Peterson, John Holway, Donn Rogosin, Jules Tygiel, James Riley Ribowsky, the staff of the Society for American Baseball Research, and others have revealed the hidden world of pre-Jackie Robinson black baseball, making it a vital part of American baseball history.

In 1972, William Brashler completed his novel *Bingo Long and the Traveling All-Stars*, which later became a successful movie starring Billy Dee Williams and James Earl Jones. After listening to hundreds of hours of taped Negro leaguer interviews, Brashler set *Bingo Long* in 1939, seeing the year as "the height of the barnstorming era."

Most of the surviving Negro league players who saw the *Bingo Long* movie (over which Brashler had little control) came away disappointed.

The movie made the black game look like a circus and its participants appear as clowns. The old players knew better. They knew that black baseball in 1939 was more than entertaining. It was great baseball. They also knew that, by 1939, the focus of the black game went beyond barnstorming, as white *and* black journalists were putting constant pressure on big league owners to break the color barrier, and the excuses offered by the owners for excluding black players seemed less and less palatable. The year proved to be more than the height of the barnstorming era. It was the year white America could no longer ignore the black game.

Black Baseball Before 1939

THE FIRST BLACK PROFESSIONAL BASEBALL PLAYER appropriately spent his boyhood in Cooperstown, New York. In 1872, after leaving the game's mythical birthplace, fourteen-year-old Bud Fowler got paid to play for a white team in New Castle, Pennsylvania, and then spent the next two decades of his life bouncing around professional baseball. Fowler offered this lament on the life of the black ballplayer at the end of a long season: "It was hard picking for a colored player this year. I didn't make a living; I just existed. If I had not been quite so black, I might have caught on as a Spaniard or something of that kind... My skin is against me."

Fowler was followed in professional baseball by Oberlin College graduate Moses Fleetwood ("Fleet") Walker. In 1884, Fleet caught for the Toledo Blue Stockings in the American Association, considered a major league at that time. Walker suffered the indignity of playing that year with Tony Mullane, Toledo's hard-throwing, 30-game-winning, racist pitcher, who refused to take signals from his black catcher. Fleet never knew what pitch Mullane intended to throw, and constantly sustained hand injuries from the pitcher's random deliveries in the days before padded catcher's mitts.

In 1885, the waiters at the Argyle Hotel in Babylon, New York, formed the first black professional team. They tried to shade their heritage by calling themselves the "Cuban Giants," though none of them were Cuban. The team barnstormed the East Coast for three years playing college and semi-pro teams, earning weekly paychecks of between twelve and eighteen dollars. The Cuban Giants were good enough to play the world champion Detroit Tigers in 1887, losing a 6-4 heartbreaker when the Tigers scored the go-ahead runs in the eighth inning.

The same year the Tigers slipped by the Cuban Giants, Hall of Fame Chicago White Stockings player-manager "Cap" Anson formalized major league baseball's color barrier by refusing to let his team play an exhibition game against Newark unless his opponent's announced black starting pitcher, George Stovey, was removed. Newspapers covered up the confrontation, attributing Stovey's absence from the lineup to illness.

By the turn of the century, most notions of integration in professional baseball had ended. One person who still held a glimmer of hope was Sol White, a late nineteenth-century black player who became an early twentieth-century historian. White's book, *History of Colored Baseball*, was published in 1906 and detailed the plight of his fellow black players since the Civil War. Despite the prejudice of Anson and others, and the existence of the "gentlemen's agreement" in place among major league owners to exclude black ballplayers from their rosters, White's book encouraged the new generation of black players:

> Baseball is a legitimate profession. It should be taken seriously by the colored player. An honest effort of his great ability will open the avenue in the near future wherein he may walk hand in hand with the opposite race in the greatest of all American games—baseball.

By the time White's book came out, at least one major league manager believed black players could compete at the major league level. Baltimore skipper John McGraw had seen light-skinned Charlie Grant play second base for Chicago's Columbia Giants, and knew Grant was good enough to start for his team. At the Orioles' 1901 spring training, in an attempt to circumvent the "gentlemen's agreement," McGraw changed Grant's name to "Charlie Tokohama" and announced to the press that his new second baseman was a full-blooded Cherokee

Indian. The Baltimore skipper then instructed Charlie that if anyone from a rival team talked to him, Grant-Tokohama was to scream "Wah-wah-wah-wah" at the top of his lungs, and grunt "Me big black Injun!"

Unfortunately for McGraw and Grant, White Sox president Charles Comiskey exposed the hoax: "If Muggsy really keeps this Indian, I will get a Chinaman of my acquaintance and put him on third. Somebody told me that the Cherokee of McGraw's is really Grant, the crack Negro second baseman, fixed up with war paint and a bunch of feathers." After Comiskey called his bluff, McGraw avoided controversy by releasing Grant before the start of the season, telling the press the second baseman wasn't good enough to make the team.

Negro professional baseball essentially did not exist from the turn of the century until 1920. During this interim, bona fide Cubans broke into the major leagues without incident when the Cincinnati Reds signed Rafael Almedo (who would play three years) and Armando Marsans (who would play eight seasons) in 1911. Booker T. Washington's Washington newspaper *The New York Age* saw hope for black ballplayers by the entry of Cuban players into the big leagues:

> Now that the first shock is over it would not be surprising to see a Cuban a few shades darker than Almedo and Marsans breaking into the professional ranks. With the admission of Cubans of a darker hue in the two big leagues it would then be easy for colored players who are citizens of this country to get into fast company. . . . Until the public gets accustomed to seeing native Negroes on big league teams, the colored players could keep their mouths shut and pass for Cubans.

In 1920, two events occurred which shaped the next quarter-century of black baseball. First, in response to the 1919 Black Sox scandal, major league owners named Chicago federal judge Landis as the game's first commissioner, a post he would hold until his death in 1944. As long as the bigoted Landis ruled, no black players would compete in the big leagues.

The second major black baseball event of 1920 was the creation of the Negro National League by Rube Foster. Historian John Holway accurately described Foster as "Christy Mathewson, John McGraw,

Connie Mack, Al Spalding and Kenesaw Mountain Landis—great pitcher, manager, owner, league organizer, czar—all rolled into one." On February 13, 1920, Foster formed the eight-team league with clubs in Chicago (which fielded two teams), New York, Detroit, St. Louis, Indianapolis, Kansas City, and Dayton. The pressures of holding the fragile league together drove Foster to the Illinois Insane Asylum in 1926 where he stayed until his death in 1930. After the passing of Rube Foster, black baseball would never have another czar.

The strongest black team in the 1920s didn't play in Foster's Negro National League. The Kansas City Monarchs had no affiliation with any league, instead touring the country to play local semi-pro teams, and, in the process, making profits for their white owner, J. L. Wilkinson. To increase the number of games the Monarchs could play in a day, Wilkinson pioneered the use of electric lights in ballgames during 1929. Rogosin described the effect of night play on Negro league life:

> Once night baseball took hold, conditions worsened for the players. The combination of a depression and portable lights encouraged the strapped owners to squeeze in as many games as possible. The Monarch bus became the home of the generator and the Monarchs themselves took to cars. As Judy Johnson later recalled, "We'd play three games at a time, a doubleheader and a night game, and you'd get back to the hotel and you were tired as a yard dog."

New black team leadership emerged in Pennsylvania in the late twenties and early thirties to strengthen the Negro National League. "Cum" Posey assembled the top East Coast black players for his Homestead Grays[1] and proceeded to dominate the black game. Posey's regime lasted until Pittsburgh numbers operator Gus Greenlee (known among his gangster friends as "Mr. Big") began pirating black baseball's best for his Pittsburgh Crawfords in 1931.

Within four years of their formation, Greenlee's Crawfords owned their own ballpark (the only Negro league team who did), and had

---

[1]Homestead was a small steel town across the Monongahela River from Pittsburgh.

five future Hall of Famers in their starting lineup—Satchel Paige, Josh Gibson (the black Babe Ruth), Oscar Charleston (the black Tris Speaker), Judy Johnson, and Cool Papa Bell. From 1935-1936, the Crawfords had the best record in the league and became known as "the New York Yankees of Negro baseball."

In 1937, believing political success would flow from having a good national baseball team, Dominican Republic dictator Rafael Trujillo borrowed pages from Posey's and Greenlee's books by bribing black players to abandon their existing Negro league contracts. Paying with upfront cash, Trujillo immediately garnered eighteen of black baseball's biggest stars (including Paige, Gibson, and seven other Crawfords) to play in the Caribbean. The raid caused Greenlee and his once mighty Crawfords to sink, though most black players only stayed with Trujillo for the 1937 season.

By 1937-1938, black and white journalists started filling their columns with venom over the exclusion of black ballplayers from the major leagues. The *Pittsburgh Courier* became the most powerful black newspaper of the era. Its principal writer was Wendell Smith, who in 1994 became the first black journalist to win Cooperstown's coveted J. G. Taylor Spink Award, presented to sportswriters who have made lifetime achievements to baseball. Among other tactics, Smith and his cronies at the *Courier*:

1. Submitted a list of black players called a "Roster of Stars" to New York Giant president Horace Stoneham in October 1937, telling him that if the Giants signed Paige, Gibson, Leonard, and Bell, his team "would be a more formidable opponent for the New York Yankees (who had just blown out the Giants in the 1937 Fall Classic) in next year's World Series." Stoneham ignored the suggestion.
2. Blasted black fans in a May 1938 article for buying tickets to major league games, and encouraged them to boycott the big leagues until the owners signed Negro league players.
3. Sent a telegram to Pittsburgh Pirate manager Pie Traynor in the winter of 1938 with a loaded suggestion. "Know your club needs players. Have answers to your prayers right here in

Pittsburgh. Josh Gibson, Buck Leonard, Ray Brown, Satchel Paige, and Cool Papa Bell are all available at reasonable figures. What is your attitude?" Traynor did not reply.

Smith's white counterparts on press row joined in the fray. In 1938, Jimmy Powers wrote articles in the *New York Daily News* explaining why black star players could lead the Giants to the pennant, and urging the Baseball Writers of America to vote for Negro league stars in their Cooperstown Hall of Fame balloting. Actually, the call for equal opportunity in baseball had started among journalists earlier than 1938. Westbrook Pegler of the *Chicago Tribune*, Shirley Povich of the *Washington Post*, and Heywood Hale Broun of the *New York Herald Tribune* had carried the torch throughout the 1930s before Powers began his crusade.

The sustained media outcry forced major-league powers to respond. In 1938, Washington Senators owner Clark Griffith acknowledged publicly that "one day" blacks might play in the big leagues, but the uncompromising Landis told the *Pittsburgh Courier*, "The time is not right for blacks in baseball... As far as I'm concerned, black fans can boycott big league games if they want."

Baseball's ugliest racial incident took place July 29, 1938. During a pregame interview, in response to a seemingly harmless question, New York Yankees utility outfielder Jake Powell told White Sox radio broadcaster Bob Elson about his offseason job. "I work as a policeman in my hometown of Dayton, Ohio, where I keep in shape by crackin' niggers over the head." Elson terminated the interview instantly, apologized for Powell, and told the huge WGN audience his station was not responsible for ballplayers' remarks.

Black America understandably went into an uproar over Powell's racist remark motivating Commissioner Landis to suspend the Yankees outfielder for ten days. Rogosin reported on the aftermath of the Powell affair:

> The story did not die. Protest groups in black organizations were formed. They demanded that Powell be banned from baseball for life. When Powell, after his suspension, returned to Chicago, he required

> a police escort and was kept out of the lineup. When Powell played in Washington, he was greeted with a hail of bottles. In New York, six thousand signed a petition supporting a lifetime ban, and the Amsterdam News suggested a one-year boycott of Ruppert's [the Yankees owner] beer.
>
> White sportswriters, sympathetic to the Negro league fight for integration, used the incident to excoriate the baseball establishment… Powell's appearance in major league parks invariably caused minor disturbances and resulted in the need for more police. In Washington, with its large black population, the bottle-throwing caused the introduction of paper beer cups. The Yankees tried to trade Powell, with no takers; and when in 1940 Powell slipped from the majors due to injury, the Yankees management was delighted.

As Jake Powell's career unwound after the 1938 season,[2] the first superstar in the Civil Rights movement prepared to sing.

The Fight and the Life Continue—1939

THE CIVIL RIGHTS MOVEMENT BEGINS

JACKIE ROBINSON'S ENTRY into major league baseball in 1947 has been celebrated by many historians (including documentary filmmaker Ken Burns) as the opening salvo of the Civil Rights movement in America. It wasn't. The movement began on the steps of the Lincoln Memorial, Easter Sunday, 1939. After being prevented from performing at Washington's Constitution Hall by the Daughters of the American Revolution (DAR), singer Marian Anderson gave a concert before seventy-five thousand white and black supporters, and a national radio audience.

When the DAR told Anderson's agent Sol Hurok there were no available dates at the concert hall in 1939 or any subsequent year for the internationally acclaimed black contralto's performance, Hurok notified the press of the exclusion. First Lady Eleanor Roosevelt promptly resigned from the DAR. Equally responsive Secretary of the Interior Harold Ickes quickly arranged for the Lincoln Memorial concert.

[2]After leaving the Yankees in 1940, Powell led a failed life leading to suicide in 1948, when he shot himself in a Washington police station after being arrested for writing hot checks.

Ickes introduced Anderson on April 9, 1939, in front of Lincoln's statue. "It is appropriate as it is fortunate that today we stand humbly at the base of this memorial to the Great Emancipator while glorious tribute is rendered to his memory by a daughter of the race from which he struck the chains of slavery. Genius like justice is blind."

When Miss Anderson began the afternoon concert with "America the Beautiful," the clouds cleared, the sun came through onto the black singer's face, and intelligent Americans realized for perhaps the first time that the second-class treatment of blacks in the "land of the free" simply could not continue.

The Black Player's Life in 1939

Marian Anderson's plight as a singer mirrored the path of the black baseball player in 1939. As Anderson had been forced to expatriate to Europe to have a concert schedule worthy of her talent, so too did many Negro league players have to leave their country. The ballplayers didn't go to Europe; they went south of the border to play in Mexico and Puerto Rico. Shortstop Willie Wells explained to the *Pittsburgh Courier*'s Wendell Smith why he left the Newark Eagles in 1939 to play for Vera Cruz in the Mexican League:

> Not only do I get more money playing here, but I live like a king… I'm not faced with the racial problems of Mexico… We live in the best hotels, we eat in the best restaurants, and can go anyplace we care to… We don't enjoy such privileges in the U.S.… I didn't quit Newark and join some other team in the United Stated; I quit and left the country… I found freedom and democracy here, something I never found in the United States… Here, in Mexico, I am a man…

In addition to Wells, future Hall of Famers Gibson, Paige, Bell, Ray Dandridge, and Martin Dihigo spent much of 1939 in Mexico and Latin America where they played with the likes of Luis Tiant, Sr., (whose son Luis, Jr., became a major league star in the 1970s) and Perucho "The Bull" Cepeda (father of 1960s National League great, Orlando Cepeda, "the Baby Bull").

As Anderson was refused the opportunity to sing in the United States' great concert halls, and could only travel the country singing in the smaller towns, so too did those black players who stayed in the country spend much of their time barnstorming. The Negro league schedule typically lasted only about 70 games a year, while teams would play twice that many games on the road taking on all comers, as Bingo Long's team did in Brashler's novel.

Hall of Fame player Buck Leonard (often called the "Black Lou Gehrig") told of the typical lodging for a black barnstormer. "Sometimes we'd stay in hotels that had so many bedbugs you had to put a newspaper down between the mattress and sheets. Other times, we'd rent three rooms because when you rented that many, you got to use the bath." Often, they just slept in their cars or pitched tents by the side of the road.

Infielder Jack Marshall described the ballplayers' diet for Robert Peterson. "Since there were so many places on the road where we couldn't eat, we'd take sardines and a can of beans and pour them into bell jars. We'd take crackers and eat out of the bell jar." When the meager food supply ran out and they had to stop at a restaurant, each team tried to include a light-skinned Negro who could often pass as white and order take-out for the team.

In 1939, most black players made anywhere from $125 to $300 a month. The nomadic, poverty-stricken lifestyle could have one of two effects on the player. Some were able to put their roles in historical perspective, as did 1939 Kansas City Monarchs first baseman Buck O'Neil. "A lot of times they'll say to me, 'Buck, you were before your time.' But I don't think so. I think I was right on time. I was right in the midst of this thing… I had something to do with them getting there. I was playing before them, and the way we held ourselves when we played back there when—that is the reason that they're playing now. Everything happens in its season."

Understandably, several players did not share O'Neil's serenity about his segregated, down-and-out circumstances. August Wilson won the 1987 Pulitzer Prize for his play *Fences* which portrayed the tortured mentality of many black ballplayers in the character of Troy Maxson (played by James Earl Jones in the opening cast on Broadway).

Baseball great John "Buck" O'Neil (National Baseball Library and Archive, Cooperstown, New York)

The fictional Maxson was a Pittsburgh garbageman in the 1950s who had been a Negro league star in the late 1930s. Playwright Wilson explained the significance of Troy Maxson: "Maxson is a composite. He stands for all of the guys, whether they were baseball players or not, who were denied opportunity–and what that does to people. It was an opportunity to show how the deprivation of possibility has an effect on a person's life and how they deal with their family."

An excerpt from *Fences* shows Maxson's basis for his torment:
BONO (Maxson's friend of last thirty years): "Troy, you just come along too early."

TROY: "There ought not never have been no time called too early! Now you take that fellow… What's that fellow they had playing right field for the Yankees back then? You know who I'm talking about, Bono. Used to play right field for the Yankees."

ROSE (Troy's Wife): "Selkirk?"

TROY: "Selkirk! That's it! Man batting .269, understand? .269. What kind of sense that make? I was hitting .432 with 37 home runs! Man batting .269 and playing right field for the Yankees! I saw Josh Gibson's daughter yesterday. She walking around with raggedy shoes on her feet. Now I bet you Selkirk's daughter ain't walking around with raggedy shoes on her feet! I bet you that!"

ROSE: "They got a lot of colored baseball players now. Jackie Robinson was the first. Folks had to wait for Jackie Robinson."

TROY: "I done seen a hundred niggers play baseball better than Jackie Robinson. Hell, I know some teams Jackie Robinson couldn't even make! What you talking about Jackie Robinson. Jackie Robinson wasn't nobody. I'm talking about if you could play ball then they ought to have let you play. Don't care what color you were. Come telling me I come along too early. If you could play… then they ought to have let you play." (Troy takes a long drink from the bottle.)

THE JOURNALISTS' RAGE

AS BLACK AND WHITE JOURNALISTS supported Marian Anderson's entitlement to operatic civil rights, so too did they attempt to advance the Negro leaguers' quest for equal opportunity. Jimmy Powers maintained his 1938 pace at the *New York Daily News*, writing a column in 1939 which said, "I have seen personally at least ten colored ballplayers I know who are good enough to be big leaguers." Shirley Povich told his *Washington Post* readers that same summer of Josh Gibson being a better catcher than New York Yankees perennial All-Star Bill Dickey.

In early 1939, after writing articles suggesting that blacks needed to organize a National Association for the Advancement of Colored People (NAACP) on behalf of black ballplayers, and then comparing American treatment of blacks with Hitler's treatment of minorities, Wendell Smith interviewed National League president Ford Frick to ask point-blank questions about baseball's closed doors. Frick told Smith: (1) baseball could not make changes until public opinion was ready for it; (2) traveling and eating with integrated teams would be difficult because many places would not accommodate blacks; and (3) these off-the-field problems would necessarily create dissension within a ballclub.

Following the Frick interview, Wendell Smith sought out forty major league players and eight managers to get their response to the National League president's perception. Eighty percent of those polled disagreed with Frick and favored integration. Despite this decided preference by the men on the field for giving equal opportunity to black players, the owners stood firm.

Smith proceeded to blast baseball's executives. "Club owners could put a few black players in their lineups and pack their parks. Can you imagine Satchel Paige pitching against Lefty Grove in an empty stadium? No! Neither can the club owners. They know Paige would pack their parks but they would rather lose money than give black boys a chance. Yet they make every appeal to the black fans to attend their lily-white shows."

Remarkably, black fans did support major league baseball in the late 1930s. Sportscaster and journalist Art Rust, Jr., described his

Famed journalist Wendell Smith, winner of the 1994 J. G. Taylor Spink Award. (National Baseball Library and Archive, Cooperstown, New York.)

experiences as a black eleven-year-old boy watching his major league heroes in his book *Get That Nigger off the Field:*[3]

> At Yankee Stadium in 1939, while leaning over the bleacher wall in right field with other youngsters seeking autographs, Washington center fielder Taft Wright called me a "black son of a bitch" when I put my scorecard in front of his face. At the Polo Grounds I was called a "black bastard" by St. Louis Cardinal left-hander Clyde Shoun when I was trying to get his autograph.
>
> I recall I used to send away to George Burke, a photographer in Chicago, who specialized in major league pictures. I had photos of every St. Louis Cardinal player from 1939 to 1942. I'll never forget Enos "Country" Slaughter signing a picture for me and walking down 8th Avenue muttering, "How did that little nigger get all those pictures?" I said to myself, "With all those crackers, ain't no way a black guy's gonna play ball in the majors."

Despite these incidents, Rust had a basis for hope. He remembered "Branch Rickey around 1939, then with the Cardinals, putting his arm around me outside the parking lot next to the Polo Grounds and telling me that one day Negro players would appear in the majors."

Thankfully, per Wendell Smith's survey, most major league players did not share the prejudice of Wright, Shoun, McGee, and Slaughter. Lou Gehrig had gone on record for breaking the color barrier in 1937. "I've seen many Negro players who should be in the major leagues. There's no room in baseball for discrimination. It is our national pastime and a game for all."

After seeing a game between Homestead and Newark in the spring of 1939, Walter Johnson told the *Washington Post,* "There is a catcher that any big league club would like to buy for $200,000. I've heard of him before. His name is Gibson... and he can do anything. He hits the ball a mile and catches so easy that he might just as well be in a rocking chair. He throws like a rifle. Bill Dickey isn't as good a catcher. Too bad this Gibson is a colored fellow."

---

[3]Rust's title came from the quote attributed to Cap Anson when he refused to play against Newark in 1887 as long as George Stovey was the pitcher.

THE NEGRO LEAGUES SEASON IN 1939

AS FOR LEAGUE PLAY DURING 1939'S REGULAR SEASON, Buck Leonard and Josh Gibson led the Homestead Grays to first place in the Negro National League. In the post-season playoff, the Baltimore Elite (pronounced "E-Light") Giants beat the Grays, sparked by the hitting of Wild Bill Wright (who won the batting title with a .402 average) and the all-around play of a young catcher named Roy Campanella. Leonard called the Grays of that late 1930s' era the greatest team he ever played on, and Homestead started moving toward the black ink in 1939 by playing their Sunday games at Griffith Stadium where the heavily black D.C. population turned out in force.

The Kansas City Monarchs, who had joined the newly formed Negro American League (NAL) in 1937, ran away with the NAL pennant in 1939. Leading the Monarchs that year were slugger first baseman Buck O'Neil and pitcher Hilton Smith.[4] Although Satchel Paige was under contract with the Monarchs, he spent most of the year on the road barnstorming with the Monarchs "B" team, called "Satchel Paige's Kansas City Colored Stars."

For the first part of the 1939 season, Paige could not pitch at all because of a dead arm he had worn out in Mexico the previous year. In his autobiography, *Maybe I'll Pitch Forever*, the great Satch explained the circumstances in Mexico which led to his sore arm:

> I worked harder and harder trying to angry up the air but my arm got mad instead. It ached all over and I couldn't hardly throw. In Mexico City you understand there ain't so much air 'cause it's up so high. If there's less air, the less can get mad and it don't shove on the ball much so it don't curve much.

When Paige's arm cratered in Mexico, no team wanted him, and at the age of thirty-two, he described himself as being "just an old man without an arm anymore." Satchel got the call from Monarchs owner Wilkinson in early 1939 and felt like he'd been resurrected. "I'd been

[4]It was Smith who pursuaded Monarchs' owner Wilkinson in March 1945 to sign an infielder by the name of Jackie Robinson.

dead. Nows I was alive again. I didn't have my arm, but I didn't even think of that. I had me a piece of work."

Aided by the massages and treatment of Monarchs trainer "Jewbaby" Floyd (whom Wilkinson dispatched to his "B" team in hopes of reviving his best-known player), Paige one day in 1939 suddenly and mysteriously regained his arm strength. Satchel told the particulars of how his arm became revitalized:

> One hot day we were playin' an exhibition in Winnipeg, Canada. I was standin' in the first base coachin' box when a ball come toward me from the bullpen. Not thinkin', I picked it up and throwed it back.
>
> 'Bout two minutes went by and my brain all of a sudden asks me, 'How did the ball get back in the bullpen?'
>
> "I throwed it," I answers.
>
> "Maybe your arm is comin' 'round,' " my brain says.
>
> "Maybe it is," I replies.
>
> I walked down to the bullpen and started warmin' up.
>
> All the Monarchs stopped play and come around to watch. "It comin' 'round, Satch, it's comin' 'round," they said like they seen a miracle.
>
> Three days later Mr. Wilkinson put me in for two innings. I struck out all six batters. "That's enough for today, Satch," he said.
>
> I been in my second childhood ever since.

Although Satchel Paige did not get back all of his overpowering velocity in 1939, he got back most of it. Coupled with his perfect control, and an arsenal of curves and changes of speed (which Paige described as "cutin' up"), the great Satch became a dominant pitcher again. Toward the end of the 1939 summer, he felt confident enough to call in his outfielders in Union Springs, Alabama, but disaster struck when a "little no account lookin' fella came up, took that big greasy swing and put my fastball where my left fielder formerly was. The polices escorted me from the field as the little man crossed home." By the fall, Paige departed for the Puerto Rican League, and "the brown arm was golden again."

As Paige's life and career got a second wind in 1939, black baseball's second-greatest player, Josh Gibson, started a decline which would lead to his early death in 1945. Author John Holway in his book *Josh and Satch* gave teammate Ted Page's account of what happened to the great catcher in 1939:

> He changed from the Josh I knew: a kid, just an overgrown kid who did nothing but play ball and eat ice cream or go to the movies. Strictly play, this was Josh. Well, that changed, all that.
>
> He started to drink. I wasn't close enough to him to have found out why, but it seems to me that his wife had misused some money, like when you're playing down in the tropics and you send some money home. If this is true, I don't know. But I would like to say this: Something caused the man to change from what he was—a congenial, big, old, young boy—to a man who was kind of bitter with somebody, or mad with somebody, he wasn't really sure who. He realized as he started to get older that his good days were behind him as a baseball player, and I feel certain that in the inside of his mind, Josh realized that he was never going to make the big leagues so who cares?

The drinking didn't keep Gibson from leading the Negro leagues in homers that year (hitting 16 in 72 games), or prevent him from being the featured player in the East-West All-Star Game[5] played at Chicago's Comiskey Park that summer before forty thousand fans.

One of Gibson's home runs in 1939 was so monstrous, the mayor of the Pennsylvania town where the game was played stopped the contest to have the field crew measure the blast. The tape stretched to 512 feet. Later in the summer, the Grays played a game at Forbes Field, and Josh hit a shot 465 feet.

Presumably, the high point of Gibson's 1939 season came when Pittsburgh Pirates president William Binswanger agreed that the

---

[5]Since there was no Negro league World Series most years, the East-West Game was the focal point of the season. It started in 1933, the year major league baseball played its first All-Star Game. By the early 1940s, the East-West game drew more than fifty thousand fans. With that kind of attendance, the picture was getting clearer to white owners that there was money to be made with black players.

Josh Gibson, the "black Babe Ruth." (National Baseball Library and Archive, Cooperstown, New York)

Pirates would allow Josh and Buck Leonard to try out for the team, only to cancel the session later. According to Binswanger, he got a call from Grays' owner Cum Posey telling him that major league baseball's signing Negro league stars would kill the black game. Posey, of course, emphatically denied the remark.

Amidst the Marian Anderson incident, the blasts by white and black journalists, and the sensational play of Negro league ballplayers in 1939, the Young Communist League of New York unintentionally damaged the plight of black players by collecting twenty thousand names on a petition demanding that the major leagues be opened to blacks. They sent the petition to Landis, who fancied himself a superpatriot, further deafening the commissioner's ears to the burgeoning sounds of integration.

After the Centennial Year, Before Jackie Robinson

THE YEAR 1940 ADVANCED NEGRO LEAGUE BASEBALL into the national limelight. *Time* magazine and the *Saturday Evening Post* ran feature stories that summer on Satchel Paige. Both magazines promoted Paige's substantial accomplishments in the Negro and Caribbean leagues and particularly emphasized his triumphs over major league players in exhibition games.

Unfortunately, but predictably, both magazines also painted a Stepin Fetchit Little Black Sambo picture of black players and their fans. *Time* quoted Satchel's childhood employer on the subject of the skinny Paige's appetite: "That boy et mo' than the hosses." The *Post* story suggested the incapacity of black ballplayers to understand Mexican currency while playing in leagues south of the border. It also described an alleged incident where a rabbit ran on the field stopping the game while Paige was pitching. "When the rabbit finally disappeared back in its silk hat, the game was resumed—until it was discovered nobody remembered the score!" White America laughed at the dialect and anecdotes in the articles, which served to confirm black America's "Amos 'n Andy" image blaring from radios across the country.

The publications shot Paige's celebrity status into orbit. Attendance at Negro league games multipled tenfold when Paige pitched after the

Time and *Post* articles ran, and his profile in the white and black communities began to equal that of Olympic gold medalist Jesse Owens[6] and heavyweight boxing champ Joe Louis.

In 1941, *Life* magazine featured Paige in an assemblage of photographs—wearing a flashy suit and fedora sitting on the bumper of a Rolls Royce; hugging New York mayor Fiorello LaGuardia; getting a haircut, shine, and manicure; in a baseball uniform pitching with his left leg kicked high over his head; and smiling at his "wife Lucy from Puerto Rico," who turned out not to be his wife. His real wife, Janet, lived in Pittsburgh at the time. Paige was making $40,000 a year by the time the *Life* story ran, more than Feller and DiMaggio, and far more than any other black player. Second-best Josh Gibson made $450 a month.

As Paige became a household name, the black and white press continued the attack on Landis and the owners. They were joined in the crusade by college newspapers and the New York Trade Union Athletic Association, which passed resolutions throughout 1940 complaining of the black player ban.

In the early 1940s, more and more black ballgames were played at major league stadiums, just as Marian Anderson was finally given the opportunity to sing at Constitution Hall in 1943. Negro league teams paid massive rents to white owners, to the tune of $100,000 a year for the use of Griffith Stadium by the Homestead Grays and the same amount by the New York Black Yankees for playing in Yankee Stadium.

In 1942, for the first time, radio covered a Negro league game. That year, there was more contact between major league baseball and black players as the White Sox gave UCLA football star Jackie Robinson an eyewash tryout. In August of 1942, Pirates president Binswanger played his second game of bait-and-switch by asking Wendell Smith to suggest four players to try out for the team. Smith recommended Gibson, shortstop Wells, outfielder Sam Bankhead,[7]

---

[6]After his Olympic triumphs, Owens made much of his living traveling with Negro league teams, where he helped the gate by serving as a pregame sideshow running races against horses. In 1939, Owens toured with the Toledo Crawfords. Surprisingly, Owens refused to race against Cool Papa Bell.

[7]His younger brother Dan pitched for the Brooklyn Dodgers at the end of the 1947 season, and then again in 1950 and 1951.

and pitcher Leon Day. Binswanger promptly reneged on the offer, as he had done in 1939.

The World War II years brought to a head the conflicting perspectives of black and white baseball. In the major leagues, with the great players serving in the military, fans got to watch the likes of Cincinnati's fifteen-year-old junior-high pitcher Joe Nuxhall (a 67.50 earned-run average in 1944) and the St. Louis Browns' one-armed outfielder Pete Gray (who hit .218 in 1945). Americans did not need to consult atomic scientists to realize that the best baseball from 1942 through 1945 was being played in the Negro leagues, and attendance at white games and black games during the war years reflected that fact.

Aware his competent players were in the military and that black players were far better than his wartime substitutes, winning-obsessed Dodgers manager Leo Durocher came out publicly in 1942 with the statement: "I'll play colored boys on my team if the big shots give the okay. Hell, I've seen a million good ones." Commissioner Landis tried to put out the fire started by Durocher, and issued an obviously false public statement: "There is no rule, formal or informal, no understanding against hiring Negro players."

After the 1942 season, baseball entrepreneur Bill Veeck thought he saw a loophole in Landis's declaration. He formulated a scheme to buy the always insolvent and hapless Phillies, and then planned to stock the lineup with Negro leaguers, leading to a certain National League pennant. When Landis and Ford Frick learned of the deal, they quickly located a more suitable buyer for the Philadelphia franchise, eliminating the troublesome Veeck's integration plans for the time being.[8]

As the war effort continued, it became clear to the country's baseball fans that to have millions of Americans fighting abroad for the preservation of our democratic system, while obviously talented black ballplayers at home were refused entry into the major leagues solely because of their race, constituted the rankest form of hypocrisy.

With the death of Landis in 1944 and the appointment of Kentucky politician Happy Chandler as baseball's commissioner in 1945, the

---

[8]According to Veeck, the new Phillies owner William Cox paid approximately half of Veeck's offered price. Cox soon became an even bigger headache to Landis than Veeck was, by betting on Phillies games during the first year of his Philadelphia regime, resulting in his banishment from the game by the commissioner.

laboratory opened for Branch Rickey's "noble experiment." At the press conference announcing Chandler's acceptance of baseball's highest position, the new commissioner proclaimed, "I'm for the four freedoms. If a black boy can make it on Okinawa and Guadelcanal, hell, he can make it in baseball." Shortly after Chandler took office, Jackie Robinson signed his first Dodgers minor league contract in August 1945, the same month World War II ended.

Jackie Robinson blazed the major league trail for black ballplayers beginning on Opening Day 1947. The great Jackie could thank his Negro league predecessors, Marian Anderson, and the crusading black and white journalists who had accelerated the momentum in 1939 for Robinson taking his place in American history.

Umpire Bill Klem, "safe at home." (Copyright: Mark Rucker, Transcendental Graphics)

CHAPTER NINE

CHARACTERS OF THE YEAR

Umpire Bill Klem and Clown Al Schacht Bring Order and Fun to the Game

THE NEGRO LEAGUE PLAYERS UNDERSTOOD BETTER than their white counterparts that professional baseball was more than an athletic contest. It was entertainment for the paying customer. A 1943 issue of *Time* magazine attributed black baseball's surprising appeal to white fans because of the players' "fancy windups, swift and daring base-running, and flashy one-handed catches."

Umpire Bill Klem (nicknamed "The Old Arbitrator"[1]) and Al Schacht (promoted as "The Clown Prince of Baseball") didn't have fancy windups, couldn't run the bases swiftly, and made no one-handed catches. In their own ways, however, they could entertain, and both of these high-profiled characters spent 1939 in the spotlight.

---

[1]Before getting to the National League, Klem worked in the American Association at a time when only one umpire called the entire field of play. A home-team representative would begin each game by calling out to the crowd the names of the starting players, and then would give the name of the umpire, always using the same traditional phrase, "...and the arbitrator's name is John Doe." Klem so liked the appelation he started referring to himself as "the Old Arbitrator" early in his career. The designation stuck.

The Old Arbitrator: Recognition and Religion in 1939

IN HIS LANDMARK BOOK *Only the Ball Was White*, Robert Peterson described how the "looseness of the Negro league structure was reflected on the field":

> It was not unusual for a player to attack an umpire with his fists and get off with a slap on the wrist. On occasion, it was worse than that. In 1938, umpire James Crump was assaulted on the field during a game in Baltimore. Crump promptly levied a twenty-five-dollar fine on a Baltimore Elite Giants player. The next day Crump got a telegram from the Negro National League's ruling board dismissing him. One of the three members of the ruling board was Elite Giants' owner Tom Wilson.

Black baseball had no Bill Klem. And if white baseball had not had umpires like Bill Klem, it likely would have suffered the same "loose structure" which plagued the Negro leagues. When Klem joined the game shortly after the turn of the century, it was not uncommon for players to fight umpires, step on their toes, and even spit tobacco juice in their face.

At the beginning of Klem's career, no less an authority on belligerence than heavyweight champion John L. Sullivan inspired the young umpire to end the attacks on the men in blue. While calling a minor league contest in 1902, Klem faced down some antagonistic players in the presence of Sullivan, who witnessed the confrontation from the grandstand. The famed prizefighter found the umpire after the game and congratulated him on his gutty performance. "Boy, you stood out there today like a champion. Don't ever let anybody make you back up. You be the boss or you can't get anywhere." Klem heeded Sullivan's advice for the next forty years.

One way an umpire could stand up to players was to enforce a prohibition on name-calling. While still in the American Association, the Old Arbitrator got a second nickname, but this one he despised. Columbus's manager Bill Clymer screamed at Klem after a disputed call, "Why, you old catfish. You can't talk, you can't smile, you can't do nothin' but move your gills." Klem gave Clymer the hook, but the "Catfish" tag stuck.[2]

When Bill Klem entered the National League in 1905, he soon realized that to gain control over the game, he had to rein in notorious umpire baiter John McGraw. After Klem made a call adverse to the Giants in his first big league season, McGraw ran up to the umpire and threatened, "You'll lose your job over this, Mr. Klem!" The confident rookie arbiter retorted, "If it's possible for you to get my job, then I don't want it."

Klem's fearless comeback at McGraw earned instant respect. Though the manager and umpire would continue to tangle during games until McGraw's retirement in 1932, they became friends and even dinner partners off the field. McGraw's approval of Klem caused the rest of baseball to follow suit. The Giants skipper went so far as to say publicly, "If there ever was a good umpire, it's Bill Klem."

Major league baseball had had more than three decades of Klem's umpiring leadership when scribes decided that recognition was in order. On February 5, 1939, at their annual dinner, the New York Baseball Writers presented Bill Klem with the National League Award of Merit for his contributions to the umpiring profession. In accepting the honor, the senior umpire laid aside his prepared speech (which had lost its bite anyway after heavy pre-dinner editing by league president Ford Frick), and spoke off the cuff.

Bill Klem told the nine hundred in attendance that night why he loved baseball in general and umpiring in particular. He projected his full-time commitment to excellence and integrity which had guided him through his major league career. Afterward, legendary sportswriter Red Smith said:

> Klem spoke of simple, familiar things. Of the invincible integrity of baseball and the umpire's position as the guardian of that heritage. He told of a man's work, and the pride of that.

---

[2]When Klem arrived in the National League in 1905, the players soon learned the nickname, and also learned to avoid using it in the umpire's presence. Chief Meyers told Lawrence Ritter in *The Glory of Their Times*, "All you had to do was call him 'Catfish' and out of the game you'd go. That's all. Just one word and you were out. I'm not sure why. Maybe it was because he had rather prominent lips, and when he'd call a ball or a strike he'd let fly a rather fine spray from his mouth. It sort of gave the general impression of a catfish, you know. He was a little sensitive about it to say the least!"

His great voice swelled with his own indomitable sincerity, and he made you see it. He made you know what it was for a man to go out to his work each day determined to do a perfect job and then go back the next day determined to do a better one.

Then he was through, and there was silence a moment, and then they tore the joint down.

As the sixty-five-year-old umpire returned to his seat amidst thunderous applause, Klem asked for quiet to permit a final statement. "Gentlemen, baseball is not a sport. It is a religion!"[3]

Klem became an umpiring evangelist that night, actually inspiring a conversion. In the audience was Philadelphia Athletics pitching coach Charlie Berry, a guest of *New York Herald Tribune* baseball writer Al Laney. When Klem sat down after accepting his award, Berry leaned over to Laney and said, "That old man's done something to me. He's shown me something I never saw before. This coaching job, where'll it ever get a guy? I like officiating anyway. I'm going to be an umpire like him." Charlie Berry soon resigned from the A's coaching staff, became a rookie umpire in the Eastern League, and by 1943 had made an American League crew.[4]

As John Houseman would have said, for his umpiring contributions to baseball, Bill Klem received the 1939 Award of Merit the old-fashioned way. He earned it. Klem innovated virtually every aspect of his profession. First, he learned (and then taught other umpires) the best way to stand at the plate. He abandoned the traditional straight-up-behind-the-catcher position, and instead utilized a leaning stance between catcher and batter (still used by all National League umpires), enabling the pitch caller to have a better view of ball location. Klem learned the new position shortly after making the big leagues. Chicago White Stockings manager Cap Anson suggested the stance to the five-foot-seven umpire

---

[3]The Old Arbitrator would use the "religion" quote repeatedly from that night on until his death in 1951. It found its way onto Klem's plaque when he and Tom Connolly became the first umpires inducted into the Hall of Fame in 1953.

[4]Berry would go on to have a twenty-year, major league career, and be named the Outstanding Umpire in the American League in 1961.

for a logical reason: "You're a good umpire, Bill, but a big catcher like Larry McLean (six-foot-five, 228 pounds) can block off your view of the plate."

Klem's next major contribution came in popularizing hand signals for an umpire's calls—a raised right arm for a strike, a sweeping thumb gesture for an out, both palms extended down for calling a runner safe on the bases, and hand-waving on foul lines to show whether a ball was fair or foul. Necessity had been the mother of these inventions. In 1906, Klem came to the ballpark one day with laryngitis. Neither the crowd nor the players could possibly hear his whispers, so he used the signals. In the days before microphones and public-address announcers, Klem immediately realized the importance of the hand signs whether he had laryngitis or not: "That guy in the twenty-five-cent bleacher seat is as much entitled to know a call as the guy in the boxes." The signals soon became standard in both leagues.

Another major improvement brought about by Bill Klem involved his securing better facilities for umpires at major league stadiums. Late in his career, Klem liked to tell his umpiring protégés that when he first arrived in the National League, he'd go to the ballpark and ask where umps were to dress. Stadium officials usually responded, "In the toilet," as there were no dressing rooms or showers for the men in blue.

The inadequacy of facilities became important because umpires had to leave the field after each game in their full blue uniforms, and found themselves riding the streetcar back to the hotel with often unappreciative fans. Klem changed that. At his insistence, no new ballpark was built after 1910 without a dressing room for the umpiring crew, thereby allowing the arbiters to maintain their necessary anonymity in post-game transit.

Beyond improving dressing facilities, Bill Klem made his profession safer by setting the standard for wearing a chest protector under his blue coat at every game. After he and the other National League umpires started wearing the interior padding on a compulsory basis, Klem twice made the mistake of opting for comfort over safety. On both occasions, when the Old Arbitrator removed his chest protector on hot days to cool off, foul tips shot back, breaking Klem's collarbones. His injuries motivated league umpires to wear chest protectors at all games from that time forward.

More important than the improved home-plate stance, the hand signals, and the upgraded facilities and equipment for his crews, Bill Klem warranted the 1939 Award of Merit by establishing controls on conduct. When a player charged him to challenge a decision, Klem drew a line in the dirt with his aluminum-toed shoes and told the loudmouth he would be ejected immediately if he crossed it. It worked. Players would stand at the Klem line like truculent schoolchildren, screaming into thin air while the umpire would turn his back and walk away.

When a manager took too long to converse with his pitcher or a player refused to leave the dugout after ejection, Bill Klem pulled out his watch and imposed a thirty-second deadline for departure. If Klem's timetable was not met, the umpire threatened the delinquent team with game forfeiture. Although there's no record of Klem ever forcing a team to forfeit a game because of a player's delay, presumably, it never occurred because no one had any doubts about the Old Arbitrator's willingness to carry out his threat.

As a result of utilizing techniques like the Klem line and the thirty-second time limit, the veteran umpire could smile and tell Red Barber during a radio interview, "I don't have any trouble at all with ballplayers or managers. Sometimes they have trouble with me."

Beyond his umpiring innovations, Bill Klem endeared himself to the New York Baseball Writers with his colorful language. When a player screamed four-letter expletives over a close play, the umpire would shoot back, "You're ill bred," "You're a counterfeit," or "You're an applehead." To an overly belligerent player, Klem would snap, "Oh, are you a fighter, too? I thought you were supposed to be a ballplayer." If a player asked too quickly whether a ball was fair or foul, the umpire replied slowly, "It ain't nothin' 'til I call it."

To prevent any appearance of fraternization, baseball's greatest umpire never called a player or manager by his first name on the field. He demanded reciprocity. Sportswriter Fred Lieb described the scene when a player tried to call the Old Arbitrator "Bill." "Klem would focus a steely eye on the offender and say, 'It's Mr. Klem to you and don't you ever forget it!' "

The strong, colorful language gave Bill Klem command over everyone at a game. Fellow crew member Beans Reardon recalled an incident in Larry Gerlach's oral history *The Men in Blue*, in which a female fan in Boston derided Klem by screaming, "If you were my husband, I'd put poison in your coffee!" Baseball's toughest umpire shot back, "Lady, if I was your husband, I'd drink it!"

The presentation of the 1939 Award of Merit was probably motivated by the desire of National League president (and former sportswriter) Ford Frick to have the veteran umpire retire. Entering baseball's centennial year, Klem would be sixty-five years old with rapidly fading eyesight[5] and limited mobility on his aging legs.

When the Old Arbitrator came to New York for the Baseball Writers dinner, he met with Frick in advance. The league president proceeded to talk with Klem about his burgeoning pension (at that time umpires earned one hundred dollars a year on their pension, and Klem had been in the league thirty-five years), and asked the senior umpire if he had ever given any thought to the $3,500. Klem snapped back, "Why, yes, Mr. Frick. I've often wondered if you would have enough nerve to offer it to me!"

Despite the exchange, the umpire would have none of Frick's none-too-subtle retirement nudge. In his acceptance speech at the February 5 dinner, Klem announced to the crowd his perception that he was "better equipped than ever, in confidence, skill, and experience to do my daily umpiring job." The February 16, 1939 issue of *The Sporting News* put the proper spin on Klem's situation as he began the 1939 season:

> Like all good things, even the umpiring days of Bill Klem must end, but probably not until the time comes when his famous retort to Frankie Frisch reaches fruition. Replying to the former second baseman's objection to a called third strike, Klem said: "When I miss the likes of that young man, I won't be out here calling them for the likes of you."

---

[5]Klem started wearing glasses privately in 1924, and, by 1932, no longer hid his off-the-field need for spectacles.

After the commencement of the 1939 season, baseball powers continued the respectful appreciation toward Klem which began at the February dinner, in a gentle attempt to encourage his retirement. The May 25, 1939 issue of *The Sporting News* promoted the idea of the Old Arbitrator being enshrined as the first umpire in the Hall of Fame. Presumably, publisher Taylor Spink figured that if the Baseball Writers' Award of Merit didn't motivate Klem to end his career, maybe a plaque at Cooperstown would.

Baseball's oldest umpire couldn't make it to the All-Star Game break in 1939. Klem was stricken with a hernia condition at Cincinnati on June 21, and he ended up in St. Louis's St. John's Hospital for surgery. By July 31, he was in good enough condition to do what he had never done before—be a spectator at a major league game. Klem sat in from the press box at Crosley Field trading stories with his sportswriter pals.

On August 8, Bill Klem returned to action at Philadelphia where he felt up to working the bases, but lacked the strength to man his favorite position behind the plate.[6] In the week after Klem's return to the field from surgery, *The Sporting News*'s Spink devoted his column to the Old Arbitrator, allowing the devout Catholic Klem to pontificate about his observations on umpiring and the national pastime:

> To me the great game of baseball means aggressiveness. Any sportsman likes to see one team battle another for supremacy and I venture to say that if you look over any umpires you will find them to be sportsmen. But disputing or arguing decisions of judgment does not come under the head of aggressiveness... The aggressive player will not fight the umpires. He may, on occasions, prompted by reasons of one sort or another, fight fellow players. The player who fights the umpire—and by the same token, the umpire who fights the player—is indicted. There is a certain definite line where aggressiveness stops and rowdyism begins...

[6]Klem perpetuated the story throughout his life of his having spent sixteen consecutive years working only behind the plate to accommodate his crew partner Bob Enslie's poor eyesight. John McGraw stated publicly he intended to put a baseball and an orange on home plate, and would defy Enslie to tell them apart. Klem said he went to then National League president Harry Pulliam before McGraw put Enslie to the orange test, offering to call every game at home plate. Pulliam's acceptance of Klem's offer purportedly added nine years to Enslie's major league umpiring career.

> Baseball took hold of the public in a big way only after the umpires had stamped out rowdyism, terrible language, and the atmosphere of the barroom. People began to realize that baseball was inexpensive, high class, grand entertainment to which they could bring their wives, sweethearts, their children...
>
> Your umpire must be allowed to guide his own conduct. He has guts. He has sight. He has honesty. And you must give him credit for the greatest of all qualities in an umpire—judgment. Here let me add that an umpire could have the guts of the lion but if he doesn't have judgment with it, his courage isn't worth a thin dime.

With no further physical flare-ups after his mid-year surgery, Bill Klem finished the 1939 regular season.[7] Despite his bad eyes, slow legs, and recent hernia, Klem insisted on signing a new contract for the 1940 season. National League president Ford Frick didn't know what to do. He knew he couldn't fire the legendary Klem without causing an umpire insurrection. The retirement decision would have to be Klem's own.

An incident at the end of the 1940 season told baseball's oldest umpire it was time to hang up his chest protector. Bill Klem had always prided himself on his capacity to "umpire the ball" and stay on his toes throughout a game, giving him the alertness and quickness to stay out of the ball's way. During a game at the Polo Grounds in the season's last week, Klem was behind first base when a ground ball hit him squarely in the leg. As he limped off the field after the contest, a young girl recognized the sixty-six-year-old legend and said sympathetically, "Tough day, eh, Pop?" Klem responded immediately to the well-intentioned remark. "When they start calling you 'Pop,' it's time to quit." And he did. Frick gave the umpire a final honor by persuading Landis to let Klem call the 1940 World Series, his major league record eighteenth Fall Classic.

---

[7]Commissioner Landis passed over Bill Klem for calling the 1939 World Series, as he had done every year since 1934. During the 1934 Classic, Klem got into a spat on the field with Detroit's Hall of Fame outfielder Goose Goslin. It got uglier in a hotel elevator after the game. Although there is no reliable account of what exactly was said in the elevator, when Landis heard about Klem's verbal explosion at Goslin, the commissioner fined the umpire fifty dollars and made a silent decision to keep the Old Arbitrator out of post-season play.

Ford Frick wanted to keep Bill Klem in the game in some capacity. In 1941, the National League president named Klem as the man in charge of all National League umpires. The retiring arbiter chose his own title, "Chief of Staff." He filled in on the field for twenty-five games in 1941, but made the decision in a contest at the end of the year never to umpire again. The chief of staff called a player out on a close play at second base, and walked away from the action telling himself, "I'm almost certain Herman tagged him." Klem then recounted for *Collier's* magazine what happened next:

> Then it came to me and I almost wept. For the first time in all my career I only "thought" a man was tagged. Frick came in the dressing room after the game and I said to him, "I started umpiring in 1902. This is 1941. I'm through."

During Bill Klem's career, a quote was attributed to him which he never said, but never denied: "I never called one wrong."[8] With the Billy Herman incident at the end of the 1941 season, the chief of staff knew his best heart-felt efforts were no longer up to major league umpiring standards.

For the remaining ten years of his life, Bill Klem's eyesight continued to fail, getting to the point where he could no longer read, but he remained the father figure to all National League umpires. He relished his paternal position to the men in blue, and two of Klem's favorite umpiring disciples, Jocko Conlan and Al Barlick, went on to have Hall of Fame careers of their own.

In his book *Walk in the Spirit*, Red Barber told of the incident when Augie Donatelli became the last umpire Klem talked to before the chief of staff left his National League office for good in 1950. Rookie umpire Donatelli walked in to Klem's office that day and asked his hero for some advice. Klem lifted his head from his desk, looked the

---

[8]What Klem actually said was, "I never missed one of those in my life," after having a stadium engineer prove that his call had been correct of a "foul" ball hitting a scoreboard near a then-unpainted foul line. When John McGraw heard of Klem's quote (which was intended to refer to the narrow circumstances of calling a ball down the line fair or foul), the Giants skipper mischaracterized the quote to impute Klem having said, "I never called one wrong," as if it referred to every umpiring call Klem ever made.

Baseball Commissioner Judge Kenesaw Mountain Landis, who needed persuading to let Bill Klem call the next year's (1940) World Series. (National Baseball Library and Archive, Cooperstown, New York)

young arbiter in the eye, and said only three words. "Save your soul." The Old Arbitrator walked out of the office without further comment and never returned.

Bill Klem's "religion" (as expressed for the first time at the New York Baseball Writers' dinner in February 1939) was more than the game to which he devoted his life. In August 1939, Klem told Taylor Spink about his other religion of saving souls and its effect on Hall of Fame second baseman Johnny Evers. "Years ago one of my chief problems was Johnny Evers, one of the greatest players of all time who fought umpires because he felt he had to put on a show to get publicity. I warned Evers that when his wonderful ability vanished, his publicity would vanish too. A dozen years later I met Evers in New York. Nobody would give him a real job. He said 'Bill, you told the truth.' Later in Cooperstown at the Centennial Celebration, we went on the air together, and Evers announced to the radio audience, 'Bill Klem is the greatest umpire of all time, in more ways than just umpiring.' "

The Clown Prince of Baseball: Fifty Thousand Miles of Laughs in 1939

AS BILL KLEM GAVE ORDER AND PERSPECTIVE to the game in 1939, Al Schacht made it fun. Baseball's first full-time clown crossed the country throughout the centennial season, bringing pantomime mockery to ballparks from Seattle to Binghamton. Schacht often told reporters his professional calling as a clown was understandable since he was born in left field—on the site in the Bronx where Yankee Stadium's left field would be located during its construction thirty-two years later.

A sensational teenage pitcher, Schacht accelerated his efforts to get to the big leagues in 1919 while pitching for Jersey City in the International League. He picked out the lowly Senators (on their way to a 56-84 season) as the team most in need of his skills, and started sending anonymous letters with enclosed Jersey City box scores to Washington owner Clark Griffith after every game he pitched.

Schacht recited his favorite self-created fan mail in his first autobiography, *Clowning Through Baseball*:

Dear Sir,
There's a pitcher with Jersey City named Al Schacht who is better than Walter Johnson. He's got just about everything. You ought to buy him right away.

Yours truly,
Just a Fan

Dear Sir,
Is it true the Yanks are after that fellow Schacht? That's what the people up here say. Hurry, hurry if you care to add this illustrious name to your roster.

Yours truly,
Just a Fan

Griffith took the bait. Washington signed Schacht at the end of the 1919 season, and Al won both games he started with a 2.40 earned-run average.

In 1920, Schacht won six and lost four as a starter and reliever, and gave his most memorable performance as a major league player. On July 1, 1920, Walter Johnson pitched the only no-hit game of his career. When it came time for the Big Train's next start, he came up with a sore arm. Griffith knew Washington fans would be livid if they paid to see Johnson pitch after his celebrated no-hitter, and then had to settle for some lesser Senators pitcher instead. Schacht surprisingly volunteered to take Johnson's spot in the rotation, and Griffith told Al, "If you win this game today, I don't care if you never win another game as long as you live, you'll always have a job with this club as long as you want it." Schacht proceeded to weather the angry crowd, win the game 4-1, and even strike out Babe Ruth with the bases loaded.[9]

By 1921, contending with a sore right arm which would end his pitching career that year, Schacht teamed up with Senators coach

---

[9]Griffith kept his word. Schacht stayed with the Senators' organization for the next thirteen years.

Nick Altrock one day for some pre-game shenanigans at Griffith Stadium. Altrock, who had already been clowning at games for years before Schacht entered the act, had a shtick composed mainly of animated pepper games and circus catches.

Al Schacht brought new routines to the shows, including melodramatic reenactments with Altrock of Jack Dempsey's championship fights, Helen Wills's tennis matches in full-petticoat regalia, and Spanish bullfights (with a rose-in-mouth Altrock playing the adoring Spanish senorita). Schacht also introduced into the act a huge baseball glove two feet in diameter with which he attempted to catch fly balls and field grounders. The oversized mitt became a staple for the remainder of Schacht's comedy career.

The Schacht-Altrock combination paid immediate dividends. The New York Giants and Yankees paid the clowns $1,000 each for performing before every game in the 1921 World Series, and they got invited back to the Fall Classic for the next dozen years.

Soon after forming the comedy partnership, Altrock unfortunately developed a case of raging professional jealousy. Schacht was an immediate hit with fans, and the big laughs always went to the newcomer. Altrock became the jealous side attraction, the set-up man, the accessory, causing him to stop pulling his punches in the pantomime boxing matches. By 1929, Altrock and Schacht were no longer speaking off the field.

When Joe Cronin left the Senators in 1934 to go to Boston as manager-shortstop, he took Al Schacht with him to be his third-base coach, thereby ending the Altrock-Schacht comedy-feud. Schacht stayed with Boston three seasons, but realized: (1) there was no real money in being a base coach; (2) "Just standing around rubbing my chin for the hit-and-run or pulling my pants for the steal wasn't very exciting"; and (3) "There's never any applause for a third-base coach."

In 1937, Schacht quit coaching to become a full-time clown, viewing all of the major and minor league baseball world as his stage. The Clown Prince's philosophy became "Laugh and the world not only laughs with you—but pays for the privilege." He hired famed New York sports agent Christy Walsh (whose other clients included

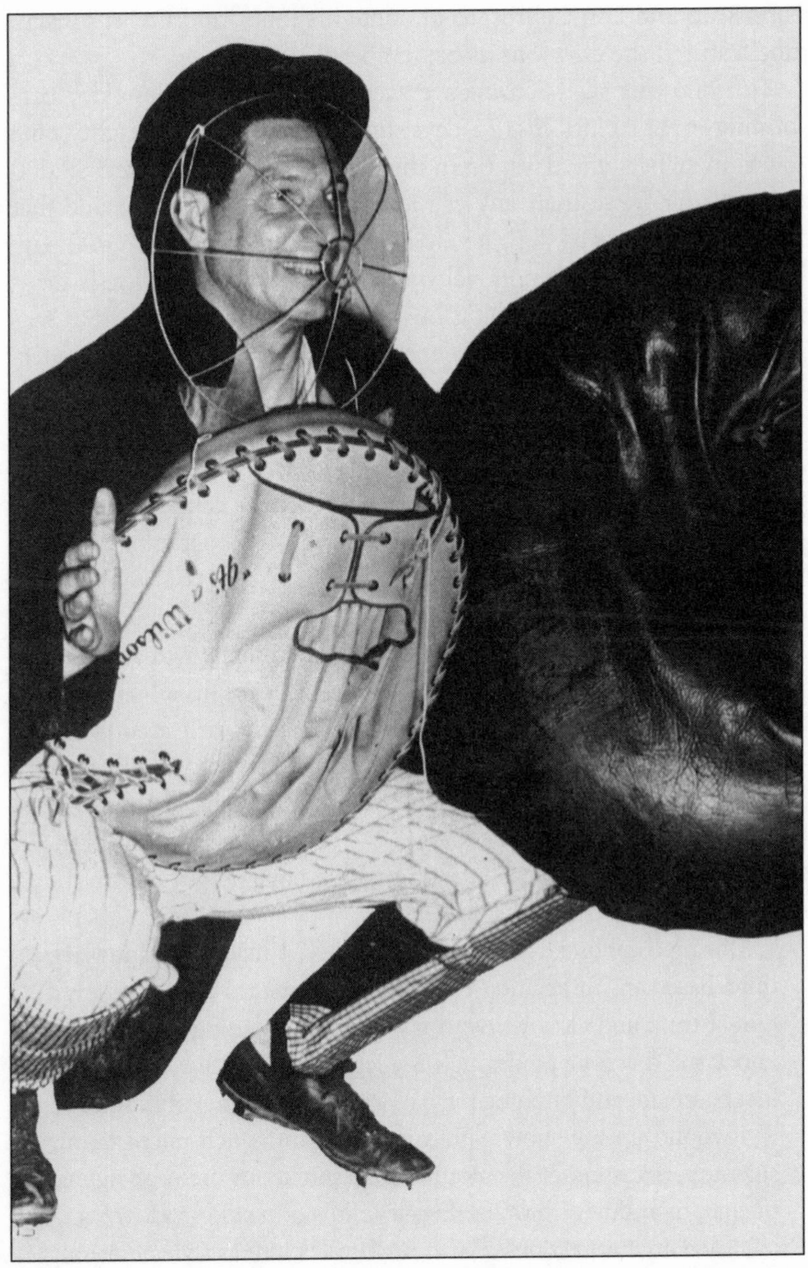

Baseball clown Al Schacht with his famous oversized catcher's mitt. (National Baseball Library and Archive, Cooperstown, New York)

Babe Ruth and Lou Gehrig) to promote his tours, and *Collier's* magazine featured the clown in its September 4, 1937 issue.

The following year, Schacht averaged four hundred miles a day, performing in 121 cities in 125 days, including a stretch of eighty-nine towns in eighty-nine days. From this constant pace, he netted $8,000 in 1938 (far more than any big league, third-base coach made that year), getting a cut of the gate on an average attendance of 4,900 paying fans. Schacht's promotional brochure distributed by Walsh mentioned that 80 percent of the Clown Prince's bookings came from second-division teams whose incompetent performance needed an entertainment boost to warrant respectable attendance during the Great Depression.

By 1939, Schacht had his promotions figured out, his comedy act in full hilarious swing, and was ready to become a centennial star. He described a standard routine in his second autobiography, *My Own Particular Screwball*:

> After being introduced I'd say a few words to the crowd and then vault into the grandstand and race around causing all kinds of havoc. I'd snatch girls and old ladies away from their escorts and show them to their seats personally, and then I'd exchange different men's hats, finally getting them all mixed up. I'd sneak up behind ladies and kiss them on the foreheads. Then I'd give away all a vendor's peanuts. Sometimes I'd bring a little boy and girl out on the field and marry them at home plate.
>
> During the home team's infield practice, I liked to shadow the third baseman, mimicking every move he made. Then I relieved him at third and clowned with my big glove—letting ground balls knock me down or go through my legs, throwing two balls to the first baseman, and catching the ball while lying on top of third base.
>
> I wound up my show with a feature stunt which might be my solo impersonation of the swell-headed pitcher or the near-sighted pitcher, or at other times, burlesque tennis or boxing. Lastly, I usually gave my impressions of various famous hitter's styles finishing with Babe Ruth's historic called home run.

Schacht's favorite gag in 1939 involved a skit where the Clown Prince served as batter and his straight man (and chauffeur) Fred Farro acted as umpire. Schacht would take a cut at an imaginary pitched ball and look into the grandstands. When Farro yelled "Foul," a local assistant secretly hired before the game would throw down twelve baseballs from the bleachers' top row onto the field.

The prank worked well throughout the centennial year until they got to Dallas. The local ball thrower there fell asleep in the bleachers at the critical time when Farro called "Foul." Schacht screamed at the assistant, "Baseballs... Baseballs," but nothing happened. Late in the Dallas game, long after Schacht's act was over, a batter hit a foul ball into the stands, and the real home-plate umpire called out "Foul." The assistant woke up, heard the ump's call, and threw the twelve balls onto the field. Fortunately, no one was hurt, but the players, umpires, and fans had no idea what was going on.

At Syracuse that summer, Schacht met more misfortune. Performing a boxing pantomime with Farro, the pre-rehearsed scene involved Schacht accidentally knocking himself out, causing mock trainer Farro to throw a bucket of water on the battered fighter. Farro accidentally threw both the water and the bucket at the unsuspecting Schacht, breaking the Roman nose of baseball's Clown Prince.

Because he took his act to the West Coast during the summer of 1939, Schacht was able to hit only 110 towns, but traveled over fifty thousand miles and performed before a half-million fans. To meet his schedule, he averaged five hundred miles a day (in the era before interstate highways), spent $1,500 on gasoline, and changed the oil in his car daily.

During the 1939 season, in addition to his minor league shows, Schacht performed at seven major league ballparks, the All-Star Game at Yankee Stadium, and the World Series at both New York and Cincinnati. Schacht so loved his life on the road, he told *The Sporting News* that summer, "Even if I were a millionaire, I wouldn't give up touring the country. The only way they can stop me is by kicking the legs from under me."

When the centennial season ended, publisher Spink profiled the Clown Prince of Baseball in an October issue of *The Sporting News*.

Schacht described his unique job and its emerging impact on the national pastime:

> I wonder if you realize how tough this racket is? Don't forget that most of my engagements are in the smaller leagues and that if a club is going well, the club owner doesn't figure he needs Al to boost the gate. I must overcome bad weather and losing clubs. And I'm not an essential. I'm the Ambassador of Goodwill. I bring in the fans and they get a show for nothing. I've proved that I bring in folks who have never before seen ballgames. They come to see me and sometimes they get the baseball habit.

Schacht kept up his clowning pace through 1940 and 1941, but then hit a snag when World War II gas rationing limited his ability to travel. Baseball's Clown Prince came up with a patriotic solution. Sponsored by the USO, Schacht took his show to America's armed forces all over the world during the next three years, doing 159 stage shows and performing in seventy-two hospitals, all of which he described in his 1945 book, *G I Had Fun*. The New York Baseball Writers presented Al Schacht with their Award of Merit in 1946 for his outstanding contributions to baseball, "with stress on his work during the war."

After 1946, Schacht kept on performing until his audiences totaled more than 68 million fans. The Clown Prince finally retired from the road in 1963 to devote full time to his successful New York City restaurant, one of the first sports bars modeled to look like a ballpark, with a stage on which Schacht could perform his comedy routines. Schacht told an interviewer he had invested almost $500,000 of his own money in the profitable club.

Al Schacht achieved success because of his uncompromising talent and total self-confidence. Like Bill Klem, Schacht (whose mother wanted her son to become a rabbi) had religion, except his was the comedy act. In an interview late in his life, Schacht described his formula for comedy. "I never rehearse. You can't rehearse pantomime. You have to go out there with a goal of who and what you're trying to impersonate. Once you're out there you have to feel who and what you're trying to impersonate as you go along—you can't stop and think. You've got to make the audience understand everything you're doing because if you lose them—even for a minute—you're going to be so humiliated that you'll want to dig a hole in the ground and crawl into it."

Though they both had successful long-term marriages, neither Bill Klem nor Al Schacht ever fathered children. Their progeny became the successors who followed them in their professional footsteps—Jocko Conlan, Al Barlick, and Augie Donatelli for Klem; Max Patkin and Ted "San Diego Chicken" Giannoulos for Schacht. Klem improved his profession and saved souls, Schacht got laughs and made money, and baseball became the beneficiary of their legacy.

Abner Doubleday, military hero and baseball pioneer. (Copyright: Mark Rucker, Transcendental Graphics)

CHAPTER TEN

THE DOUBLEDAY MYTH

How Cooperstown Got the Hall of Fame

WE SHOULD ALL BE GRATEFUL to Abner Doubleday. Little did he or the group that was with him in Cooperstown, New York, in 1839, realize the boon they were giving to the nation in devising baseball... General Doubleday was a distinguished soldier both in the Mexican and Civil Wars, but his part in giving us baseball shows again that peace has her victories no less renowned than war.

—Franklin Roosevelt, 1939

The only thing Major General Abner Doubleday ever started was the Civil War, when he answered the Confederate Beauregard by firing the first shot from Fort Sumter.

—Branch Rickey, 1965

The formal dedication of the National Baseball Hall of Fame and Museum building in Cooperstown, New York, on June 12, 1939, served as the sport's focal point for its centennial celebration. The location of the Hall cemented the mythology for at least baseball's second hundred years that Abner Doubleday invented the game at Cooperstown in 1839.

Regrettably, but accurately, historians have concluded that Doubleday was the wrong man, Cooperstown the wrong place, and

1839 the wrong year. The historical consensus for the last half-century has been that baseball was not "invented," but rather evolved from the British game of rounders. If there has to be an "inventor" and a place and time of "invention" for the American game, it was not Doubleday at Cooperstown in 1839, but rather Alexander Cartwright at Elysian Fields, Hoboken, New Jersey, in 1845 with assistance from his Knickerbocker teammate Daniel "Doc" Adams.

Despite its dubious origin, Abner Doubleday's place in baseball history survives. Without Doubleday, Cooperstown (population 2,500) would be just another little scenic New York lakefront community. Because of the Doubleday myth, it has become a major tourist center, attracting four hundred thousand baseball fans every year, many of whom *still* believe they're walking on hallowed ground.

Mythology scholar Joseph Campbell surely would have perceived Cooperstown as baseball's "sacred place" or its "bliss station," as he defined those terms in response to Bill Moyers's question:

> Moyers: "It's not just the past that moves you when you go there, is it?"
>
> Campbell: "No, it's the present... It's a place for meditation, just walking around, just sitting, just looking at those beautiful things."

In this century, one man, A. Bartlett Giamatti, fully grasped the significance of baseball's mythology—its heroes, patterns, and lessons. The late commissioner trained for his final role on earth with decades of scholarship in Greek mythology and Renaissance literature. Because of his background, Giamatti became baseball's poet laureate, sharing "the green fields of his mind," and constantly teaching how the game mirrors life. As Joseph Campbell perceived the typical mythological hero's path marked by "departure, fulfillment, and return," so Giamatti saw application to the baseball field, saying:

> Sometimes I think baseball was invented just to remind us of things. It's a living memory, and it has an epic quality—you can't get away from it. Think of the man at the plate, and what he wants to do up there—travel that long way around, and all just to get back

> where he started from—back home. He's a pioneer. He has to wander and explore, but it's dangerous out there and he remembers the other need as well—the need to get back home. You can die at second base.

Furthermore, Giamatti's metaphorical perspective on the game acknowledged the mythological connection:

> The prism through which I see things is the prism that understands baseball as an enormously important American institution with long and deep roots whose deep purpose is to provide pleasure and fun for the American people, and whose integrity and authenticity are essential in order to provide that pleasure. The pace of the game allows for rumination even at the moment instead of just in retrospect, and it is a game with a history and methodology so intricately connected to America that in some idealized and *mythological* sense, it is virtually synonymous with America.

Giamatti imbibed Cooperstown's sacredness. In a letter to the village's Glimmerglass Opera in June 1989, he wrote, "I won't go into all my feelings about the birthplace of baseball, but it is obviously the Mecca to which we all must make a pilgrimage." The commissioner chose for the dust jacket of his final book *Take Time for Paradise* a picture of himself in Cooperstown's Doubleday Field grandstands. His colleagues chose for the cover of their "Remembering Giamatti" December 1989 issue of *Yale Alumni Magazine* another Giamatti-at-Doubleday-Field pose, with the green "earthly paradise" ballpark in the background.

The Yale Renaissance scholar found something mystical in the Cooperstown region surrounding Lake Otsego, named appropriately (for baseball purposes) "place of the meeting" by the once-resident Iroquois. Giamatti's lifetime goal was to "conserve something of purpose in a world of confusion… and praise something other than the giddy headlong rush," making it natural for him to bond with the area described by hometown novelist James Fenimore Cooper as a place of "solemn solitude and sweet repose… with a placid view of heaven."

To the commissioner-mythologist, the historical inaccuracy of the Doubleday-Cooperstown-1839 centennial myth became irrelevant in the overall scheme of things.

Using Giamatti as baseball's mythological mentor, the fiction of Abner Doubleday creating baseball in Cooperstown in 1839 is not troublesome. The issue is not whether the myth is true, but whether it served a historical purpose and made the baseball world a better place. Abner Doubleday may not be a baseball hero, but he is an American hero (using *Webster's* definition of the word) in the same noble mold as Lou Gehrig. Pastoral, idyllic Cooperstown serves as a more scenic location for the game's birthplace than industrialized, grimy Hoboken. And, using hindsight's assistance, having a focused, front-page centennial celebration in 1939 (when our national concerns were limited to a fading Great Depression and a troublesome but still distant German dictator) was clearly preferable to waiting until 1945 when FDR's death, two atomic bombs, and the Axis surrender would have appropriately put recognition of baseball's first one hundred years in the background.

Joseph Campbell concluded, "Mythology is not a lie, mythology is poetry, it is metaphorical... It is the penultimate truth—penultimate because the ultimate cannot be put into words." The Doubleday myth is also not a lie, but poetry, and its popularity highlighted baseball's centennial euphoria.

The Mills Commission: The Story Behind the Myth

IN 1939, THE STANDARD COMPANY-LINE RESPONSE to the questions "Why Abner?" "Why Cooperstown?" "Why 1939?" was "because of the Mills Commission's findings." On December 30, 1907, after almost three years of alleged research, a seven-man committee chaired by former National League president Abraham G. Mills issued a written report of its findings regarding baseball's beginning. The Commission's findings formalized the Doubleday-Cooperstown-1839 pronouncement of the game's commencement.

Presiding baseball patriarch Albert G. Spalding had pulled strings with the league presidents to appoint the Mills Commission in 1905 to resolve the dispute over the game's origin. For years, he had engaged in the "creation of the game" debate with Henry Chadwick, the British-born editor of Spalding's annual *Official Baseball Guide*. By 1905, Albert had had his fill of debating and sought to end the dispute with the appointment of the Commission.

Chadwick had written an essay in the 1903 *Spalding's Guide* supporting his conclusion that baseball evolved from "the English game of rounders." Shortly before the Mills Commission's appointment, Big Albert fired back in the 1905 *Guide* with his own essay defending baseball as a purely American game, based largely on observations during his 1888-89 baseball-around-the-world tour with the National League's top players. On that excursion to Australia, Egypt, and everywhere in between, Spalding saw many varieties of ballgames being played with a mallet or club, but determined none of them bore even a slight resemblance to baseball. In England, he watched "that asinine pastime" of rounders, and found it "as exciting as a game of Ring-Around-the-Rosy."

Upon the baseball ambassadors' return to New York City in 1889 after their six-month tour, three hundred VIPs (including Theodore Roosevelt, Mark Twain, and Chauncey DePew) attended a banquet in the ballplayers' honor at Delmonico's Restaurant. According to historian Harold Seymour, when Abraham Mills addressed the gathering to deliver Spalding's stirring patriotic assessment that baseball had a purely American heritage, "the audience greeted this announcement with enthusiastic cries of 'No Rounders!' "

The die was cast. No amount of historical research by Chadwick could turn the tide after the Delmonico's banquet. When the aging editor for *Spalding's Guide* reared his ugly British head in print with the 1903 essay, he was no match for Spalding, who propped up his American creation of baseball convictions with the financial power of his emerging sporting-goods empire and a cavalry of obedient yes-men led by Abraham Mills.

Despite baseball fans' knowledge of Spalding's predetermined attitude toward the game having an American origin (as he had written in his 1905 *Guide*), Albert and the league presidents represented to the world that the Mills Commission's members were an absolutely impartial group of distinguished citizens and knowledgeable baseball people. In addition to Chairman Abraham Mills, other commissioners were James E. Sullivan, Alfred J. Reach, George Wright, N. E. Young, and United States Senators Morgan G. Bulkeley (Connecticut) and Arthur P. Gorman (Maryland).

The members of the Mills Commission might have been distinguished, but they were not impartial. Sullivan was president of a Spalding subsidiary, The American Sports Publishing Company. Reach and Wright, former ballplayers, were both presidents of other sporting-goods companies in which Spalding owned interests. "Nick" Young and Senator Bulkeley, (like Mills), were former National League presidents, and thus kowtowed to Spalding. Senator Gorman, who died before the issuance of Mills's report, had been president of the Washington baseball team before entering politics and also recognized Spalding's control over the sport.

Spalding handpicked Abraham Mills to lead the Commission. Mills had served in the Union Army during the Civil War, attained the rank of colonel, and distinguished himself primarily as a baseball player in uniform. Mills packed his bat and ball with a rifle as part of his standard equipment and played in the famous game attended by forty thousand between Duryea's Zouaves and a team of soldier/baseball All-Stars on December 15, 1862, in Hilton Head, South Carolina.

After the war, Mills became an accomplished Chicago lawyer and represented prominent businessman and ultimate National League organizer William A. Hulbert. Mills brought stability to baseball's early team-jumping days by drafting the "National Agreement," which required professional players in the National League and the competing American Association (formed in 1882) to honor their existing contracts. His moral commitment to the sanctity of contracts motivated his resignation as National League president in 1885, after the league voted to reinstate players who had breached their contracts with teams in other leagues. Upon resigning, Mills abandoned baseball to pursue a career with the Otis Elevator Company and had no further official contact with the game until he agreed to head the Commission twenty years later.

By the time Abraham Mills met Albert Spalding in the mid-1870s, he had already commenced the most important friendship of his life.

In 1873, at the Lafayette Post of the Grand Army of the Republic in New York City, Civil War Colonel Abraham Mills changed the course of baseball history by encountering retired Major General Abner Doubleday.

Doubleday as Hero

ABNER DOUBLEDAY HAD AN ENVIABLE FAMILY TREE and a studious boyhood. His grandfather Abner fought in the American Revolution at the Battle of Bunker Hill and served under "Mad" Anthony Wayne. His father Ulysses, a printer and newspaper editor, served as a congressman from New York during Doubleday's youth. Abner Doubleday's primary boyhood pastimes were reading, map-making, and mathematics in his hometowns of Ballston Spa (near Cooperstown[1]) and Auburn. If he ever played baseball, there is no credible record of it.[2]

In 1838, young Doubleday commenced his engineering and military studies at West Point, where his classmates included Ulysses Grant and William Tecumseh Sherman. Army records described Doubleday as being "correct in deportment, social and communicative with his companions... but adverse to outdoor sports." As a young plebe in 1839, per West Point's rules, Doubleday wouldn't have been able to obtain leave to go home to invent baseball or for any other purpose.

After his 1842 graduation, Doubleday's first major military service involved fighting in the Mexican War under Zachary Taylor from 1855-1858. Following that, he fought Indians with Stonewall Jackson in the American West.

By 1860, Doubleday had attained the rank of captain and was stationed at Fort Moultrie, South Carolina. On December 26 of that year, his commander, Major Robert Anderson, moved Doubleday

---

[1]Major General Abner Doubleday had a younger cousin named Abner Doubleday who actually grew up in the village of Cooperstown.

[2]Doubleday kept an extensive diary, which ended up being forty-one volumes by the time of his death. There is no mention of baseball in any of them.

(second-in-command) and the rest of the battalion to nearby Fort Sumter. Following South Carolina's secession from the Union in late 1860, and Lincoln's inauguration on April 4, 1861, the newly formed Southern army fired the first shot at Fort Sumter on the morning of April 12, 1861. In Doubleday's own words, Confederate cannon fire "penetrated the masonry and burst very near my head. We took breakfast early before going to the guns. I aimed the first gun on our side in reply to the attack on Fort Sumter." The battle was joined, the Civil War was on, and Doubleday had played a major role in starting it. For the remainder of his life, Doubleday often accompanied the signing of his autograph with the introductory assertion, "Armed treason must be answered from the mouth of the cannon."

After surrendering Fort Sumter on April 14, 1861, (and, fortunately, not being taken prisoner), Doubleday's military career took him to every important location in the War Between the States except Appomattox. Doubleday led regiments at Bull Run, Fredericksburg, Chancellorsville, Antietam, and Gettysburg. Not only did he serve with bravery in fighting off Pickett's Charge at Gettysburg[3] (now commemorated by a statue of Doubleday on that battlefield), Doubleday later accompanied President Lincoln to the battle site and sat on the speaker's platform when Lincoln delivered the Gettysburg Address in November 1863. After the war, Doubleday authored two books, *Forts Sumter and Moultrie in 1860-1861* and *Chancellorsville and Gettysburg*.

Before retiring from the Army, while stationed in San Francisco from 1869-1871 as a recruiting service general supervisor, Doubleday observed the obvious difficulties of horse-drawn transportation through the city's steep hills. Utilizing his West Point engineering training, Doubleday proceeded to design and obtain the charter for the cable car street railway.

Because of Doubleday's distinguished military record, when retired Colonel Abraham Mills sidled up to retired Major General Doubleday

---

[3]The eloquent Doubleday later wrote of his Gettysburg infantry platoon: "An awful thunderstorm brooded over the Republic; but amidst the flashes of lightning, the roll of thunder, and the sweep of the hurricane, the men stood firm for liberty and law, for the Constitution, and for the right of every man to be paid for his labor. They did their part to obliterate the last vestiges of slavery and barbarism from the land.

at the Lafayette Post for the first time in 1873 to begin their twenty-year friendship, the junior officer got the opportunity to hear first-hand from his mentor about the most important people and events of the nineteenth century.

Abner Doubleday had more to offer the friendship than mere accomplishments. He had an humble, yet engaging personality, making no mention of his considerable heroics in either of his Civil War books. Doubleday was eloquent, capable of quoting poetry for hours (and did while leading his troops to battle), and was always in great demand as a public speaker. Doubleday followed a physically and morally pure lifestyle, avoiding tobacco, alcohol, expletives, and infidelity. In retirement, he remained a concerned citizen, publishing articles on municipal water supply. Doubleday filled his final years reading Spanish and French literature, playing chess, and studying the Hindu language of Sanskrit, which mythology expert Joseph Campbell described as "the great spiritual language of the world."

Mills Honors His Hero

When Abner Doubleday died in 1893,[4] Abraham Mills made sure his best friend received proper tribute. First, he orchestrated the memorial service permitting Doubleday's body to lay in state at New York's City Hall where the caskets of Lincoln and Grant had been displayed. Next, Mills assembled thirteen Army generals to serve in Doubleday's honor guard. As a final honor, the Colonel arranged for Major General Doubleday's burial at Arlington National Cemetery.

Mills's greatest contribution to the legacy of his late, great friend was yet to come. Exactly what the Mills Commission did during its almost three years of existence remains a mystery. It appears only Mills and James Sullivan did anything at all. Mills charged Sullivan with assembling research on the topic of baseball's origins, and Sullivan did advertise that the Commission was gathering evidence on the creation of baseball, inviting anyone with pertinent information to offer it.

[4]In his book *Baseball in America: The Heroes of the Game and the Times of Their Glory*, Donald Honig wrote, "When Abner Doubleday died, he didn't know a baseball from a kumquat."

After Sullivan completed the gathering of his evidence (composed almost entirely of letters responding to his advertisement), a fire destroyed The American Sports Publishing Company, where Sullivan's research was stored. The fire probably saved the Commission from public embarrassment, as all circumstantial evidence regarding Mills's and Sullivan's diligence and scholarship reflects their having done only one meaningful thing. The Mills Commission's single historically significant act entailed its accepting letters Spalding submitted—and to which Spalding asked the Commission to give "special attention"—prepared by septuagenarian Abner Graves, whom Mills described in his report as "a respectable gentleman." After writing his famous letters to Spalding, "respectable gentleman" Graves later murdered his second wife (after she refused to sign a bill of sale conveying their homestead) twenty years later, and spent his final years at the Colorado State Insane Asylum.

Graves could prove he had lived near Cooperstown in the 1830s.[5] Graves said in his letters that at three different Cooperstown locations (including Elihu Phinney's cow pasture), Doubleday had taught the game to him and other boys by modifying an early nineteenth-century pastime called town ball. Graves's letters described Doubleday's alleged adjustments to town ball, including reducing the number of players on a team, positioning the players on the field so each would have responsibility for his own territory, and eliminating wooden posts from the field and replacing them with flat stones he called "bases."

With Graves's letters, Spalding had what he needed. There was no further need for research or investigation. For years, he had reflected on the circumstances of baseball's beginnings and had decided (as he reported in his 1905 rebuttal to Chadwick) that, once upon a time, there was "an ingenious American lad" who got baseball rolling. Doubleday could be that lad, and as a Civil War hero whose life at that time had not motivated a biographer, he was the ideal deceased mystery candidate whose boyhood achievements had not previously been documented. No record existed to disprove Graves's letters, and the

---

[5]Presumably, as a child, Graves might well have encountered Major General Doubleday's cousin, also named Abner Doubleday.

humble major general (who would have been the last person to welcome unmerited fame) was not around to dispute anything.

Spalding relished the idea of tying his favorite sport to war, by metaphor or otherwise, since this accentuated his American-origin-of-baseball hypothesis. Major General Doubleday being the game's inventor made the link between war and baseball that much stronger. Spalding's own book, *America's National Game*, published in 1911, repeatedly reflected this preoccupation. Baseball was "combative," while British cricket was "genteel." Spalding expounded upon the analogy:

> Baseball, I repeat, is War! and the playing of the game is a battle in which every contestant is a commanding General, who having a field of occupation must defend it; who, having gained an advantage, must hold it by the employment of every faculty of his brain and body, by every resource of his mind and muscle.

His book also repeatedly stated his titled premise, that the game was purely and obviously American. Sounding almost like a nineteenth-century Giamatti, Spalding waxed eloquent with alliteration on the second page of his book:

> I claim that Base Ball owes its prestige as our National Game to the fact that as no other form of sport it is the exponent of American Courage, Confidence, Combativeness; American Dash, Discipline, Determination; American Energy, Eagerness, Enthusiasm; American Pluck, Persistency, Performance; American Spirit, Sagacity, Success; American Vim, Vigor, and Virility.
>
> Base Ball is the American Game par excellence, because its playing demands Brain and Brawn, and American manhood supplies these ingredients in quantity sufficient to spread over the entire continent.

With such an overloaded patriotic spirit, it is no surprise when Spalding sent the Graves letters to the Mills Commission, his transmittal note mentioned, "It certainly appeals to an American's pride to have had the great national game of Base Ball created and named by a major general in the United States Army." The December 30, 1907 Mills Commission report, prepared with succinct precision by contract lawyer Mills, stated the desired conclusions:

> First—That Base Ball had its origin in the United States.
>
> Second—That the first scheme for playing it, according to the best evidence obtainable to date, was devised by Abner Doubleday, at Cooperstown, New York, in 1839.

Had the Commission not reached its first conclusion, Spalding likely would have court-martialed his lieutenants, and they knew that. Had the Commission not reached its second conclusion, Mills would have lost his last great opportunity to honor his mentor, Abner Doubleday.

Surely, Mills recognized the irony of his best friend being credited with inventing the national pastime, in the context of Doubleday never having discussed baseball with Mills during their twenty-year relationship. Nonetheless, Mills did not know Graves, had no reason to question the veracity of the man whose letters Boss Spalding ordered the Commission to give "special attention," and surely delighted in the chance to supplement Doubleday's place in history. Neither Mills nor Sullivan had any real interest in investigating and correcting Graves's obvious error of giving credit to Abner Doubleday being in Cooperstown at a time when the West Point plebe could not have been in the village.

Spalding published the Mills Commission's report in his 1908 *Guide*, and Henry Chadwick conveniently died in April of that year to end the debate... for a while.[6] Compared to prior pronouncements regarding baseball's beginnings, the Commission's findings had the loudest ring of authenticity, boosted by Spalding's substantial publicity of Mills's report. Cooperstown's citizens sensed the new Doubleday-Mills Commission circumstances might lead their village toward further historical recognition, and the promotional percolating began.

---

[6]The most important research which essentially obliterated the Doubleday myth came, ironically, during the 1939 centennial year upon the publication of New York librarian Robert Henderson's research. Henderson's well-documented conclusions were so airtight as to be beyond any meaningful criticism as he cemented for all time the determination of baseball's evolution from rounders.

How Cooperstown Got the Hall of Fame

SUCCESSFUL POLITICAL CAMPAIGNS usually combine grass-roots support, substantial financial backing, and creative and effective marketing to support an electable candidate. The campaign to formalize Cooperstown as the birthplace of baseball succeeded because of the fulfillment of that formula. The citizens of Cooperstown provided unified support. The Clark family, as beneficiaries of the Singer Sewing Machine fortune, gave the money. Clark family employee Alexander Cleland[7] served as the marketing and organizing wizard. And the scenic beauty of the Glimmerglass area coupled with the Mills Commission's Doubleday conclusion made Cooperstown the perfect candidate.

Following the publication of Mills's report in the 1908 *Spalding Guide*, a decade of incubation passed among the Cooperstown residents. Finally, in 1917, Arthur Richardson, Deke White, Michael Fogarty, George Oliver, and Patrick Fitzpatrick from the village's surrounding area commenced the movement to honor Cooperstown's serving as the site for the first game. The five men started their Cooperstown baseball effort by digging deep into their trouser pockets, and each contributed twenty-five cents to provide the corpus for building a Doubleday memorial. Though they lacked the necessary money, the men had the good sense to realize their dream would die unless they shared it. They contacted *New York Journal* sportswriter Sam Crane (a former major league player) and told the journalist their goal.

Crane visited Cooperstown and proved himself to be a normal human being by immediately falling in love with the place. He spent the next eight years promoting Cooperstown among the *Journal*'s readers, thereby starting to expand the support base for the village as baseball's birthplace.

During the next two decades, the citizenry never wavered in its commitment to making a permanent place in baseball history for its hometown. The chamber of commerce, led by local dentist Ernest Pitcher,

---

[7]All baseball historians, including this author, are indebted to Utah history professor James Vlasich and his 1990 book, *A Legend for the Legendary*, published by the Bowling Green State University Popular Press, which virtually single-handedly illuminated Cleland's vital role and other pertinent facts in the formation of the National Baseball Hall of Fame and Museum.

raised more than $3,700 to acquire a lease on the alleged site of Elihu Phinney's cow pasture (one of Doubleday's baseball stomping grounds, per Graves) to be used as the site for Doubleday Field.

Sportswriter Crane and local leaders attracted the attention of major league baseball to the Doubleday memorial, enticing then National League president (and former umpire) John Heydler to come to Cooperstown to witness the local fervor. Doubleday Field opened with a contest between Cooperstown's hometown nine against arch rival Milford on September 6, 1920, and League president Heydler was there to call the game.

By 1923, Cooperstown's residents voted to impose a tax for the village to use in purchasing the Doubleday Field property from Phinney's descendants, thereby stopping the leasing limbo. Additional grandstands were built around the ballpark until the Great Depression hit town. The Works Progress Administration (WPA) finished the Doubleday Field project in 1934.

The WPA's completing the ballpark dovetailed with the commencement of the Clark family's interest in a baseball venture at Cooperstown. Edward Clark, patent lawyer turned millionaire sewing machine entrepreneur, married a Cooperstown girl and summered in the village from the mid-nineteenth century until his death in 1882. Lawyer Clark had one child, Alfred, who inherited $40 million from his father's estate. Alfred and his wife had four sons who each received equal shares in the family fortune which had reached $120 million upon Alfred's passing in 1896.

Three of Alfred's sons had no progeny, but each of the three left a dramatically different legacy. Robert Sterling Clark assembled a massive art collection still on display at the Sterling and Francine Clark Art Institute in Williamstown, Massachusetts. Frederick Ambrose Clark devoted his adult life to the raising of thoroughbred horses at sizable ranches on Long Island and Cooperstown. Bachelor Edward Severin Clark built Cooperstown's two most important non-baseball structures—the still grand Otesaga Hotel and the imposing stone barn located on property once owned by James Fenimore Cooper, and which now houses the Farmer's Museum.

Only eldest son Stephen Carlton Clark produced children, and his empire (estimated by *Forbes* magazine in 1989 to be worth in excess of $400 million) is now controlled by his grandchildren. Stephen Clark's vision and fortune allowed Cooperstown to achieve its most lasting recognition. After returning from distinguished service in World War I, Stephen Clark decided on two seemingly contradictory pursuits. First, he wanted to bring tourists to the dormant Cooperstown area to boost the local economy. Second, he wanted the area to remain unspoiled.

During the 1920s, Stephen Clark began his quest to make the Otsego area a tourist attraction by developing museums devoted to farming, pioneer settlement, and art. Clark knew museums would motivate outsiders to come to the community, and, after arriving, the area's pristine grandeur would captivate even the weariest traveler. Hall of Famer Bill Terry, whose countenance was described as being consistently sour, came to Cooperstown for the centennial in 1939. Upon spending time at Lake Otsego, and retreating to his boyhood memories by skimming stones across the lake, he proclaimed, "This is the most pleasant day I've ever experienced. Right now I love everybody!" Terry's reaction to Cooperstown's splendor was (and is) the rule rather than the exception, and Stephen Clark recognized the potential pull of this local paradise before anyone else did.

In 1931, Clark encountered a charitable crusader named Alexander Cleland. This native Scot, who came to America in 1903 at the age of twenty-six, spent his first three decades in the United States assisting indigent immigrants.[8] Stephen Clark was one of the leading benefactors to the plight of foreigners' transition, and Clark House in New York City served as a regional center for immigrant assistance. Clark hired Cleland as the director of Clark House in 1931, and, for three years, they limited their conversations to charitable activities.

On a spring Saturday in 1934, Stephen Clark invited Cleland to his home in Cooperstown to discuss immigrant relief business. Cleland rode the train up from New York City to the village, had his meeting

---

[8]In his autobiography, Ford Frick described Cleland as "a stocky, red-faced little Scotsman, with the broad burr of the highlands in his speech and the missionary ardor of John Knox in his soul."

with Clark, and then planned to take the train home. After the completion of the business meeting, on Cleland's walk from Clark's home to the Cooperstown train station, he encountered a WPA worker finishing up at Doubleday Field. The rest is history. The ballpark worker apparently bubbled with enthusiasm about his work on the field and the prospect of the coming 1939 baseball centennial. That contagious enthusiasm sparked Cleland to lose his Clark House immigration focus on the train ride home and think about a new kind of museum "...where a collection of all past, present, and future data of the game could be shown."

The following Monday, knowing of his boss's interest in creating museums, Cleland delivered a memorandum to Stephen Clark which spelled out his vision for the development of a baseball museum in Cooperstown. The idea engaged Clark from the outset. Soon Clark and Cleland hired an architect to design the museum, directing that the building should achieve two objectives—blend in with the surrounding community, and be absolutely fireproof to provide comfort to donors of irreplaceable memorabilia.

Clark and Cleland knew they would need the full support of Major League Baseball for the centennial celebration and the baseball museum project to succeed. They began finding that support during the summer of 1934 through a Clark Foundation contact, prominent New York lawyer and Brooklyn Dodger director Walter "Dutch" Carter.

To put pressure on baseball's leadership to jump on the centennial bandwagon, Carter subtly tried to embarrass them into participation by having the *New York Evening Post* publish his letter describing organized baseball's Cooperstown oversight. The letter read, "The powers of baseball should be not only willing but anxious to make this cradle of our greatest game a shrine." As a follow-up, Cleland and Carter sent a memorandum regarding the need for organized baseball to take part in the movement to National League president Heydler, who distributed it to Commissioner Landis and American League president Harridge. Sadly, nothing happened among the triumvirate at the top.

Major league baseball's inertia toward the Cooperstown movement ended in late 1934 when Heydler retired and National League owners named Ford Frick as his successor. Frick, a former newspaper reporter and advertising agent in Colorado, came to New York to be a sportswriter for the *New York American* in 1921. He then emerged as a sports radio personality and became director of the National League's Service Bureau for the first nine months of 1934 before being named league president.

Stephen Clark knew of the National League president's attraction to Cooperstown based on Frick's recent article on the village which had appeared in the *New York American*. Clark sent Cleland to meet with Frick, seeking to accomplish what Cleland and Dutch Carter had failed to accomplish with Heydler—engage the active participation of Major League Baseball in the Cooperstown 1939 baseball centennial.

At the 1935 meeting between Cleland and Frick, the former advertising-whiz-turned-National-League-president proceeded to raise the bar for the centennial. He suggested to Cleland that in addition to a baseball museum in Cooperstown, there should be a Baseball Hall of Fame created, modeled after New York University's Hall of Fame for Great Americans organized in 1901. Cleland and Stephen Clark embraced the idea immediately.

While Frick's leadership brought Major League Baseball into the Cooperstown baseball centennial project, in early 1935 at the nearby Otsego County hamlet of Fly Creek, a battered trunk reportedly containing "reputable gentleman" Abner Graves's boyhood mementos was discovered in a farmhouse attic. In the trunk was an old baseball. Upon hearing of the discovery, shrewd trader Stephen Clark immediately bought the ball from the depression-desperate farmer for five dollars. Steve Wulf of *Sports Illustrated* described the ball in his 1989 article on the Hall of Fame's fiftieth anniversary:

> It is an ugly little thing that looks more like a fossilized chaw of tobacco than a baseball. The cross seams on one side of it have come apart, revealing some kind of cloth stuffing that resembles dirty yarn. Hard to believe anybody saved the thing in the first place.

Because of the Mills Commission's Graves-Doubleday connection, Cooperstown newspaper editor Walter Littell labeled Clark's purchase "the Doubleday ball," and Clark promoted it as baseball's missing link, proving forever the tie between Doubleday, Cooperstown, and the invention of baseball.

By early 1935, the unified citizens of Cooperstown, led by the trustees of the Historical Association and the chamber of commerce, formed a corporation they called "The National Baseball Museum, Inc." and stated in their corporate paper filings that they formed the company "for the purpose of collecting and preserving pictures and relics reflecting the development of the national game from the time of its inception through the ingenuity of Major General Abner Doubleday in 1839 to the present." Cleland served in the position of the corporation's secretary and was empowered to do whatever was needed to achieve the corporate purpose.

Immediately after forming, the museum corporation decided to start assembling and displaying baseball artifacts at Cooperstown's Village Club which served as the museum's home until the Hall of Fame and Museum building was completed and opened in 1939. Beginning in 1935, tourists to Cooperstown could observe the Doubleday Ball, Stephen Clark's collection of baseball art, and other old memorabilia.

With the missing-link Doubleday Ball under glass at the temporary headquarters of the aggressive museum development and the Clark-Cleland-Cooperstown commitment to provide a Hall of Fame in addition to a museum, Ford Frick was satisfied. In August 1935, with the blessings of all Major League Baseball executives, and on behalf of organized baseball, Frick formally endorsed the National Baseball Hall of Fame and Museum at Cooperstown. From that point forward, the deal was closed, leaving for the next four years only Cleland's strong promotion of the necessary follow-up activities: raising funds, constructing the building, acquiring the artifacts, advertising the Cooperstown centennial celebration, and commencing the Hall of Fame selection procedures.

In 1926, eighteen years after the publication of his Commission's report, Abraham Mills had put everything regarding Cooperstown in its proper historical perspective. When asked by a reporter, "What conclusive evidence do you have that the first game was actually played in Cooperstown?" Mills replied:

> None at all, young man. None at all, so far as the actual origin of baseball is concerned. The committee reported that the first baseball diamond was laid out in Cooperstown. They were honorable men, and their decision was unanimous. I'm willing to let the matter rest right there. This we do know. We know that baseball developed through long processes of evolution. We know that it developed as a rural game for ours was basically a rural nation. We know that once the diamond was devised and the game standardized, it was taken up eagerly by thousands of youngsters, in hundreds of typical American villages and hamlets scattered over thousands of miles of pioneer American countryside. I submit to you, gentlemen, that if our search had been for a typical American village, a village that could best stand as a counterpart of all the villages where baseball might have originated and developed—Cooperstown would best fill the bill. Unless and until new evidence is developed, or a more typical spot is discovered, I'll stand with Cooperstown—and the committee.

The sacred-place-bliss-station of Cooperstown got the Hall of Fame because of a mythological thread tying together Doubleday, Spalding, Mills, Graves, the village residents, sportswriter Crane, the WPA worker, Cleland, Clark, and Frick over the course of a century. In his autobiography, *Games, Asterisks, and People*, Ford Frick concluded the chapter on the Hall of Fame with the observation:

> The most intriguing thought of all: without a battered trunk, an ancient ball, and a packet of time-stained letters, baseball would have been without its greatest monument.
>
> In the box score of baseball history, a kindly Providence should be credited with at least an assist.

An evolution allowed the consummation of baseball's centennial and the opening of the Hall of Fame and Museum in 1939. Mere mortals cannot determine whether the evolution occurred due to a series of coincidences created by mere chance, or because of the orchestration by a higher authority.

Perhaps Bart Giamatti now knows.

Babe Ruth holds court at the 1939 dedication of the Baseball Hall of Fame. (National Baseball Library and Archive, Cooperstown, New York)

CHAPTER ELEVEN

THE BIRTHDAY PARTY

Baseball Celebrates Its Centennial

After almost five years of organization by Alexander Cleland and the residents of Cooperstown, baseball's centennial finally arrived. Major League Baseball demonstrated its commitment to the game's one-hundredth birthday by having each league produce a film. The two movies emphasized what Cleland, Landis, and everyone involved in the game wanted the public to know about the national pastime—baseball had a rich history and a rigidly enforced integrity which bonded generations; it was good exercise for boys, and helped teach them about life; and, at the major league level, the game was played by highly skilled, decent people.

The American League Film: *The First Century of Baseball*

THE FIRST PUBLIC SCREENING OF A LEAGUE FILM took place January 5, 1939, in Philadelphia at the annual Athletics banquet. Both league presidents attended, and American League chief Will Harridge told the press he saw the showing of his league's movie as "the opening gun of the 1939 centennial celebration." Sponsored by General Motors,[1] the

[1]GM's interest in promoting baseball films has continued, serving as the primary sponsor of Ken Burns's *Baseball* documentary in 1994.

American League called its thirty-nine-minute motion picture *The First Century of Baseball*.

To demonstrate the game's timelessness, the American League film opened with a gray-haired grandfather on a couch reading baseball history to his two grandsons from a large picture book. As Grandpa read aloud about the evolution of the game, a scene from colonial America was pictured with children in tricorn hats playing Old Cat games with a ball and a cricket-type mallet.

But Old Cat games weren't good enough for American youth. The next segment had a road sign marked "Cooperstown," followed by a scene of boys playing town ball. As the players tried to catch the ball, they crashed into each other, and the narrator explained, "The game needed a clear head to bring order into it." Up walked Abner Doubleday in a top hat and suit. The West Point cadet told the boys they needed to maintain fixed positions in the field and assume responsibility for their territories, which would result in fewer collisions. Because of Doubleday's directions, "baseball first took form."

After a brief interlude showing baseball played at all levels, from Iowa high schools to intercollegiate rivalries to the sandlots, the history resumed with a scene involving Alexander Cartwright and his New York Knickerbocker team. Per Cartwright's rules, an umpire was shown instructing pitcher Candy Cummings to throw underhanded pitches to the location where the batter indicated. With the hitter having all the advantage, Cummings expressed understandable frustration. The next day, Cummings found himself standing in a pool hall and got an idea watching billiards players applying different spins to balls making them curve. At the next ballgame, Candy Cummings threw the first curveball in baseball history, and the batter ducked out of the way as the pitch crossed the plate. The initially confused umpire eventually called the pitch a strike. With the advent of the curveball, the game had now changed, and pitchers had a more equal chance when they battled the hitter.

Having covered the history angle, the American League film next became instructional. Pitching stars Bob Feller, Lefty Gomez, Ted

Lyons, Buck Newsom and others[2] were shown gripping curveballs, knuckleballs, and fastballs—and throwing overhand, three-quarters, and sidearm. Hitters then displayed their techniques, as Joe Cronin, Jimmy Foxx, Lou Gehrig, Joe DiMaggio, Charlie Gehringer, and Hank Greenberg demonstrated slow-motion form.[3] Next came lessons on infield play and base running. Joe Cronin was shown tagging a runner sliding into second with his bare hand gripping the ball, and the narrator said Cronin's method (which risked having the fielder's hand torn apart by an aggressive base runner) was the proper way to tag. Finally, the Philadelphia Athletics' Bill Werber[4] performed a variety of slides for the camera.

The film then returned to Grandpa as he recalled for his adoring grandsons the founding of both leagues (National in 1876 and American in 1901), and the first World Series in 1903. Some players from the old man's days were still around, and the film showed retired stars Ed Walsh, Tris Speaker, and Cy Young at old-timers' games.

The American League next reminded the viewer how truly great its players were, showing highlights from the 1938 All-Star Game (mentioning that the American League had taken four out of the six from the National League in the Mid-Summer Classic) and the 1938 World Series (won by the American League for the third consecutive year).

Not only were American League players skilled, they were also wholesome. The next scenes depicted Norman Rockwell America scenes of ballplayers off the field. George McQuinn was shown driving up to Pete Fox's home and talking pleasantly. Joe Gordon signed autographs for children. Luke Sewell agreed to show a boy how to throw if the child would promise to stay away from traffic in the street. Former teammates Mel Harder and Joe Vosmik remained

---

[2]Monty Stratton, the White Sox's 15-game winner in 1938, was one of the film's featured pitchers. Stratton would have his leg blown off in a hunting accident before the start of the 1939 campaign, thereby ending his major league career.

[3]Of course, by the time the film was shown throughout the 1939 season, Gehrig's best real-life swing was in slow motion.

[4]Werber would move to the National League's Reds by the time the film was shown.

friends and were featured hunting together. Not only were the players good folks, the gray-haired owners appeared as kindly as old Grandpa. Connie Mack and Clark Griffith were shown reminiscing about how many games they had been through together in their combined 108 years of baseball. The wholesome image of the national pastime continued with a segment on spring training—plenty of sunshine, healthy exercises, friendly conversations between current and former players, patient instructors with eager students, interested owners, and spirited pepper games.

Then came an attempt to put the umpire's difficult job into perspective. The film showed a series of close plays run at full camera speed, always ending in a cloud of dust, and the narrator almost threatening the viewer with, "You be the umpire!" Slow-motion replays gave correct calls in an attempt to encourage a healthier appreciation for the job done by the men in blue.

As the *First Century of Baseball* approached its ending, Yankee manager Joe McCarthy offered America his paternal advice: "Give a boy a bat, a ball, and a place to play, and he'll make little trouble for you." As Grandpa closed the book, he smiled and told his grandsons, "A hundred years is a long time, but the game's going to go right on forever."

The National League Film: *The National Game*

The National League called its General-Mills-sponsored movie *The National Game*. Although this film had no public grand opening like *The First Century of Baseball*, *Spalding's Official Baseball Guide* for 1939 devoted three full pages to the forty-two-minute film and told its readers how to obtain a copy for showings to "banquets, smokers, civic and social luncheons, chamber of commerce meetings, boys clubs, YMCA meetings, Army and Navy bases, Legion posts, in hospitals and sanitariums, and just about everywhere, in fact."

The National League film opened showing youth all over the world ("Youth in Italy...Youth in France...Youth in Germany," etc.) marching in military uniforms, and "being dumbly obedient to diplomatic stupidity." When it came time for "Youth in America," boys on a sandlot were shown choosing up sides, laughing, and playing ball.

The National League promoted the game's appeal for all ages with a scene showing a gruff businessman taking a phone call at the office resulting in an invitation to the ballgame that afternoon. After hanging up the phone, the executive became transformed, smiled, and even whistled as he tipped the office boy fifty cents on his way out the door. The businessman was then shown enjoying a hot dog at the ballpark, and smiling at the office boy who had somehow gotten to the game himself.

The game didn't just change the mood of city folks. The next *National Game* scene showed a gathering of older men and boys on the front porch of a country store, playing checkers, and arguing about politics. In the background sat a big radio. When the ballgame came on, all gathered round, differences were put aside, and the group cheered together.

The National League then tried its own 1839 Cooperstown reenactment. Natty Abner Doubleday was shown sitting with a formally attired friend his same age, observing a game of town ball in progress. Doubleday said to his companion, "You know, Graves,[5] I'm going in the Army soon, and what makes the Army fascinating to me is the offensive and defensive strategy—matching my brains and men against your brains and men. And that's what my new game does." After Graves encouraged Doubleday to try out his new game on the boys, Doubleday called the players together, and drew a diamond in the dirt while explaining the rules. As Doubleday and Graves watched the boys playing Doubleday's new game, they realized the team on offense had an unfair advantage because the bases were too close together. Graves proceeded to tell Doubleday, "What you need is an engineer to determine where to put the bases, because the essence of the game lies in the distance the boys must run against the speed of the ball."

After Doubleday's scene, the camera went straight to young "civil engineer" Alexander Cartwright's "scientifically" setting the proper

[5]One of the main holes eventually poked in Abner Graves's letters to the Mills Commission was the fact that they read as if he and Doubleday were the same age when, in fact, Abner Doubleday was almost fifteen years older than Graves.

distances between bases for his Knickerbocker club,[6] followed by his becoming the game's first missionary, teaching baseball while leading a wagon train across the country to join the gold rush.

Next came a Civil War campground segment, as generals were shown trying to communicate with a distracted President Abraham Lincoln. The military leaders wanted to talk about the war, but all Abe could think about was baseball, as he wondered about the outcome of a nearby game between the New York regiment and Illinois soldiers. When the generals challenged the president's priorities, Lincoln explained that baseball games between soldiers were important "to make people take their minds off war." A messenger suddenly rode up and handed the president what appeared to be an important document. Abe read the report, slapped his knee, and then exclaimed to his generals, "Men, Illinois beat New York!... Gentlemen, you want to do something important. Get the men in both armies back home where they can play ball on their own ground."

After the Civil War scene, the National League film showed the effect of the Industrial Revolution, bringing large groups of men together to work in factories, thereby making games easier to organize. City teams played well, but often lacked discipline and integrity, leading William Hulbert and other businessmen to gather in a New York hotel. Hulbert was shown telling the group his vision for a league of teams representing each major city, and playing clean games under the governance of a constitution. The future National League president advised those in the room he had locked the doors and no one could leave until an agreement was reached regarding the formation and governance of the league.

The achievement of athletic purity became the film's next theme. Hulbert and Al Spalding were shown sitting in a room talking about the state of the game when in walked an unshaven, red-eyed ballplayer previously discharged from the game for gambling. The broken man pleaded with the league executives to acknowledge the genuineness of his repentance and allow him to play again. Benevolent league

---

[6]Cartwright might have been gifted in determining the distance between bases, but he was not a civil engineer. His biographer Harold Peterson listed Cartwright's pre-baseball occupations as bank teller, bookstore owner, and fireman.

president Hulbert observed the player's obvious down-and-out condition and handed him fifty dollars, but admonished the bum, "You sold the game! I can never trust you again!" After the player left the room, the good-hearted but firm Hulbert was shown telling Spalding, "That's the hardest thing I've ever done."

Since the National League had little to brag about in its recent performances in World Series and All-Star Game competition, the film next stressed the league's innovations—Ladies Days at Wrigley Field, and night baseball in Cincinnati and Brooklyn "allowing the working man to go to the game."

If National League players couldn't match American Leaguers in performance, at least they measured up in clean living. Cub third baseman Stan Hack was shown at his home coming downstairs to find breakfast prepared by his attractive wife, who was feeding their baby in a high chair. In addition to acknowledging the ballplayers as good family men, the narrator proclaimed, "Ballplayers have wholesome hobbies," as Braves infielder Tony Cuccinello was shown fishing, and Phillies pitcher Claude Passeau hunting.

History and goodness exhausted, next came scenes showing the nature of the game itself. Baseball was fun—Gabby Hartnett's pepper game looked like a Marx brothers' comedy routine. Baseball was caring—the Chicago Cub trainer was shown rubbing down pitcher Larry French. Baseball required a clear head and a healthy body—the camera looked into Ducky Medwick's sharp eyes, and then showed his strong grip and smooth swing.

Now, it was instruction time. The film slow-motioned the hitting technique of the league's best batters—Mel Ott, Ernie Lombardi, Lloyd Waner ("You don't have to be big to be a great hitter."), Frank McCormick, Arky Vaughan, Billy Herman, and others. Durocher showed how to bunt and play the infield. Vince DiMaggio demonstrated outfielding form. Then came pitching tips, and the viewer got to observe the different styles of the Giants' Carl Hubbell (who displayed perfect control by breaking four panes of glass in each quarter of the strike zone), the Reds' Johnny Vander Meer and Paul Derringer, the Cubs' Bill Lee, and the Dodgers' Freddie Fitzsimmons. Pepper Martin, and Rabbit Warstler showed how to slide, though the narrator cautioned, "The head-first slide is not recommended." Al Lopez, Mickey Owen, and Ernie Lombardi showed how to catch with two hands. Dolf Camilli demonstrated how a first baseman properly shifts his feet and stretches from the bag. By the end of the National League film, an attentive audience was presumably prepared to play every position in the field, pitch, and hit at a major league level.

The National Game closed with the explanation, "Baseball, with its emphasis on playing to win, helps youth to play the game of life." Children in grandstands were shown clapping together and screaming in unison, "We want baseball, we want baseball," as the film ended.

Doubleday Makes it Through the Year

SINCE FORD FRICK HAD LED MAJOR LEAGUE BASEBALL IN 1935 to endorse the Hall of Fame's being located in Cooperstown, both leagues' films gave full credit to Abner Doubleday as the game's creator. In addition to the leagues, respected sportswriters on the order of Ken Smith, Dan Daniel, J. G. Taylor Spink, and Fred Lieb all signed off during 1939 on the acceptance of Doubleday as baseball's inventor. *Newsweek* magazine put the Civil War hero on its June 19, 1939 cover with the explanation, "General Doubleday fathered baseball one hundred years ago." The June 1939 issue of *Baseball Magazine* and the annual *Sporting News Record Book* for 1939 did the same. The cover of *Spalding's 1939 Official Baseball Guide* had as its subject baseball's founders, with Abner pictured at the top. Perhaps most significantly, President Franklin D. Roosevelt gave Doubleday a presidential seal of approval with his letter delivered to the February 5, 1939 New York Baseball Writers' Dinner.

As far as 1939 went, Alexander Cartwright never had a chance. Though Cartwright's mid-1840s Rules and Knickerbockers had motivated Commissioner Landis and league presidents Frick and Harridge (the then sole members of the Hall of Fame's Veterans Committee) to put Cartwright into the Hall in 1938, and Cleland held an Alexander Cartwright Day at Cooperstown to help appease the Cartwright family on August 26, 1939, baseball's centennial year belonged to Abner.

At the Baseball Writers' February 5 dinner (where Bill Klem gave his "Baseball is religion" quote), Postmaster General James A. Farley announced that for the first time, the United States Post Office would honor an American sport by issuing a postage stamp to commemorate baseball's centennial. Farley said, however, that no choice had yet been made as to whom or what would be on the stamp. Following the dinner, a national NBC radio program polled its listeners on the appropriate image for the stamp. Abner Doubleday narrowly beat out Christy Mathewson and John McGraw, while Alexander Cartwright got no votes at all.

At the same dinner, writers Arthur Daley, Fred Weatherly, and Lon Effrat affirmed the proposition of Doubleday as the game's creator by putting on a skit entitled "Looking Backward on Abner Doubleday's Dilemma." The plot involved Doubleday and Cartwright encountering a swami in 1839, and then listening to the fortune teller predict baseball's future. On the horizon, the game would motivate millions of fans to eat something called hot dogs (which sounded canine to the baseball pioneers) and one day would be ruled by a czar (i.e., Landis) as powerful as any Russian leader. When Doubleday heard what was ahead for his game, he tore up the rules, and told his friend, "No, Mr. Cartwright, I will not invent the game."

Baseball's centennial dedication to Doubleday was most passionately reflected on the morning of April 17, 1939, when Joe McCarthy and Clark Griffith took their Yankees and Senators teams to Arlington National Cemetery for a memorial service at Doubleday's grave.

The Centennial Postage Stamp

THE LEAGUES, WRITERS, MAGAZINES, FANS, AND PLAYERS had accepted Abner Doubleday as the hero of the centennial despite the emerging body of persuasive (and, ultimately, indisputable) evidence that the Civil War major general had had nothing to do with the game. Postmaster Farley decided by the commencement of the 1939 season that he couldn't ignore the reliable historical accounts by New York librarian Robert Henderson and sportswriter Frank Menke disputing the Mills Commission's finding. To avoid the potential embarrassment of honoring Doubleday for something he possibly didn't do, Farley

Baseball's centennial stamp of 1939. (National Baseball Library and Archive, Cooperstown, New York)

chose for the baseball centennial stamp image a scene of boys (some with shoes, some without) playing baseball on a sandlot with no umpire or parents in sight. Farley's press release said the stamp aimed "to typify the heritage of American youth."

The idea for the issuance of a baseball centennial stamp had come at the suggestion of Ford Frick. The National League president had been an avid philatelist since childhood, and his collection exceeded fifteen thousand stamps. Farley accepted Frick's suggestion, and the stamp's 450,000 first-day issue from Cooperstown became the largest in post office history. The Cooperstown postmaster had to hire an extra twenty-five employees just to handle the demand. Ultimately, 65 million baseball centennial stamps were issued during 1939.

The United States Post Office had a quixotic goal for the stamp. Third Assistant Postmaster General Ramsey Black wrote in a May 1939 letter to the president of the Middle Atlantic League, "This stamp is intended primarily to stimulate on the part of youngsters, the citizens of tomorrow, a greater appreciation of outdoor sports, particularly baseball... and will mean much toward stimulation of outdoor athletics." In 1939, Farley's troops apparently thought a boy seeing a postage stamp would somehow motivate him to run to the sandlot and organize a baseball game.

The stamp's first day of issue was June 12, 1939, the day the National Baseball Hall of Fame and Museum opened its doors at Cooperstown. Farley entered the Cooperstown Post Office that morning and sold the first stamp to Commissioner Landis, who handed over three pennies. The purchase of the stamp began the most important day in the history of Cooperstown.

The Centennial Promotion

IN 1938, MAJOR LEAGUE TEAM OWNERS had voted to spend $100,000 in connection with celebrating the centennial. To supervise the fund's proper administration and all the year's activities, Kenesaw Landis appointed the blue-ribbon National Baseball Centennial Commission. Desiring a select group he could wrap in red, white, and blue, Landis chose World War I hero General John Pershing to headline the Commission, and then added as commissioners the Army chief of staff, the commandant of the Marines, the Navy's chief of naval operations, the commissioner of the U.S. Office of Education, the national commander of the American Legion, the commander of the Veterans of Foreign Wars, the commander of Disabled American Veterans, the president of the U.S. Chamber of Commerce, the director of the Boys Clubs of America, the president of the National Collegiate Athletic Association (NCAA), the president of the Baseball Writers Association, the president of the National Association of Broadcasters, J. G. Taylor Spink of *The Sporting News*, and Alexander Cleland.

After picking the honorary commissioners, Landis selected Steve Hannagan, a prominent New York public relations specialist, to spread the baseball centennial gospel. Among other things, Hannagan designed several different brochures, tens of thousands of which his office sent to civic leaders, chambers of commerce, American Legion posts, high school coaches, amateur teams, and major league franchises. The Hannagan brochures told "How to Conduct Invitational

Baseball Tournaments," "How to Conduct a High School Baseball Day," "How to Conduct a Public Baseball Clinic," and "How to Conduct Extended Junior Baseball Schools."

Beyond attempting to motivate the organization of baseball schools and tournaments, Hannagan also prepared brochures that contained complete prototype baseball centennial speeches to be delivered at townwide celebrations or over the radio. Per the opening of the National League's centennial film, Hannagan's orations expressed that while Europeans engaged in war, Americans engaged in baseball. An excerpt from one of the speeches found in the publicist's brochures delivered the "Baseball Over War" pitch:

> It must be regretfully admitted that there is a lot of dangerous talk abroad in the world today. We can thankfully add that most of this talk is going on beyond three thousand miles of ocean. Over here, we are talking baseball, talking it up like an infield when the bases are full with a "clean-up man" at the bat. We are celebrating baseball's one-hundredth birthday. Perhaps there never was a time when baseball stood America in better stead than today. The Old World is resounding with the clank of arms and the rattle of guns. On this side of the Atlantic and the Pacific, far from the smoke and horror of war, I hope we are listening for other sounds. For good, healthy excitement, give me, anytime, the resounding crack of a hard hit line drive.

Repeatedly, Hannagan worked into his centennial spiel the story of Abe Lincoln playing baseball with friends in Springfield. When a delegation arrived from the 1860 Republican National Convention to tell Lincoln he had been nominated for the office of President, Lincoln told the group's advance man, "Tell the gentlemen they will have to wait until after I have had my turn at bat." *Newsweek* accepted the Lincoln-baseball connection and featured the story in its June 19, 1939 Doubleday cover issue.[7]

---

[7]The truth of the Lincoln story has been widely disputed. The appendix to this book gives this author's analysis of the incident's historical accuracy.

Hannagan left no marketing stone unturned, going so far as soliciting President Franklin Roosevelt to promote baseball centennial events at high schools—for the boys, an oratory contest with a prize for the best rendition of "Casey at the Bat"; for the girls and boys, an essay contest on the subject, "The Contribution of One Hundred Years of Baseball to the Spirit of American Sportsmanship." Although FDR failed to endorse the contests, the President did send a letter to the Hall of Fame which *The Sporting News* published in its entirety on June 1, 1939:

> It is most fitting that the history of our perennially popular sport should be immortalized in the National Baseball Museum at Cooperstown, where the game originated and where the first diamond was devised a hundred years ago.
>
> Baseball has become, through the years, not only a great national sport, but also the symbol of America as the melting pot. The players embrace all nations and national origins and the fans, equally cosmopolitan, make only one demand on them: Can they play the game?
>
> It seems to me that the museum will be a place of special interest, particularly in this centennial year of baseball.

Throughout Hannagan's promotions, the Baseball Centennial emblem appeared on virtually all stationery, brochures, and advertising. The design was chosen from a competition sponsored by Landis and the Commission and was the creation of New York artist Marjori Bennett. The colors in her poster image matched the Commission's patriotic constituency—red, white, and blue. In the background, four red vertical stripes were separated by three white stripes representing four balls and three strikes. A red-and-white uniformed right-handed batter finishing his swing was superimposed over a white baseball with blue seams in the middle of the picture, which was in turn placed in the center of a blue baseball diamond on top of the background red-and-white stripes. Above the diamond were the years "1839" and "1939" in blue, and below it were the words "Baseball Centennial" in red and blue. Professional baseball so approved of Ms. Bennett's image

Baseball's centennial patch of 1939, pictured with commemorative stamp and Hall of Fame. (Major League Baseball Properties)

that all major and minor league players wore a patch with the emblem on their uniform sleeves throughout the 1939 season,[8] becoming the first patch ever to be worn on all uniforms in a given year.

June 12, 1939: The Opening of the Hall of Fame and Museum

COMMISSIONER LANDIS, POSTMASTER GENERAL FARLEY, league presidents Frick and Harridge, virtually all of baseball's surviving legendary figures, three national network radio teams, dozens of the country's leading sportswriters, two players from the current roster of each of the sixteen teams, and, in all, more than ten thousand people converged on Cooperstown for the opening of the Hall of Fame and Museum on June 12, 1939. Weed-covered train tracks came into

[8]The patch had such visual appeal that almost fifty years later, the filmmakers who produced the movie *The Natural* starring Robert Redford put it on the uniforms of the mythical New York Knights and all of their opponents, although Bernard Malamud's novel made no mention of his story being set in a particular year.

Cooperstown from the south, but no train had traveled the route from New York City since 1934. The dedicated village residents got out their hoes and cleared the railroad path, allowing the mid-morning arrival of the celebrity guests.

The keynote event for the day was the platform ceremony, which took place in front of the Hall of Fame building. Sportswriter (and later Hall of Fame Director) Ken Smith gave his impression of the building constructed during the Great Depression at a cost of $100,000:

> You can sense in the spiral lines of the Hall of Fame ever so slight a suggestion of an early American Colonial church, just enough to provide the reverence called for by the nature of the foundation. It is a square-rigged American Revolutionary style building but the overall impression is one of warmth and friendliness.

The ceremonies scripted by Hannagan began at noon with a local band playing "My Country 'Tis of Thee." Baseball Writers' Association president Charles Doyle presided as master of ceremonies and introduced the many assembled VIPs. After the band played the obligatory "Take Me Out to the Ballgame," Cooperstown Mayor Rowan Spraker welcomed the largest assemblage of tourists in the history of the village.

Kenesaw Mountain Landis next came to the microphone. The Commissioner acknowledged the thirteen pioneers[9] "who were the moving spirits of the game in its infancy" already chosen by the Hall of Fame's Veterans Committee, and the twelve greatest retired players[10] elected by the Baseball Writers Association. Despite the twenty-five inductees' contributions to the national pastime, Landis told the crowd in Cooperstown and the national radio audience, "I should like to dedicate this museum to all America... to lovers of good sportsmanship...

[9]Morgan Bulkeley, Ban Johnson, Connie Mack, John McGraw, George Wright, Alexander Cartwright, Henry Chadwick, Cap Anson, Charles Comiskey, Candy Cummings, William Ewing, Hoss Radbourne, and Albert Spalding.

[10]Ty Cobb, Walter Johnson, Christy Mathewson, Babe Ruth, Honus Wagner, Nap Lajoie, Tris Speaker, Cy Young, Grover Cleveland Alexander, Eddie Collins, Willie Keeler, and George Sisler.

healthy bodies... and keen minds. It is to them, rather than to the few who have been honored here, that I propose to dedicate this shrine of sportsmanship."

Upon concluding his remarks, Landis gave Frick and Harridge a pair of scissors. After cutting the ribbons in front of the museum, the three executives followed Cooperstown Centennial Committee Chairman Theodore Lettis up the stairs to the building's entry, where Lettis unlocked the door, and then handed Landis the key.

The officials returned to their seats, and emcee Doyle began the introduction of the twenty-five members of the Hall of Fame, beginning with George Wright. After the reading of each pioneer's name, there was a ruffle of drums. Only one of the thirteen pioneers was alive in 1939, and Doyle read his name last. "Cornelius J. McGillicuddy, Connie Mack!" The Philadelphia A's legend stepped out from behind the museum's door and walked down the steps to the platform, while the crowd cheered and the band again played "Take Me Out to the Ballgame."

Following the thirteen pioneers came the introduction of the twelve players elected by the writers. Announced first were Keeler and Mathewson, the only deceased player inductees, and as their names were called, the band played "Taps." The ten surviving players present were introduced next and they each gave the crowd a brief welcome, with Babe Ruth getting the biggest ovation. Of the living players, only Cobb was not there for the introduction, purposefully arriving late to avoid being photographed with his longtime enemy Landis. At the conclusion of the program, Landis announced, "I now declare the National Baseball Museum and the Baseball Hall of Fame in Cooperstown, New York, home of baseball—open!"

Between the ceremony's closing and the start of the parade at 2:30 P.M., the crowd had time to tour the museum. The limited artifacts and pictures could easily be observed in a thirty-minute tour of the facility. As it existed in 1939, the nucleus of the museum's collection was the Doubleday Ball (described in chapter 10). Other Doubleday material (donated by Washington Senators owner Clark Griffith) on display were a portrait of the late major general as well as a Civil War landscape scene of "General Doubleday Crossing the Potomac River." To counter-balance the Doubleday emphasis, the

1939 Hall of Fame baseball game program. (Major League Baseball Properties)

Cartwright family had given Cleland a good sampling of Alexander's mementos, including his diary and receipts showing Knickerbocker earnings collected from losing teams.

Cleland had also gotten the player inductees to make contributions. Cy Young donated one of his gloves and the ball with which he won his 500th game. Nap Lajoie gave the bat used for his 3,000th hit. Babe Ruth delivered a uniform, his 60th-home-run bat from 1927, and a collection of milestone balls. Christy Mathewson's widow gave his glove and uniform.

Though the years following the centennial would enrich the museum until it housed the greatest collection of baseball memorabilia in the world, the inventory of relics was not impressive when the building opened. Sportswriter Dan Daniel wrote in the June 22, 1939 issue of *The Sporting News*, "The museum is disappointing. To be sure the proposition is new and the committee is combing the country for memorabilia of the game, but the collection is much too meager."

The afternoon parade began at 2:30 P.M. from the steps of the Hall of Fame and went down Cooperstown's Main Street to Doubleday Field. In the parade were two players from every major league team (Landis had scheduled no games for June 12) as well as the Hall of Famers themselves. At the head of the parade were soldiers dressed to play a game of baseball in the pre-Civil War Knickerbocker era, followed by Cooperstown's adolescents dressed in costumes from the 1830s ready to re-enact a game of town ball, with both games to be officiated by an umpire wearing a stovepipe hat.

Upon the parade entering Doubleday Field, where eight thousand fans jammed the grandstands, the program began with an address from Doubleday's descendant Lieutenant Daniel Doubleday followed by another brief Landis speech. After the remarks and the ten-minute exhibitions of nineteenth-century baseball, it was time for the real thing. Honorary team captains Honus Wagner and Eddie Collins grabbed a bat and chose up sides. Nine future Hall of Famers[11] played in the game, as did legendary names Johnny Vander Meer, Moe Berg,

---

[11]Lloyd Waner, Billy Herman, Mel Ott, Hank Greenberg, Dizzy Dean, Arky Vaughan, Charlie Gehringer, Joe Medwick, and Lefty Grove.

and Cookie Lavagetto. The only member of the Hall of Fame inductees who tried to play was pinch hitter Babe Ruth, and for one of the few times in his life, the Bambino disappointed the crowd by popping up to the catcher. By the end of the seventh inning, umpires Bill Klem of the National League and Eddie Romel of the American League had to call the game to an end, allowing the players and other celebrities to catch the train back to New York City.

Other Activities of the Year

BESIDES THE MAJOR CELEBRATION ON JUNE 12, Cooperstown stayed busy throughout 1939. In recognition of Doubleday's career in the military, the first game played at Doubleday Field that year took place on May 6 between military schools Manlius Academy and Albany Academy. Christy Mathewson's widow (accompanied by John McGraw's widow) came to the village on May 27 to unveil a bust of the legendary pitcher at the museum, followed by a matchup between Bucknell (Mathewson's alma mater) and St. Lawrence College.

After June 12, the most important day in Cooperstown took place on July 9 when the Cooperstown Centennial Committee and the National Association of Professional Baseball Leagues joined to host Minor League Day. One player from each of the forty-one minor leagues operating in the United States and Canada came to Cooperstown to play in an exhibition game that day, and the two teams of minor league All-Stars were named "the Doubledays" and "the Cartwrights." In addition to the game, the high point of Minor League Day was the dedication of the Hall of Fame Library.

By the end of 1939, the National Baseball Hall of Fame and Museum had attracted almost thirty thousand people from thirty-one countries and every state in the U.S. except Wyoming. It had set a Hall of Fame standard soon followed by other sports and American institutions. During his illustrious baseball career, one-time-sportswriter Ford Frick had ghostwritten for Babe Ruth, served as National League president when Jackie Robinson broke the color barrier, and been Commissioner when baseball moved to the West Coast and entered the big-dollar television era. Despite those baseball achievements, shortly before his death in 1978, Frick said he regarded his role in the founding and development of the Hall of Fame as his greatest accomplishment.

The nation took part in centennial festivities outside of Cooperstown. On March 19, 1939, NBC Radio ran an hour-long national program called "The Cavalcade of Baseball," tracing the first one hundred years of the game's history. On May 7, the National Semi-Pro Baseball Congress organized the playing of 12,500 games all over the country simultaneously. On May 27, the Army dedicated its own Doubleday Field at West Point in honor of its most distinguished baseball alumnus. Throughout the summer, communities gathered to reenact baseball games played under Cartwright's Knickerbocker rules[12] sponsored by the National Association of Professional Baseball Leagues. The NAPBL's director of publicity, L. H. Addington, even wrote a poem read on Opening Day 1939 at baseball fields all over the country and published in *Baseball Magazine*, entitled "Baseball's Centennial":

One hundred years of baseball,
Turn back historic pages;
The game that's now a century old
Has flourished through the ages.

A hundred years of wholesome sport,
Replete with skill and action;
A game that knows no boundary lines
Of race or creed or faction.
A game that's thrilled the rich and poor,
The mighty and the humble;
Each knows the joy of sparkling play,
The tragedy of fumble.

The melting pot of human souls,
Where elbows rub together;

---

[12]Eleven players per team; the pitcher forty-five feet from home plate throwing underhanded; no gloves; and the first team to score 21 aces won.

Where banker cheers with tradesman
At the crash of bat and leather.

One hundred years of baseball
May it thrive a thousand more;
May it show a winning record
When posterity asks the score.

The films, the Doubleday-Cartwright debate, the stamp, the Hannagan brochures, the Bennett emblem and player patch, the opening of the Hall of Fame, and all of the centennial activities throughout the country led *The Sporting News* to declare in its January 4, 1940 issue that 1939 had been the greatest year in baseball history. Total attendance in professional baseball had reached its highest level with the minor leagues drawing three million more fans than ever before.

The country and its national pastime had risen to the occasion in 1939, fulfilling Alexander Cleland's vision. The celebration of baseball history would not be equaled again on a national level until a PBS viewing audience estimated in the tens of millions watched Ken Burns's documentary *Baseball* in September 1994.

Little League founder Carl Stotz talks baseball with his two nephews in 1940. (Photo courtesy of the Stotz family)

CHAPTER TWELVE

THE FUTURE BEGINS IN WILLIAMSPORT

Carl Stotz Forms Little League Baseball to Keep His Promises

SIX DAYS BEFORE THE NATIONAL HOOPLA over the Hall of Fame's opening, an obscure twenty-nine-year-old lumberyard clerk from Williamsport, Pennsylvania, named Carl Stotz started a movement which would become baseball's most important new development during its second hundred years. On June 6, 1939, at the corner of a local park, the team sponsored by Lundy Lumber Company beat the Lycoming Dairy Farm boys, 23-8, in the first Little League baseball game ever played. Stotz that day began fulfilling the promises he had made to himself as a child and to his nephews the summer before.

Before Stotz started Little League, American boys played their baseball largely on sandlots, as depicted in the opening of the National League's 1939 film and on James Farley's baseball centennial postage stamp. Author Wilfrid Sheed gave his perspective on the pre-1939 need for an organized boys' baseball program in his book *Baseball and Lesser Sports*:

> Little League has been much maligned as being far too organized and parent-dominated. But as a kid I would have given my Wally Moses and even my Arky Vaughn bubble gum cards for such organization. The way it was then we used to spend the best part of

Saturday trying to scrape together enough players just for one o'cat and when you finally had them, there was no place legal to play.

Starting in 1937, the Kellogg Company sponsored the first "free baseball schools" for boys, beginning the movement away from the sandlot in favor of organization. Hall of Famer Tris Speaker and former American League batting champion Lew Fonseca taught baseball fundamentals to young players at the schools, which started in Chicago. They became so popular, Kellogg soon sponsored the program in other cities. In addition to improving the boys' knowledge of baseball, the schools had the side benefit of reducing juvenile delinquency wherever they were conducted. The drawback to Kellogg's program was it did not provide the game competition necessary to fully develop a young ballplayer. Speaker recognized the schools' limitation in his April 1939 article in *The Rotarian* magazine. After heralding Kellogg's program, Baseball's Grey Eagle acknowledged the need for what Carl Stotz was already doing something about in Williamsport:

> The diamonds on which the boys play (tin-can sandlots) are still rough enough in many places. (A chance there for adults to help provide better ones!) And the boys themselves are only diamonds in the rough.

The Promises

CARL STOTZ'S IDEA FOR CREATING LITTLE LEAGUE began on a Williamsport sandlot in 1938. One summer afternoon, Carl (nicknamed "Uncle Tuck") saw his six- and eight-year-old nephews Jimmy and Major Gehron being excluded from playing in a pick-up game because of their size.

What was happening to the Gehron boys had happened to Uncle Tuck twenty years before. Stotz remembered his childhood frustration at not getting to play enough baseball either due to his small size[1] or because of the difficulty in organizing a game with eighteen boys. As

[1]The slender Stotz stayed small his entire life, reaching an adult height of only five-foot-six.

a teenager, Carl felt the frustration again. His Williamsport Lutheran church had a Sunday School men's league team, but the adolescent Stotz sat on the bench while adults got most of the playing time.

As he watched his nephews, Stotz also remembered his childhood fantasy of being a big league player in front of cheering crowds at a ballpark, wearing a complete uniform, and using all new equipment. Carl had made a childhood promise to himself that when he grew up and "got rich," he would have his own baseball team, and turn the dream into a reality.

To soothe the Gehron boys' frustration in the summer of 1938, "Uncle Tuck" played catch with his nephews. While running to get an errant throw one Saturday, Carl stepped on the stems of a lilac bush and scraped his ankle. As he sat on his neighbor's steps evaluating the cut, Stotz began a brief but historic conversation with Jimmy and Major: "How would you boys like to play on a regular team with uniforms, a new ball for every game, and bats you can really swing?" The excited nephews responded: "Who would we play? Would people come to watch us? Do you think a band would ever come to play?" Carl Stotz then made "the promise" to his nephews of bringing the idea to fruition, thereby keeping the promise he had made to himself as a child.

Stotz went forward with his boys' baseball plan on two fronts. The first challenge was to set up rules for the game. From the outset, Carl wanted his Little League to be only for boys less than thirteen years old. To allow older boys to play would squeeze out the playing time of those smaller kids for whose benefit Stotz had designed the program.

In starting a league for pre-adolescent boys, Carl realized his players lacked the strength to pitch from a mound more than sixty feet from home plate or throw a ball from third to first base on a field with bases ninety feet apart. A boy's attempt to make such long throws risked injury to an underdeveloped physique. In his book (written with Kenneth Loss) entitled *A Promise Kept*, Stotz described the problems faced by young boys playing on men's fields in the years before 1938:

> When I'd begun to play sandlot ball twenty years earlier, when I was nine, nothing was geared to children. The pitcher was too far

> away to throw hard enough to be effective, so he simply aimed the ball over the plate. The catcher, without a mask, chest protector, or shin guards, stooped over near the backstop, when there was one. The ball usually came to him on a bounce, making him more of a retriever than a catcher.

Uncle Tuck, his nephews, and other neighborhood kids spent their 1938 summer evenings at Williamsport's Max M. Brown Memorial Park running tests to measure how far boys could throw on a line, how quickly they could run, how fast they could pitch, and how far they could hit so as to determine the best dimensions for a Little League field. Presumably, Alexander Cartwright and his Knickerbockers did essentially the same thing at Hoboken's Elysian Fields almost one hundred years before.

Stotz described the process in his book:

> After I placed the newspapers around the field to represent home plate and each base, I positioned the boys around the infield while I served as pitcher. From time to time, I changed the distance between the bases. I was trying to find out what distance would enable the boys to throw a runner out from third base or shortstop while still giving the batter a fair chance to beat it out, depending on where he hit the ball.
>
> Night after night I squeezed the boys into my black 1934 Plymouth two-door sedan—it was quite a crowd—and took them to practice in the park. Each evening, I continued experimenting with the distance between bases. When I finally had what I thought was the ideal distance, I stepped it off and used a yardstick at home to measure my strides. The distance was so close to sixty feet that I set that as the distance we would use thereafter.

As a result, Carl set up his Little League field at exactly two-thirds the size of the standard diamond. The bases were sixty (rather than ninety) feet apart, and the pitcher's mound was forty feet, four inches (rather than sixty feet, six inches) from the plate. Stotz first set the mound at less than forty feet from home plate to accommodate the four seven-year-old boys who played Little League the first year, but soon moved it to the exact two-thirds' distance of forty feet, four inches.[2] To maintain the two-thirds' standard for Little League, Stotz made each game last six innings. The only other two rules imposed by Stotz different from traditional baseball were his requirements that (1) a base runner intending to steal couldn't leave his base until the pitched ball crossed home plate, and (2) a batter couldn't run to first base if the catcher dropped a third strike.

In addition to establishing the new rules, Carl's second task in keeping his promises was finding money to support the league. Stotz had not achieved his boyhood goal of getting rich, so he solicited Williamsport businesses to provide funding for league expenses. He prospected through fifty-six local merchants before finally striking gold with Lycoming Dairy Farm manager Floyd Mutchler, who gave the program thirty dollars (although many accounts list the original contribution at thirty-five dollars). With the money, Stotz bought a dozen baseballs, two bats, a catcher's mitt, and some uniforms. However, Stotz knew he needed more funds. He then went to the heads of Lundy Lumber and Jumbo Pretzel, who agreed to contribute some money, though less than Lycoming Dairy. With the additional funds, Stotz bought more uniforms, field equipment, and shirt emblems. Having the necessary equipment and uniforms, and then lining up brothers George and Bert Bebble (both of whom were previously unknown to Stotz) to coach the other two teams, Carl Stotz had everything in place for Little League to begin in the summer of 1939.

After establishing the field's dimensions and getting funding from the team sponsors, Stotz developed rules to guide the program from its inception:

A It would have the name "Little League."[3]

---

[2]In the late 1950s, Little League moved the pitcher's mound back an additional three feet, eight inches, to forty-four feet from home plate. This was done because pitchers had come to dominate too many of the boys' games and after a rash of batters got hit with pitches.

[3]Stotz's original idea was to call his program "Junior League Baseball," but decided that name would be confused with the national women's service organization, The Junior League.

B The basic unit of organization would be the league and not the teams comprising the league.

C Teams would be selected from a common pool of players from well-defined geographical areas.

D The playing field would have the scaled-down size dimensions.

E The sponsors would have no voice in any matter pertaining to the operation of the league or teams.

F The players would be selected solely on the basis of ability without regard to race, color, or creed.

G Boys with a complete cross section of ages (between eight and twelve) would be placed on each team.

H All funds contributed by sponsors would be placed in a common treasury for the equal benefit of each team.

I The program would not be exploited by commercial interests.

Rule (c) was perhaps the most intriguing. In 1949, Arthur Daley described its workings in his *New York Times* column:

> Perhaps the most novel thing about the leagues is the way the players are assigned to the various teams. A community call is issued each spring to every tiny tot who thinks he can play ball. There are tryouts staged in the presence of the various managers who appraise all talent. Then comes the "purchase" of the players.
>
> Each manager is given 36,000 credits (presumably the equivalent of $36,000)[4] for buying the junior-size athletes. An auction is held among them with what's called a Player Agent in charge. Anyone can bid as high as he wants for any performer but he has to be careful that he doesn't get too extravagant so that his credits are exhausted. Once a player is thus "purchased" he becomes the property of his "owner" for the duration of his Little League career, the same as the Big Leagues. Once all credits are exhausted, the managers draw numbers from a hat until rosters are filled.

[4]Originally, in 1939, each manager got twenty thousand credits, and the number expanded over the years.

Daley pointed out an additional advantage of the selection program in addition to its creating league balance: "The players' pool becomes a community melting pot. The rich boy from the hills plays alongside the lad from the wrong side of the railroad tracks... The pool cuts across all lines."[5]

In addition to training boys in the fundamentals of baseball, Stotz wanted Little League to teach sportsmanship for boys and their parents.[6] An umpire was to eject any player saying a cuss word or who challenged the arbiter's call. If a fan booed, the umpire was to stop the game until the booing ended.

Little League in the Stotz Years: 1939-1955

STOTZ COMPOSED THE FIRST LITTLE LEAGUE of three[7] evenly matched, ten-player teams[8] which battled through a twelve-week season. If all ten boys showed up for a game, the coach played four outfielders, so no kid had to warm the bench. Each team played six-inning, twilight games umpired by a lone volunteer who made all his calls standing behind the pitcher. Teams shared gloves, bats, and one catcher's mask. With his prized pocketknife, Stotz personally carved the home plate and the pitcher's mound out of some black rubber he found in his father's basement. His sister Laurabelle made the bases out of either cheap material filled with excelsior or old feed bags stuffed with straw.

---

[5]Arthur Daley's intrigue with Little League Baseball motivated him to write articles about the program, not just for the *New York Times* in 1949 and 1952, but also for *Parade* magazine and *Reader's Digest* in 1950, and *American* magazine in 1951.

[6]In his book, Stotz told of a game during the inaugural 1939 season, when a fan started disputing an umpire's call. The volunteer ump decided he didn't have to take it and simply walked off the field to stand with the other spectators. With that, the game had no arbiter. Stotz left his coaching post, walked to the pitcher's mound, exhorted the crowd to refrain from booing the umpire, and asked for a volunteer to finish the game. A Lundy Lumber employee came forward and the game proceeded without further problem.

[7]Stotz had aspired to have four teams in 1939, but couldn't make up a fourth team, because (1) he didn't find a fourth sponsor, (2) he had only three managers, and (3) his player pool was too small the first year.

[8]The three teams' records in 1939 of 9-7, 8-8, and 7-9 reflected the even distribution of talent.

Stotz's inaugural Lycoming Dairy team of 1939. (Photo courtesy of the Stotz family)

During the inaugural season, the teams played their games at Park Point, located at a corner of Memorial Park (where the 1938 tests were run), but the first Little League field had no fences, dugouts, bleachers, or loudspeakers. Stotz carried a small blackboard from game to game, which became the league's official scoreboard.

The 1939 Little League season proved a success. Adults who weren't even parents came out to watch the boys' games. Every week, the *Williamsport Sun-Gazette* put up the boys' scores on the wall of its building in addition to covering the games in the paper. It was the enhancement of father-son relationships, however, which became the most important aspect of the young program's success.

William "Mac" McCloskey was a pipe-smoking British immigrant living in Williamsport before the war who knew nothing about America's national pastime, when Stotz started Little League. Mac's son Dalton begged his father to let him try out for Stotz's team, although the boy lacked the necessary coordination to be even an adequate player. McCloskey decided to abandon his British heritage (rounders, cricket, and the like) and jumped headfirst into fulfilling his son's dream. The overachieving father devoured every baseball instructional book he could find and began working with Dalton daily to improve his skills. By the time the McCloskeys worked together a few years, the boy's skills improved to the point of becoming the best pitcher and hitter on his Williamsport Little League team, with the side benefit that father and son had forged a permanent bond.[9]

Before the summer of 1940, Carl Stotz and the Bebble brothers decided the teams should have an official, properly outfitted field of their own. They cleared two hundred trees from a lot at the corner of Demerest and Memorial Avenues and built Little League's first ballpark.[10] Sufficient demand caused the creation of a fourth team in Stotz's league by the start of the 1940 season. As the years passed, Williamsport became a better place because of Little League. The program's spread throughout the community caused a 50-percent reduction in juvenile delinquency there from 1945 to 1948.

From the inception of Little League in 1939, Stotz imposed a strict geographical limit on each team.[11] As the program became more popular each year, new areas wanted their own leagues, resulting in its spreading outside of Williamsport to other areas of Pennsylvania during the war years. By 1946, there were twelve leagues in the state with a total of forty-eight teams. In 1947, New Jersey became the first state outside of Pennsylvania to field a Little League team.

---

[9]Mac McCloskey maintained his commitment to the program after his son graduated. He became the Lou Gehrig of Little League official scorekeepers, scoring 1,327 consecutive games over a period of twenty-eight years. In his book, Stotz called McCloskey "the most faithful and loyal person I have ever known."

[10]The 1940 park was eliminated in 1942, because the space was needed for a war factory. Stotz and his supporters built a new field in 1942 at Max Brown Memorial Park, where Stotz had run the boys through the 1938 tests. This field hosted the Little League World Series until the 1959 construction of Howard J. Lamade Stadium, where the Series still is played.

[11]Per the local school-zone districts, one team could not represent an area having more than fifteen thousand people.

Heartwarming stories of the boys' games spread nationally, accelerating parents' desires to have Little League programs in their own areas. In his 1989 book, *Growing Up at Bat*, author Harvey Frommer told his favorite story from the league's early years:

> A big playoff game was scheduled in Williamsport in 1947. Two boys, lifelong friends, were the opposing pitchers in this game. They traveled to the big game on the same bicycle; one pedaled while the other perched on the bike's crossbar. Each was dressed in his team's uniform. When they got to the ballfield, they parked the bike, wished each other well, and separated toward opposite dugouts.
>
> The game began and moved on. Inning after inning each pitcher took his turn on the mound, holding the opposition scoreless. It was a nail-biting affair. The game moved into the final inning. Not a run had been scored by either side. Then the youth who owned the bicycle came to the plate to face his friend. Their eyes met for an instant. On a pitch that some said was out of the strike zone, the batter swung and hit a home run. The final score was 1-0.
>
> The game concluded, the two youths left the field as they had arrived. The winning pitcher pedaled; the losing pitcher sat on the crossbar, tears streaming down his cheeks.

With the program's expansion outside of Pennsylvania, Stotz decided he should host a Little League World Series (which he first called the "National Little League Baseball Championship Tournament") in the summer of 1947, to name a champion from the seventeen leagues and sixty-eight teams. Williamsport's own Maynard Midgets became the first Series champions in 1947, and a national press syndicate covered the event for seven hundred newspapers.

Following the 1947 Series, Carl Stotz sought a solution to a recurring problem. Because Little League boys all played in sneakers, they couldn't dig in at the plate or change directions quickly in the field. Metal spikes worn by major league players were clearly too dangerous for children, so Stotz decided someone should manufacture a rubber-cleated shoe. As he thought about the need for the special shoe, Stotz

Every Little League team has its own version of a "Murderer's Row." (National Baseball Library and Archive, Cooperstown, New York)

also decided he needed a corporate sponsor to fund the expenses for future Little League World Series. The New York-based United States Rubber Company, (now Uniroyal), with a plant in Williamsport, solved both of Stotz's problems.

After sending dozens of letters, Stotz got an audience in December 1947 with U.S. Rubber executive Charles Durban. The meeting began with Carl describing the formation and development of Little League Baseball. Stotz again followed in the footsteps of Alexander Cartwright (as he had done in establishing the field's dimensions) by becoming a baseball missionary that day. Durban later recounted his immediate reaction to the program. "I liked the basic lessons of Little League ball... of giving the small boys a chance to play... drawing no social or economic lines... showing the value of teamwork, discipline, and fair play... and all of it adding up to a mighty good lesson in Americanism."

After the meeting, U.S. Rubber wrote a check for $8,000 to Little League for the upcoming 1948 World Series, and got exclusive rights to manufacture the official Little League shoe. In 1949, the company raised its financial commitment, providing sufficient funds not only to cover the World Series, but also to give Stotz a salary, allowing him to devote all his time to Little League.

With Stotz working full time, the year 1949 cemented Little League's importance in American life. The May 14, 1949 issue of the *Saturday Evening Post* carried an article entitled "Small Boy's Dream Comes True," and profiled Stotz. It told of Williamsport's spectacular boys' field which featured bleachers, a pressbox, an electric scoreboard, a clubhouse with showers, and a fence circling the outfield in an arc 180 feet from home plate. Little League had become so popular it was outdrawing the ever-popular Class A Williamsport Tigers, who played in the Eastern League. By the close of that summer, *National Geographic* magazine also featured the program, and *Life* magazine did a photo spread in 1950.

From 1949 to 1955, the Little League movement grew from 867 teams in twelve states to 16,554 clubs (made up of 248,310 boys) in forty-six states. During that time, Stotz and U.S. Rubber incorporated Little League Baseball, Inc. as a nonprofit corporation, and Stotz accelerated the program's growth by speaking to representatives of 2,600 leagues all over the country. His friend Cy Young added credibility and prestige to Little League by attending every World Series during Stotz's final five years with the organization. By 1951, *Baseball Magazine* announced it would commit to an annual December feature printing the box score and play-by-play account of the Little League championship, "because we feel the program has reached the stage of importance where it deserves our recognition."

The movement became international in the early fifties, with Montreal the first foreign team to play in the World Series in 1952, and ten countries having programs by 1954. Arthur Daley in the May 25, 1952 issue of *The New York Times* hailed the development of Little League Baseball as "the biggest thing in sports since Abner Doubleday outlined his baseball diamond at Cooperstown in 1839."

Driving this mushrooming international phenomenon was a seemingly simple man. On the surface, Carl Stotz started the program to become the world's greatest uncle, working day and night to make his nephews' dreams come true. When the *Saturday Evening Post*'s Harry Paxton interviewed Stotz for the 1949 Little League article, the writer described Stotz as being "no hot-eyed zealot, but unassuming and amiable of manner and slight of build. The hot-eyed characters have a way of burning out, but Carl Stotz had the patience and persistence to stick with his dream, day in and day out, year after year, until, little by little, it became real." *Lycoming Ledger* reporter Pamela Rockerman later said Stotz had "a wonderful sense of humor and a charming personality." Stotz's strong religious faith also fueled a morally pure lifestyle. He didn't smoke, drink, or use profanity, and he tried to motivate all involved with Little League to do the same.

Like most people, however, Stotz had an ego. Knowing he would never be a financially successful businessman, his life and career in the business world appeared to be consistent with his boyhood sandlot bench-warming days until Little League took off. In 1949 and the years following, this short, skinny, lumberyard clerk suddenly found himself pictured in the *Saturday Evening Post* and *National Geographic*, and profiled in *The New York Times*, *Parade*, and *Reader's Digest*.

Evidence of the program's success having an effect on Stotz came when Carl joined with Williamsport's M. W. Baldwin to write a children's book in 1952 called *At Bat with the Little League*. The book was written through the eyes of boys from the fictional town of "Haywood," who took their team all the way to the Little League World Series. When the Haywood team arrived in Williamsport for the series, Stotz and Baldwin portrayed the Little League founder as the kindly Little League Baseball commissioner, there to greet the Haywood team in person. When the big game finally arrived, Haywood's team chaperone thought to himself, Wonder what Carl Stotz feels like right now? If this knocks me out, what must it do to him to see on his own field champion teams from every corner of the United States?

When the fairytale Haywood team made it to the championship game, the authors described the pregame ceremonies. On the field were the governor of Pennsylvania, the president of U.S. Rubber Company, Ford Frick (commissioner of baseball by 1952), the vice president of the Baseball Hall of Fame, the president of the Eastern League, and others. After listing the Series' VIPs in attendance, Stotz and Baldwin wrote, "Then Carl Stotz walked out on the field to make his bow. The tremendous ovation from the crowd and from the boys on the field was heart-warming and unforgettable." When Haywood lost the championship game, the team was consoled by two men hurrying to the Haywood dugout. "The boys stared. They knew who Ford Frick was—national commissioner of big-league baseball! And for Carl Stotz they had admiration just this side of idolatry."

The growth, the praise, and the glory for Carl Stotz came to a screeching halt after the 1955 season. From the time it came on board as the program's corporate sponsor, U.S. Rubber wanted Little League to get bigger, and became more and more in control of it to further that end. Stotz, a stickler for details, saw himself losing control of all aspects of his creation and becoming essentially a ceremonial figurehead. To him, the program seemed to be moving away from its fundamental sandlot flavor and becoming an international big business at the behest of U.S. Rubber executive Peter McGovern, who had joined Little League's board of directors in 1953.

Stotz's problems with McGovern were brought to a head in 1955. He returned from an international Little League promotional tour to find that McGovern had fired Stotz's longtime secretary while he was gone. This personnel change came on the heels of the board of directors' changing Little League's by-laws to reduce Stotz's powers as commissioner.

Unwilling to accept his changed circumstances, and, by his own admission, "not being an especially tactful or diplomatic person," Stotz filed a federal court lawsuit against McGovern and U.S. Rubber in 1955 alleging breach of contract arising from his "no longer having a representative voice in Little League policy decisions." He alleged in his complaint he had suffered actual damages of $300,000. After losing several hearings, and being financially unable to continue the suit, Stotz ended up withdrawing the litigation, but its filing led McGovern and the board of directors to remove the game's founder from the program permanently. Carl Stotz left Little League's employment to later become the tax collector in the Old Lycoming township section of Williamsport for twenty-odd years, never to see another boys' baseball game played under the auspices of Little League Baseball, Inc. Stotz's commitment to youth baseball prompted his maintaining a connection with his original four-team league in Williamsport (known as "Original Little League," permitted because of the Original League's severing all ties with Little League Baseball, Inc.)

Little League After Stotz

WITH CARL STOTZ OUT, Peter McGovern resigned from U.S. Rubber to assume full-time Little League duties. The new head of the program attempted to effect a smooth transition out of the Stotz era.

The public seemed little disturbed by the change in leadership, and Little League's incredible growth continued. From 1955-1963, the program doubled in size, going from 16,554 teams to 33,180. McGovern accentuated the commitment of his new regime to the organization's historic patriotic fervor by creating the Little League Pledge soon after Stotz's departure. Each team was to recite the Little League Pledge before each game:

> I trust in God
> I love my country and will respect its laws
> I will play fair and strive to win
> But win or lose
> I will always do my best.

By July 16, 1964, Little League's national influence had grown to the point of its becoming the only sports organization to obtain a federal charter. The charter gave the program a tax exemption and put it in the same league as the Boy Scouts of America. The legislative justification for Little League's tax exemption was that it was given in return for "using the disciplines of the native American game of baseball to teach spirit and the competitive will to win, physical

Peter McGovern, for 31 years the president and board chairman of Little League Baseball. (Williamsport Sun-Gazette)

fitness through individual sacrifice, the values of team play, and wholesome well-being through healthful and social association with other youngsters under proper leadership." Baseball centennial publicist Steve Hannagan couldn't have said it any better.

Like Abner Doubleday, Little League even got a presidential seal of approval. Former President Herbert Hoover wrote a letter to the Williamsport headquarters April 4, 1954 (published later that year in *Little League Baseball* magazine), saying, "I am interested in Little Leaguers for just two reasons. First, team sports are the greatest training in morals second only to religious faith. Second, it is one of the greatest stimulants of constructive joy in the world." By 1959, in celebration of its twentieth anniversary, the program received the blessing of President Dwight Eisenhower, who issued a proclamation naming the second week in June "National Little League Week." John F. Kennedy did the same in 1961.

Criticism of Little League began in the mid-1950s following the Stotz litigation. The *Philadelphia Inquirer* said the lawsuit caused Little League "to lose its innocence." New York Yankees great Tommy Henrich said in the August 1957 issue of *Sport* magazine he saw Little League as a game run for the enjoyment of adults resulting in the fun being taken away from the kids. Following Henrich's lead, educators and psychologists published articles regularly on their fear of Little League creating an obsession for winning as a higher priority than a boy enjoying the game and learning its skills. Red Sox slugger Ted Williams gave his view in an August 1961 issue of *Look* magazine: "In Little League, never mind instructing the kids, instruct the parents."

Some critics of the program came from unlikely places. Joey Jay gained national attention in 1953 for becoming the first Little League player to make the major leagues. By 1965, because of his seven-year-old son's bad experience, Jay published an article in *True* magazine, "Don't Trap Your Son in Little League Madness," which described boys getting ulcers and organizers putting together "tryout schedules and tournaments run like an IBM machine."

A 1954 issue of *Little League Baseball* magazine featured Philadelphia Phillies star Robin Roberts. In 1975, Roberts' "My Turn" essay in *Newsweek* entitled "Strike Out Little League" opened with: "It says in 1939, Little League baseball was organized by Bert and George Bebble and Carl Stotz. What they had in mind in organizing this kid's baseball program I'll never know, but I'm sure they never visualized the monster it would grow into." Before giving his suggestions for change, Roberts described the program's disruption of families' evening schedules, the inefficiency of most Little League coaches as instructors, and his impression that "more good young athletes are turned off by the pressure of organized Little League than are helped."

Despite the justified criticism, as well as substantial bad publicity coming from Little League's ultimately failed attempts in 1974 to exclude both girls (who won the right to play in a New Jersey lawsuit brought by the National Organization of Women) and foreign teams (the board revoked the prohibition on foreign teams in 1975), the program continued to flourish.

Little League Baseball celebrated its first fifty years in 1989, and Bart Giamatti went to Williamsport in June to address the gathering assembled for the anniversary of the game between Lycoming Dairy and Lundy Lumber. During the course of his speech, the commissioner announced that more than two-thirds of the players on major league rosters had played Little League. The program's link to Major League Baseball became even further solidified on July 23, 1989, when Carl Yastrzemski became the first Little Leaguer ever inducted into the Baseball Hall of Fame in Cooperstown.

Since 1939, Little League had grown from Stotz's thirty boys to a program with 2.5 million players in 1989. Media coverage had gone from the *Williamsport Sun-Gazette* as lone correspondent in 1939 to ABC-TV's live television coverage of the Williamsport World Series in the summer of 1989,[12] broadcast to forty countries around the world.

As part of the fifty-year publicity campaign, Little League formed a Challenger Division allowing handicapped children to participate in baseball. That same year, as a sign of the unfortunate changing times, the program also promoted a Drug and Alcohol Education Program

---

[12]ABC first televised the Little League World Series on a delayed basis in 1963, and first showed it live in 1985.

headed up by Los Angeles Dodgers pitching ace Orel Hershiser, himself a former Little Leaguer.

The biggest event on the organization's schedule in 1989 came when President George Bush, a former Midland, Texas, Little League coach, welcomed the program's current Chairman Creighton Hale (who had succeeded McGovern)[13] to the White House on July 7. Dan Quayle joined the President at the ceremonies in recognition of being the first vice president to have played Little League Baseball. President Bush accompanied Hale the next day for the presentation of the first four boys' baseball charters in Poland.

Carl Stotz stayed home in the summer of 1989, unwilling to participate. Taiwan had honored him in 1987 and Canada in 1988 for his contribution to boys' baseball, but no meaningful recognition came from the current powers of Little League Baseball, Inc. Hale had his lieutenants make periodic reconciliation overtures to Stotz through the years, but he refused any settlement advances unless they came from the boss himself, which Hale refused to do.

In 1982, Little League Baseball completed construction of the Peter McGovern Little League Museum in Williamsport, but Stotz refused to let McGovern and Hale have any of the relics he had kept from the program's early years. Stotz made his backyard into a private personal museum far superior in its collection to what the organization could display in its facility. Upon Stotz's death in 1992, his daughter inherited the Little League memorabilia, and apparently has no intention of turning it over to the Williamsport brass who broke her father's heart.

The citizens of Williamsport treated Carl Stotz better than McGovern and Hale did. They renamed the Max Brown Memorial Park (where the 1938 tests were run) the Carl E. Stotz Field. In the Old Lycoming township part of Williamsport, residents named a recreational park after Little League's founder, and the owner of the facility where the tax office was located named his building the Carl Stotz Office Building to recognize Stotz's more than two decades of service as the local collector.

---

[13]Peter McGovern died in 1984.

An elderly Carl Stotz shares a laugh with the Woodrich All-Stars after presenting them championship certificates in 1990. (Williamsport Sun-Gazette).

In Conclusion

UNIVERSITY OF CHICAGO PROFESSOR NORMAN MACLEAN saw life in the context of a river and turned that metaphor into a novel, which became the subject of a Robert Redford-directed movie. MacLean concluded his story with the observation which became the book's title: "Eventually, all things merge into one, and a river runs through it."

Cooperstown, the focal point of baseball's first one hundred years, is located at the source of the Susquehanna River. The forces of nature drive the Susquehanna in a southwesterly direction almost two hundred miles to Williamsport, the home of baseball's most important development during its second hundred years. From there, the river flows south to Harrisburg and then turns southeast where it runs to its mouth at the Chesapeake Bay.

Like the Susquehanna River, baseball's centennial of 1939 ran from Abner Doubleday to Carl Stotz; from the sudden, tragic retirement of quiet Lou Gehrig to the jump-start of brash Ted Williams; from the reminiscence for the rural sandlot to the emerging technology of television; from segregated bigotry to the suddenly realistic hope of integration. All converged in 1939, when baseball turned like a river from the Golden Age to the modern era.

APPENDIX

THE FOLLOWING ARTICLE APPEARED in the Opening Day 1993 issue of *Elysian Fields Quarterly*, as assessed by Thomas Schwartz, curator of the Henry Horner Lincoln Collection at the Illinois State Historical Library in Springfield, Illinois.

Lincoln and Baseball: The Truth

Copyright 1992 by Talmage Boston

> *TELL THE GENTLEMEN they will have to wait a few minutes 'til I get my turn at bat.*
> —ABRAHAM LINCOLN, after being interrupted on a sandlot to be told he had won the nomination for the presidency, 1860.

The quote and its circumstances first came to my attention ten years ago when I came to February 12 on a calendar. Abe Lincoln had always been my kind of president, but this told me he was my kind of guy. I hung the quote on my office wall.

My friend Richard Brock and I decided recently that the quote might open a business opportunity in the form of hiring an artist to depict the famous Lincoln-baseball scene, and then selling it as a limited edition print. Before going forward with it, however, we wanted to verify that it was truth and not legend.

The quote popped up all over our research. *Newsweek* reported it in its June 19, 1939 Baseball-Centennial Issue. The *Dallas Morning News* quoted it twice in the last six months. Tulsa sportswriter Mike Sowell mentioned it in his new book, *July 2, 1903*, but cautiously labeled it "a popular tale." The June 1939 issue of *Baseball Magazine* not only described the incident, it reported that "a famous newspaper cartoon drawn by Homer Davenport" depicting the event hung on the wall of Lincoln's Springfield home.

We changed our plan of hiring an artist, and decided to locate and then reproduce the Davenport cartoon. "Quick, call Lincoln's Springfield home!" No luck. The tour guides knew nothing of it and suggested we contact Thomas Schwartz at the Illinois State Historical Library since "he knows everything there is to know about Lincoln."

Tom Schwartz said he thought he had heard about the cartoon, but had never seen it. He acknowledged that he had also heard the baseball-nomination story, but had never researched its accuracy. He agreed to see what he could find in the library.

We received from Schwartz a copy of a document dated March 24, 1860 (two months before Lincoln's nomination), reflecting that twenty-three Springfield businessmen, including Lincoln's law partner William Herndon, had organized to clear certain lots "for the purpose of playing ball and other suitable exercises." Surely, we reasoned, this must have been the site of the baseball game, and Lincoln likely would have played in a game with his law partner.

We also received a story by Clinton Conkling published in 1909 (the centennial of Lincoln's birth), entitled "How Mr. Lincoln Received the News of his First Nomination." Conkling wrote that while Lincoln awaited the Republican convention's results, he "occasionally, joined in a game of hand ball, the then favorite pastime of the professional men of the town." Yes! Surely, "hand ball" was an 1860 synonym for baseball. Based on the March 24 document, twenty-three men would not organize to clear a field for what we now know as handball. Cartwright's *Rules of 1845* used the terms "hands" or "hand outs" for what we now know as "outs," and games lasted until one team scored "twenty-one counts" (i.e., handball scoring). Finally, we strengthened our hypothesis that Conkling was talking about baseball after we found an 1860 political cartoon showing Lincoln holding a bat and characterizing his political position in baseball lingo.

Unfortunately, Conkling went on to say that on May 18, 1860, he learned of Lincoln's receiving the nomination and became the first to tell Abe the news on a Springfield street. A setback. Our baseball story sounded apocryphal.

The Conkling article cited the *Illinois State Register* of February 12, 1909, "in which T. W. S. Kidd tells what Lincoln himself told him about where he was nominated and who first brought him the news." I asked Schwartz to locate Kidd's article.

In the meantime, we called around the country trying to locate the famous Davenport cartoon, came up empty, and proceeded to give our artist the go-ahead.

We received Kidd's article. He acknowledged the existence of the baseball story, but said it was false. Kidd himself had asked Lincoln where he first learned of his nomination, and Lincoln's account jived with Conkling's. Kidd then said that years later, he encountered a Mr. Powers, then custodian and historian of the Lincoln Monument (who sounded to us like a reliable source), telling monument visitors the baseball-nomination story. Kidd rebuked Powers for misrepresenting history, and an altercation ensued.

I resumed my conversation with Schwartz, asking, "If the baseball story is legend, why did the Davenport cartoon hang in Lincoln's home? Why did typically reliable news sources, such as *Newsweek*, report it as fact?" Schwartz acknowledged that the evidence was certainly conflicting.

I retreated to the local bookstore to browse away my gloom over the possibility that Abe's quote might not be the real stuff. I came across A. G. Spalding's re-issued 1911 classic, *Base Ball: America's National Game*. There, on page 233, was the lost Davenport ark: Abe holding a bat, in front of two baseball players, with the messenger trying to interrupt the game.

I showed the cartoon to Richard, and he then analyzed how all the apparently contradictory evidence could be reconciled. Lincoln learned of his nomination from Conkling on a Springfield street after a long night waiting on telegrams. The next day, he relaxed with his friends playing baseball in the commons. As his time at bat approached, he was interrupted by a messenger leading the convention delegation, coming to advise him *officially* of his nomination. The transaction with the delegation would be a formality, since Abe already knew he had won. He chose to complete the game and delay the formality and communicated his choice with his immortal words. Kidd and Powers, both knowledgeable Lincoln people, had fought because each man knew he was right, and he was. Spalding's text accompanying the Davenport cartoon confirmed our construction of the seemingly conflicting accounts:

> In the year 1860, when the Chicago Convention Committee which nominated Lincoln for the Presidency visited his home at Springfield, to notify him *formally* of the event, the messenger sent to apprise him of the coming of the visitors found the great leader out on the commons, engaged in a game of Base Ball.

The key word is "formally." Even the most fanatical baseball fan finding himself in a situation waiting to hear whether he would be a presidential nominee, surely would have dropped his bat to find out the convention's results. That same fan, however, enjoying the camaraderie of a spirited game, already knowing the convention's outcome, would likely refuse to mix with politics until his brief interlude enjoying the emerging national pastime had passed.

Peter Levine's critically acclaimed biography *A. G. Spalding and the Rise of Baseball* satisfied any doubts about Spalding's knowledge of the incident by revealing that Spalding's father had been one of the founders of the Republican Party in Illinois and Abraham Lincoln's personal friend. Stephen Lehman, editor of *Elysian Fields Quarterly*, recently observed history's process:

> Whatever evidence remains behind for the analysis of historians is inevitably sketchy, its survival often the result of chance or serendipity, and its actual significance almost always problematic. Finding meaning in the debris of history's scrap heap is a

> process of tedious digging and sorting followed by imaginative and intelligent conjecture.

Amen! Lincoln's quote still hangs in my office. I can now say "Abe Lincoln was my kind of guy" with a historian's conviction.

ILLINOIS STATE HISTORICAL LIBRARY

A DIVISION OF THE ILLINOIS HISTORIC PRESERVATION AGENCY
Old State Capitol • Springfield 62701 • 217-782-4836

July 13, 1993

Mr. Talamage Boston, Esq.
Payne & Vendig
3700 Renaissance Tower
1201 Elm Street
Dallas, Texas 75270

Dear Mr. Boston:

Many thanks for your article on "Lincoln and Baseball: The Truth." It will be catalogued and added to the collection. Your research helped to clear up the incident in my mind. Thanks again for your thoughtfulness.

Sincerely,

Thomas F. Schwartz
Curator, Henry Horner Lincoln Collection
(217) 785-7954

TFS:cl

ACKNOWLEDGMENTS

Taking on a major project is only possible with support on the homefront. Spending several hundred hours over a period of two years to write a baseball history book in a soft sports book market involves a substantial financial sacrifice. My wife Claire never expressed regret over my going forward with the project, and for that I owe her my first expression of thanks.

Elysian Fields Quarterly editor Stephen Lehman gave me the confidence to write this book in the first place. Stephen was the first literary figure to think my writing worthy of publication, supported the idea for the book from the outset, published the McKechnie chapter as the cover story in the Summer 1994 issue of *EFQ*, and even came up with the book's title.

Jeff Guinn started out as my book-writing mentor and ended up my editor. Jeff's editorial assistance made every chapter better. His most important contribution involved going to bat for me with my publisher, The Summit Group, whom I wanted from the outset since it had done a nice job on Jeff's two baseball books. What he saw in the summer of 1992 to merit his continuous dedication to this book is still a mystery, but I thank God for Jeff's two years of advice and support.

Several respected baseball figures and writers were nice enough to read chapters along the way and give me important feedback. The most notable of these were Bill Gladstone, Bobby Brown, Robin Roberts, Bobby Bragan, Tim Kurkjian, David Pietrusza, Mike Sowell, Dewayne Staats, Rob Neyer, and Paul Rogers. In addition, James Vlasich answered my questions and Tom Heitz gave me important feedback on the Doubleday-Cooperstown chapter, as did Robert Creamer on the Red Barber chapter, Jack Moore on the DiMaggio chapter, Larry Gerlach on the Bill Klem chapter, Buck O'Neil on the Negro league chapter, and Kenneth Loss on the Little League chapter. Special thanks to John Thorn and Michael Gershman for their thoughts on virtually every aspect of the commercial side of publishing a baseball book. I will always be indebted to Buck O'Neil for his magnificent foreword.

The assistance I received from my research associate Rob Neyer gave me confidence in knowing I had left no material stone unturned. Rob's vast storehouse of knowledge permitted an instant focus on the logical sources of information, thereby shortening my research time considerably. Locally, Paul Rogers and John Mayeron made available their substantial baseball libraries in Dallas whenever I needed them.

The staff at The National Baseball Hall of Fame and Museum Library was extremely helpful. Tom Heitz, Bill Deane, the late Gary Van Allen, and Bob Browning provided help for my research needs during my time in Cooperstown, as well as in the dozens of follow-up phone calls.

Len Oszustowicz, president of The Summit Group, stood up for my book and made it come to pass. Len's encouragement and, above all, his moral perspective on what is important in books gave me comfort to know I had chosen the best possible publisher.

The lawyers at my firm Payne and Vendig, P.C., were remarkably understanding. In particular, Bob Payne and Lee Vendig supported the project and seemed to understand how important all of this was to me.

My secretary, Sara McCord, gritted her teeth, typed the multiple revisions of each chapter, and somehow kept her sanity. Certainly, I could never have completed this work without her daily assistance.

In addition to my wife, Claire, son Scott, and daughter Lindsey, friends and family members provided necessary encouragement along the way—particularly, sister and brother-in-law Ann and Larry Faber, brother and sister-in-law, Dr. James and Terry Boston, parents Paul and Mary Jean Boston, grandparents "Happy" and Lucile Durham, parents-in-law J. D. and Henry Esther Lindsey, cousin Donn Boston, brother-in-law Rick McDowell, best friend Marvin Blum, lifelong friends Austin and Mary Anne McCloud, and special friends Peter Haveles, Dave Wexler, Randy Avery, Rev. Jim Turley, Dr. Joe Washington, Duncan Fulton, Richard Brock, Webb Spradley, Alan Perkins, John Peper, John Blair, the late Bill Armstrong, Pat Bolin, Scott Frost, Bob Townsend, John Jackson, Frank Fleming, Bob Sharp, Jim Young, Myra Robinson, and Dr. John Ledbetter.

Finally, I praise God, from whom all blessings flow.

BIBLIOGRAPHY

In addition to pertinent issues of *The Sporting News*, which are referenced throughout the book, and *The Baseball Encyclopedia* set forth below are the main sources of information used for the respective chapters.

Chapter One: The Iron Horse Corrodes

Dahlgren, Babe. "Gehrig's Last Day." *Yesterday In Sport: A Sports Illustrated Book*. New York: Time-Life Books, 1968.

DiMaggio, Joe. *Lucky To Be A Yankee*. New York: Grosset & Dunlap, 1947.

Durso, Joseph. *Baseball and the American Dream*. St. Louis, Missouri: *The Sporting News*, 1986.

Gallico, Paul. *Lou Gehrig: The Pride of the Yankees*. New York: Grosset & Dunlap, 1942.

Gehrig, Eleanor and Joseph Durso. *My Luke and I*. New York: Thomas Y. Crowell Company, 1976.

Graham, Frank. *Lou Gehrig, A Quiet Hero.* New York: G. P. Putnam's Sons, 1942.

Henrich, Tommy, and Bill Gilbert. *Five O'Clock Lightning.* New York: Birch Lane Press, 1992.

Honig, Donald. *Baseball America.* New York: MacMillan Publishing Company, 1985.

Honig, Donald. *Baseball When Grass Was Real.* New York: Coward, McCann & Geoghegan, 1975.

Hubler, Richard G. *Lou Gehrig, The Iron Horse of Baseball.* Boston: Houghton Mifflin Company, 1941.

Lieb, Frederick. *Baseball as I Have Known It.* New York: Coward, McCann & Geoghegan, 1977.

Robinson, Ray. *Iron Horse: Lou Gehrig in His Time.* New York: W. W. Norton & Company, Inc., 1990.

Williams, Joe. *The Joe Williams Baseball Reader*, edited by Peter Williams. Chapel Hill, North Carolina: Algonquin Books of Chapel Hill, 1989.

Chapter Two: The Kid Arrives at the Show

Baldassaro, Lawrence. *The Ted Williams Reader.* New York: Simon & Schuster, 1991.

Cramer, Richard Ben. *Ted Williams: The Seasons of the Kid.* New York: Prentice Hall Press, 1991.

Hirschberg, Al. "Handsome Bad Boy of the Boston Red Sox." *Cosmopolitan Magazine* (1956).

Holway, John. *The Last .400 Hitter.* Dubuque, Iowa: William C. Brown Publishers, 1992.

Honig, Donald. *The Boston Red Sox: An Illustrated History.* New York: Prentice Hall Press, 1990.

Johnson, Dick, and Glenn Stout. *Ted Williams: A Portrait in Words and Pictures.* New York: Walker and Company, 1991.

Lieb, Frederick G. *The Boston Red Sox.* New York: G. P. Putnam's Sons, 1947.

Linn, Edward A. *Hitter: The Life and Turmoils of Ted Williams.* New York: Harcourt, Brace & Co., 1993.

Robinson, Ray. *Ted Williams.* New York: G. P. Putnam's Sons, 1962.

Seidel, Michael. *Ted Williams: A Baseball Life.* Chicago: Contemporary Books, 1991.

Williams, Ted, and John Underwood. *My Turn at Bat: The Story of My Life.* New York: Simon & Schuster, 1969.

Williams, Ted, and John Underwood. *The Science of Hitting.* New York: Simon & Schuster, 1970.

Chapter Three: The Lip at the Helm

Allen, Lee. *One Hundred Years of Baseball.* New York: Bartholomew House, 1950.

Alexander, Charles C. *Our Game—An American Baseball History.* New York: Henry Holt and Company, 1991.

Broeg, Bob, and William J. Miller, Jr. *Baseball from a Different Angle.* South Bend, Indiana: Diamond Communications, 1988.

Durocher, Leo, and Ed Linn. *Nice Guys Finish Last.* New York: Simon & Schuster, 1975.

Durocher, Leo. *The Dodgers and Me.* Chicago: Ziff-Davis Publishing Company, 1948.

Einstein, Charles. *The Baseball Reader.* New York: Bonanza Books, 1989.

Eskenazi, Gerald. *The Lip—A Biography of Leo Durocher.* New York: William Morrow and Company, 1993.

Golenbock, Peter. *Bums.* New York: G. P. Putnam's Sons, 1984.

Graham, Frank. *The Brooklyn Dodgers.* New York: G. P. Putnam's Sons, 1945.

Honig, Donald. *Baseball America.* New York: MacMillan Publishing Company, 1985.

Koppett, Leonard. *The Man in the Dugout.* New York: Crown Publishers, 1993.

Meaney, Tom. "Always on the Spot." *Sport Magazine* (April 1947).

Okrent, Daniel. *Baseball Anecdotes.* New York: Oxford University Press, 1989.

Pope, Edwin. *Baseball's Greatest Managers.* Garden City, New York: Doubleday, 1960.

Powers, Jimmy. *Baseball Personalities.* New York: Rudolph Field, 1949.

Warfield, Donald. *The Roaring Redhead.* South Bend, Indiana: Diamond Communications, 1987.

Chapter Four: The Deacon of Cincinnati

Allen, Lee. *The Cincinnati Reds.* New York: G. P. Putnam's Sons, 1948.

Allen, Lee, and Tom Meaney. *Kings of the Diamond.* New York: G. P. Putnam's Sons, 1965.

Bartel, Dick. *Rowdy Richard.* Berkeley, California: North Atlantic Books, 1987.

Bloodgood, Clifford. "Crafty Craft." *Baseball Magazine* (January 1939).

Costello, James, and Michael Santa Maria. *In the Shadows of the Diamond.* Dubuque, Iowa: Elysian Fields Press, 1992.

Daniel, Dan. "Miracle Man McKechnie." *Baseball Magazine* (July 1938).

Durocher, Leo, and Ed Linn. *Nice Guys Finish Last.* New York: Simon & Schuster, 1975.

Frommer, Harvey. *Baseball's Greatest Managers.* New York: Franklin Watts, 1985.

Hirshberg, Al. *The Braves: The Pick and the Shovel.* Boston: Waverly House, 1948.

Honig, Donald. *Baseball When The Grass Was Real.* New York: Coward, McCann & Geoghegan, 1975.

Knack, William. "The Razor's Edge." *Sports Illustrated* (May 6, 1991).

Koppett, Leonard. *The Man in the Dugout.* New York: Crown Publishers, 1993.

Lake, Austin. "Return of McKechnie: A Break for Young Red Sox Hurlers." *Baseball Digest* (1952).

Langford, Walter M. *Legends of Baseball.* South Bend, Indiana: Diamond Communications, 1987.

Lieb, Fred. *The Pittsburgh Pirates.* New York: G. P. Putnam's Sons, 1948.

Pope, Edwin. *Baseball's Greatest Managers.* Garden City, New York: Doubleday, 1960.

Van Blair, Rick. "Harry Craft: Speedy Outfielder Played for Two N. L. Champs." *Sports Collector's Digest* (April 30, 1993).

Van Blair, Rick. "Junior Thompson and the 1939, 1940 Reds." *Sports Collector's Digest* (July 9, 1993).

Werber, Bill. *Circling the Bases.* Self-published, 1978.

Williams, Joe. "Deacon Bill McKechnie." *Saturday Evening Post* (September 14, 1940).

"McKechnie Glimpses a Vision of 1914." *Baseball Magazine* (October 1933).

Chapter Five: The Redhead in the Catbird Seat

Abodoher, N. J. "Baseball Via the Ether Waves." *Baseball Magazine* (November 1929).

Allen, Mel, and Ed Fitzgerald. *You Can't Beat the Hours.* New York: Harper & Row, 1964.

Barber, Lylah (Mrs. Red). *Lylah.* Chapel Hill, North Carolina: Algonquin Books of Chapel Hill, 1985.

Barber, Red. *1947 —When All Hell Broke Loose in Baseball.* Garden City, New York: Doubleday & Company, Inc., 1982.

Barber, Red, and Robert Creamer. *Rhubarb in the Catbird Seat.* Garden City, New York: Doubleday & Company, Inc., 1968.

Barber, Red. *The Broadcasters.* New York: The Dial Press, 1970.

Barber, Red. *The Rhubarb Patch,* with pictures by Barney Stein. New York: Simon & Schuster, 1954.

Barber, Red. *Walk in the Spirit.* New York: The Dial Press, 1969.

Barber, Red. "Can Baseball Be Saved?" *Reader's Digest* (April 1969).

Broeg, Joe, and William J. Miller, Jr. *Baseball From a Different Angle.* South Bend, Indiana: Diamond Communications, 1988.

Chad, Norman. "Everybody Knew it Was the Beginning of Something Big." *Washington Post* (August 19, 1989).

Edwards, Bob. *Fridays With Red.* New York: Simon & Schuster, 1993.

Golenbock, Peter. *Bums.* New York: G. P. Putnam's Sons, 1984.

Hubler, Richard G. "The Barber of Brooklyn." *Saturday Evening Post* (March 21, 1942).

Minzeshiner, Bob. "Barber Always a Pro, Never a Fan." *USA Today* (October 23, 1992).

Scully, Vin. "Unforgettable Red Barber." *Reader's Digest* (April 1993).

Sheed, Wilfrid. *My Life as a Fan*. New York: Simon & Schuster, 1993.

Smith, Curt. *Voices of the Game*. South Bend, Indiana: Diamond Communications, Inc., 1987.

Warfield, Don. *The Roaring Redhead*. South Bend, Indiana: Diamond Communications, 1987.

"Compliments of Wheaties, et al." *Time* (April 17, 1939).

Chapter Six: The Greatest Player in His Greatest Year on the Greatest Team

Alexander, Charles. *Our Game—An American Baseball History*. New York: Henry Holt & Company, 1991.

Allen, Lee, *100 Years of Baseball*. New York: Bartholomew House, 1950.

Allen, Lee, and Tom Meaney. *Kings of the Diamond*. New York: G. P. Putnam's Sons, 1965.

Allen, Maury. *Where Have You Gone, Joe DiMaggio?* New York: E. P. Dutton & Co., 1975.

Allen, Mel, and Ed Fitzgerald. *You Can't Beat the Hours*. New York: Harper & Row, 1964.

Astor, Gerald. *Hall of Fame 50th Anniversary Book*. New York: Prentice Hall Press, 1988.

Broeg, Bob. *Superstars of Baseball*. St. Louis, Missouri: *The Sporting News*, 1971.

Busch, Noel F. "Joe DiMaggio, Baseball's Most Sensational Big-League Star." *Life Magazine* (May 1, 1939).

Creamer, Robert. *Baseball in '41*. New York: Viking, 1991.

Daniel, Dan. "Inside Joe DiMaggio." *Baseball Magazine* (February 1952).

De Gregorio, George. *Joe DiMaggio: An Informal Biography*. New York: Stein and Day, 1981.

Durso, Joseph. *Baseball and the American Dream.* St. Louis, Missouri: *The Sporting News*, 1986.

Henrich, Tommy, and Bill Gilbert. *Five O'Clock Lightning.* New York: Birch Lane Press, 1992.

Honig, Donald. *Baseball America.* New York: MacMillan Publishing Co., 1985.

Honig, Donald. *Baseball in the '30's.* New York: Crown Publishers, 1987.

Koppett, Leonard. *The Man in the Dugout.* New York: Crown Publishers, 1993.

Lane, F. C. "The Greatest Rookie of the Decade." *Baseball Magazine* (September 1936).

Linn, Ed. *The Great Rivalry: The Yankees and the Red Sox 1901-1990.* New York: Ticknor & Fields, 1991.

Moore, Jack B. *Joe DiMaggio—Baseball's Yankee Clipper.* New York: Greenwood Press, 1986.

Ritter, Lawrence, and Donald Honig. *The Image of Their Greatness.* New York: Crown Publishers, 1979.

Seidel, Michael. *Streak: Joe DiMaggio and the Summer of '41.* New York: McGraw-Hill, 1988.

Sher, Jack. "DiMag, The Man Behind the Poker Face." *Sport Magazine* (September 1949).

Sheed, Wilfred. *Baseball and Lesser Sports.* New York: Harper Collins, 1991.

"The Big Guy." *Time Magazine* (October 4, 1948).

The DiMaggio Albums. Editor: Richard Whittingham. New York: G. P. Putnam's Sons, 1989.

Chapter Seven: Rapid Robert Hits His Stride

Bloodgood, Clifford. "Has Another Walter Johnson Come Along?" *Baseball Magazine* (March 1937).

Boudreau, Lou, and Russell Schneider. *Covering All the Bases.* Champaign, Illinois: Sagamore Publishing, 1993.

Bryson, Bill. "Iowa's Favorite Son." *Best of Baseball.* New York: G. P. Putnam's Sons, Sidney Offit, editor, 1956.

Cannon, Jimmy. "Feller Legend Bows to Materialism." *Baseball Digest* (1947).

Cobbledick, Gordon. "Faster Than Feller Talked." *Baseball Digest* (1947).

Cobbledick, Gordon. "Is It True About Bob Feller?..." *Sport Magazine* (June 1948).

Eyman, Scott. "Bob Feller: Still In There Pitchin." *Cleveland Sunday Plane Dealer Magazine* (October 1, 1978).

Feller, Bob, and Bill Gilbert. *Now Pitching—Bob Feller.* New York: Birch Lane Press, 1990.

Feller, Bob. *Strikeout Story.* Grosset & Dunlap, 1947.

Feller, Virginia. "He's My Feller!" *Baseball Digest* (May 1952).

Fitzgerald, Ed. "Feller Incorporated." *Sport Magazine* (June 1947).

Flaherty, Vincent X. "Feller Goes To Sea." *Baseball Digest* (March 1943).

Gilbert, Bill. *They Also Served: Baseball and the Home Front, 1941-1945.* New York: Crown Publishers, 1992.

Graham, Frank. "And Then McCarthy Brought In Feller." *New York Sun* (July 12, 1939).

Hayes, Gayle. "Fanning with Feller." *Baseball Magazine* (December 1938).

Honig, Donald. *Baseball: When the Grass Was Real.* Coward, McCann & Geoghegam, 1975.

Kirksey, George. "When a Feller Needs a Fella." *Baseball Magazine* (June 1938).

Lebovitz, Hal. "Bob Feller's Disappointment." *Sport Magazine* (October 1959).

McAuley, Ed. "Feller's a Whiz Promoting Two." *Baseball Digest* (September 1946).

Powers, Jimmy. *Baseball Personalities.* New York: Rudolph Field, 1949.

Shippy, Dick. "Still Pitching." *The Beacon Journal* (November 14, 1982).

Smith, Ira. *Baseball's Famous Pitchers.* New York: A. S. Barnes & Co., 1954.

Stockton, J. Roy. "Bob Feller—Storybook Ball Player." *Saturday Evening Post* (February 20, 1937).

Chapter Eight: Moving Toward the Day

Bankes, James. *The Pittsburgh Crawfords.* Dubuque, Iowa: William C. Brown Publishers, 1991.

Beasley, Maurine Hoffman. *Eleanor Roosevelt and the Media.* Urbana, Illinois: University of Illinois Press, 1987.

Brashler, William. *The Bingo Long Traveling All-Stars and Motor Kings.* Urbana, Illinois: University of Illinois Press, 1973.

Brashler, William. *Josh Gibson: A Life in the Negro Leagues.* New York: Harper & Row, 1978.

Bruce, Janet. *The Kansas City Monarchs.* Lawrence, Kansas: University of Kansas Press, 1985.

Chadwick, Bruce. *When the Game Was Black and White.* New York: Abbeville Press, 1992.

Clark, Dick, and Larry Lester. *The Negro Leagues Book.* Published by The Society of American Baseball Research, 1994.

Craft, David. *The Negro Leagues.* New York: Crescent Books, 1993.

Donovan, Richard. "The Fabulous Satchel Paige." *Collier's* (1953).

Folliard, Edward T. "75,000 Acclaim Miss Anderson." *The Washington Post* (April 10, 1939).

Holway, John B. *Blackball Stars.* Westport, Connecticut: Meckler Books, 1988.

Holway, John B. *Josh and Satch.* Westport, Connecticut: Meckler Publishing, 1991.

Holway, John B. *Voices from the Great Black Baseball Leagues.* New York: De Capo Press, 1975.

Paige, Satchel, and Hal Lebovitz. *Pitchin' Man—Satchel Paige's Own Story.* Westport, Connecticut: Meckler Publishing, 1992.

Paige, Satchel, and David Lipman. *Maybe I'll Pitch Forever.* Lincoln, Nebraska: University of Nebraska Press, 1993.

Peterson, Robert. *Only the Ball Was White.* Old Tappan, New Jersey: Prentice-Hall, 1970.

Ribowsky, Mark. *Don't Look Back.* New York: Simon & Schuster, 1994.

Riley, James A. "88 Years Before Jackie Robinson." *The Diamond Magazine* (January/February 1994).

Rogosin, Donn. *Invisible Men.* New York: MacMillan, 1983.

Ruck, Rob. *Sandlot Seasons: Sport & Black Pittsburgh.* Urbana, Illinois: University of Illinois Press, 1987.

Rust, Art, Jr. *Get That Nigger Off the Field.* Brooklyn, New York: Book Mail Services, 1992.

Seymour, Harold. *The People's Game.* New York: Oxford University Press, 1990.

Shane, Ted. "Chocolate Rube Waddell." *Saturday Evening Post* (July 27, 1940).

Tygiel, Jules. *Baseball's Greatest Experiment.* New York: Oxford University Press, 1983.

Veeck, Bill, and Ed Linn. *Veeck—As in Wreck.* New York: G. P. Putnam's Sons, 1962.

Vehanen, Kosti. *Marion Anderson: A Portrait.* New York: McGraw-Hill, 1941.

Weaver, Bill L. "The Black Press and the Assault on Professional Baseball's 'Color Line.' " *Phylon, The Atlanta University Review of Race and Culture,* vol. XL, no. 4. (Winter 1979).

Wiggins, David K. "Wendell Smith, the *Pittsburgh Courier-Journal* and the Campaign to Include Blacks in Organized Baseball, 1933-1945." *Journal of Sports History,* vol. 10, no. 2. (Summer 1983).

Wilson, August. "Fences." *Three Plays.* Pittsburgh, PA: University of Pittsburgh Press, 1991.

"The Colored Athlete and Professional Baseball." *Baseball Magazine* (May 1929).

"Satchel Paige, Negro Ballplayer, is One of the Best Pitchers in Game." *Life Magazine* (June 2, 1941).

"Satchelfoots." *Time* (June 3, 1940).

"She Let Freedom Sing." *Newsweek* (April 19, 1993).

Chapter Nine: Characters of the Year

BILL KLEM:

Barber, Red. *Walk in the Spirit.* New York: The Dial Press, 1969.

Conlan, Jocko, and Robert Creamer. *Jocko.* Philadelphia, Pennsylvania and New York: Lippincott, 1967.

Daley, Arthur. *Inside Baseball.* New York: Grosset & Dunlap, 1950.

Daley, Arthur. "Klem Self-Styled Umpire." *The New York Times* (February 26, 1969).

Evan, Billy. *Umpiring From the Inside.* Self-published, 1947.

Fitzgerald, Ed. "Play Ball! The Story of Bill Klem." *Sport Magazine* (January 1948).

Frick, Ford C. *Games, Asterisks, and People.* New York: Crown Publishers, 1973.

Gerlach, Larry. *Men in Blue.* New York: Viking, 1980.

Gorman, Tom. *Three and Two.* New York: Scribners, 1979.

Kahn, James M. *The Umpire Story.* New York: Putnam, 1953.

Klem, Bill, and William J. Slocum. *Collier's* (April 14, 1951).

Lane, F. C. "The Dean of All World Series Umpires." *Baseball Magazine* (October 1933).

Levy, Sam. "The Ol Arbitrator." *Baseball Digest, condensed from The Milwaukee Journal* (November 1951).

Ritter, Lawrence. *The Glory of Their Times.* New York: McMillan, 1966.

Smith, Red. "Klem's Oratory Converts Berry Into Umpire—For Al!" *Baseball Digest, condensed from The Philadelphia Record* (April 1943).

Smith, Red. "For Hall of Fame: Bill Klem." *Baseball Digest, condensed from The Philadelphia Record* (October 1943).

AL SCHACHT:

Amman, Larry. "The Clown Prince of Baseball." *Baseball Research Journal*, XI (1982).

Cunningham, Bill. "Clown Prince." *Collier's* (September 4, 1937).

Lieb, Fred. *Comedians and Pranksters of Baseball.* St. Louis, Missouri: *The Sporting News*, 1958.

Molen, Sam. *They Make Me Laugh.* Philadelphia: Torrance & Co., 1947.

Povich, Shirley. *The Washington Senators.* New York: G. P. Putnam's Sons, 1954.

Powers, Jimmy. *Baseball Personalities.* New York: Rudolph Field, 1949.

Ribalow, Harold. *Jew in American Sports.* New York: Bloch, 1959.

Schacht, Al. *Clowning Through Baseball.* New York: A. S. Barnes, 1941.

Schacht, Al. *G I Had Fun.* New York: Putnam's Sons, 1945.

Schacht, Al. *My Own Particular Screwball.* Garden City, New York: Doubleday & Co., 1955.

Chapter Ten: The Doubleday Myth

Bartlett, Arthur. *Baseball and Mr. Spalding.* New York: Farrar, Straus, and Young, 1951.

Bryson, Bill. "In Defense of Doubleday." *Baseball Magazine* (June 1939).

Daniel, Dan. "Doubleday, Baseball's Patron Saint." *Baseball Magazine* (June 1939).

Frick, Ford C. *Games, Asterisks, and People.* New York: Crown Publishers, 1973.

Holzman, Robert S. *General Baseball Doubleday.* New York: Langmans, Green and Co., 1955.

Heldman, Fred. "The Doubleday Myth: Why is Baseball Afraid to Face the Truth?" *The Washington Star* (January 26, 1977).

James, Bill. *The Politics of Glory.* Macmillan Publishing Company, 1994.

Peterson, Harold. *The Man Who Invented Baseball.* New York: Charles Scribner's Sons, 1969.

Salvatore, Victor. "Abner's False Rep." *American Heritage Magazine.* Reprinted Eastern Review (August 1983).

Scollan, David. "Doubleday Served U.S. 35 Years." Auburn, N.Y. newspaper (July 24, 1964).

Seymour, Harold. *Baseball: The People's Game.* New York: Oxford University Press, 1990.

Seymour, Harold. *Baseball: The Early Years.* New York: Oxford University Press, 1960.

Shumway, Harry Irving. "Abner Doubleday: Father of Baseball." *Famous American Athletes of Today*. Boston: L. C. Page & Company, 1940.

Smith, Ken. *Baseball's Hall of Fame.* New York: A. S. Barnes, 1947.

Spalding, Albert G. *Base Ball: America's National Game.* Original copyright 1911. San Francisco: Revised edition Halo Books, 1991.

Spalding's Official Guide for 1939.

Vlasich, James. *A Legend for the Legendary: The Origin of the Baseball Hall of Fame.* Bowling Green, Ohio: Bowling Green State University Popular Press, 1990.

Wolf, Andrew. "The Myth of Abner Doubleday." *U.S. Air Magazine* (September 1981).

Wulf, Steve. "The Stuff of Legend." *Sports Illustrated* (June 12, 1989).

Chapter Eleven: The Birthday Party

Bryson, Bill. "In Defense of Doubleday." *Baseball Magazine* (June 1939).

Daniel, Dan. "Doubleday, Baseball's Patron Saint." *Baseball Magazine* (June 1939).

James, Bill. *The Politics of Glory.* New York: MacMillan Publishing Co., 1994.

Smith, Ken. *Baseball's Hall of Fame.* New York: A. S. Barnes, 1947.

Vlasich, James. *A Legend for the Legendary: The Origin of the Baseball Hall of Fame.* Bowling Green, Ohio: Bowling Green State University Popular Press, 1990.

"Doubleday Field Association Organized at Meeting Held In Cooperstown." *Otsego Farmer* (April 12, 1935).

Spalding's Official Baseball Guide for 1936.

Chapter Twelve: The Future Begins in Williamsport

Addie, Bob. "Little Leagues Are a Waste of Time." *Baseball Magazine* (July 1956).

Brosnan, Jim. *Little League to Big League*. New York: Random House, 1968.

Bucher, Dr. Charles A., and Tim Cohane. "Little League Baseball Can Hurt Your Boy." *Look Magazine* (August 11, 1953).

Cohane, Tim. "Juvenile Parents Hurt Little League Baseball." *Look Magazine* (August 1, 1961).

Daley, Arthur. "Baseball in Miniature." *New York Times* (1949).

Daley, Arthur. "30,000 Little Big Leaguers." *American Magazine* (April 1951).

Daley, Arthur. "The Little League is Big Time." *New York Times Magazine* (May 25, 1952).

Frommer, Harvey. *Growing Up at Bat*. New York: Pharos Books, 1989.

Henrich, Tommy, and Bob Feller. "Is Little League Baseball Good for Kids?" *Sport Magazine* (August 1957).

Jackson, Shirley. "It's Only a Game." *Harpers Magazine* (May 1956).

Jay, Joey. "Don't Trap Your Son in Little League Madness." *The Third Fireside Book of Baseball*. New York: Simon & Schuster, 1968.

Kehoe, Bill. "Uncle Tuck's Legacy." *Grit Magazine* (1954).

Lilly, Joseph. "Watch Little League Grow." *Baseball Magazine* December 1951.

Paxton, Harry T. "Small Boy's Dream Come True." *Saturday Evening Post* (May 14, 1949).

Roberts, Robin. "Strikeout Little League." *Newsweek* (1975).

Rockerman, Pamela. "Little League Founder Ignored by Nation." *Lycoming Ledger* (October 24, 1985).

Speaker, Tris. "Diamonds in the Rough." *Rotarian Magazine* (April 1939).

Stotz, Carl E., and Kenneth D. Loss. *A Promise Kept*. Jersey Shore, Pennsylvania: Zebrowski Historical Services Publishing Company (1992).

Stotz, Carl E., and M. W. Baldwin. *At Bat With the Little League*. Philadelphia: Macrae South Company, 1952.

Woodberry, Clarence. "Better Baseball for Your Boy." *Women's Home Companion* (July 1950).

"Little League Baseball, Inc.: A $2 Million-a-Year Business." *Philadelphia Inquirer* (August 21, 1977).

INDEX